CW00458337

MESSIAH MODI?

MESSIAH MODI?

A Tale of Great Expectations

Tavleen Singh

HarperCollins *Publishers* India

First published in India in 2020 by
HarperCollins *Publishers*
A-75, Sector 57, Noida, Uttar Pradesh 201301, India
www.harpercollins.co.in

2 4 6 8 10 9 7 5 3 1

Copyright © Tavleen Singh 2020

P-ISBN: 978-93-5357-594-6
E-ISBN: 978-93-5357-595-3

The views and opinions expressed in this book are the author's own and
the facts are as reported by her, and the publishers are not in any
way liable for the same.

Tavleen Singh asserts the moral right
to be identified as the author of this work.

All rights reserved. No part of this publication may be reproduced,
stored in a retrieval system, or transmitted, in any form or by any means,
electronic, mechanical, photocopying, recording or otherwise,
without the prior permission of the publishers.

Typeset in 11/15.2 Sabon LT Std at
Manipal Technologies Limited, Manipal

Printed and bound at
Thomson Press (India) Ltd

MIX
Paper
FSC FSC® C010615

This book is produced from independently certified FSC® paper to ensure
responsible forest management.

'The highest morality for a king is that his kingdom should prosper'
– *Arthashastra*

Contents

Prologue

IT is in times of dark despair that people hope for a messiah. And at the time that India celebrated her 66th birthday as an independent nation in 2013 it felt as if despair had made a place in India's soul. The dreams of the freedom movement were dead. The political party that led the freedom movement had reduced itself to a private limited company with a woman born in a foreign country as its Chairman and Managing Director. Sonia Gandhi, credited with having saved the Congress Party when she became its president in 1997, had come to be seen as someone who entered politics mainly to save her family's right to rule India. Her children were her closest advisors and she made it clear when Rahul Gandhi entered electoral politics in 2004 that her sole aim was to ensure that he inherited what she seemed to believe was his birthright: India.

So politically feeble were the men and women she surrounded herself with that everyone in the Congress Party fell in line and accepted that although she was not officially Prime Minister she was India's real ruler. The Prime Minister she chose at the beginning of her first term in power (if not office) was not embarrassed to admit publicly that any time Rahul Gandhi wanted his job he was happy to give it to him. Dr Manmohan Singh was a good Prime Minister in his first term in office but when his job was reduced to being that of regent till Sonia's heir grew up he seemed to lose confidence in himself and his policies. He accepted every new humiliation with quiet grace and did not object even when Rahul declared that the ordinance his government brought, permitting convicted political leaders to stand for high office, should be thrown into the garbage bin.

This ultimate public humiliation of India's Prime Minister happened on September 27, 2013. Rahul Gandhi barged melodramatically into a press conference being addressed by a senior Congress Party leader, who was trying sincerely to defend a bad idea, when the Heir to India suddenly appeared and said the ordinance was 'complete nonsense' and should be 'torn up and thrown away'.

The Prime Minister was in Washington at the time and unable to defend himself, which made the timing of this public humiliation of India's Prime Minister look really bad. A general election was less than six months away. This made it worse. But by those last months of 2013 most Indians had accepted that India's real ruler was not the Prime Minister. They had accepted that he was not appointed to serve India so much as to serve the interests of India's most powerful political dynasty. It had been a bad year for India and an especially bad year for the government that Sonia Gandhi ran by remote control. Her chosen Prime Minister was the hero of the economic reforms that changed the character of the Indian economy when it was brought to the verge of bankruptcy in the early '90s. As Finance Minister in the Congress government that took office immediately after the assassination of Rajiv Gandhi he initiated the first steps to end the licence raj.

This was at the height of India's socialist era when the state controlled all the major levers of the economy, keeping private investors on a leash through licences, quotas and permits. Dr Manmohan Singh, once a socialist himself, ably defended the decision to change India's economic direction in the forums of the world, explaining that the faith India had placed in socialism had not brought the dividends India hoped for. And this was the reason why it had become necessary to change India's economic direction and orient it towards free markets and more liberal policies.

He continued the process of reforming the economy in his first term as Sonia's chosen Prime Minister. But once Rahul Gandhi entered politics Sonia took personal charge of his government, albeit from behind the scenes and without accountability. She was never officially part of Dr Singh's Cabinet but played the role of an extra-constitutional Prime Minister with her own unofficial Cabinet. In her private Cabinet were a caboodle of socialists and NGO types, mainly leftists and statists, who advised her to take India back in a socialist direction. The National Advisory Council, of which they were members, was in every sense more powerful than the Cabinet that Dr Manmohan Singh headed, so his ministers were forced to bow to the wishes of Sonia's NGO friends. They did this without demur, even sending government files to Sonia's residence for her to examine and alter, though this was officially denied.

On the advice of her NGO friends she decided that the way forward was to go backwards to the kind of socialism that made her mother-in-law such a popular leader. So she began to spend vast amounts of taxpayers' money on schemes that would bequeath to 'the common man' cheap food grain and a hundred days of work a year. These were suggestions that came from her leftist friends whose fundamental belief, like that of all socialists, is that they have a right to spend other people's money until it runs out. By the end of 2013 the economy was in the doldrums and the government was broke. The project to make Rahul Gandhi Prime Minister was not doing well either.

Some time in the middle of that last year of the government Dr Manmohan Singh ran at Sonia Gandhi's behest, her son and heir was invited to address India's richest businessmen at an event in Delhi organized by the Confederation of Indian Industry (CII). This was his first chance to explain his 'vision' from an important public platform and it did not take him long to make it clear that if he had a 'vision' for India it was disturbingly confused. He said India was not a country but 'an energy' that came from the sacred rivers that 'we worship'. His audience of powerful businessmen was just beginning to digest this mysterious comment when he added that his vision for India was formed by talking to ordinary Indians. He had taken a night train from Gorakhpur to Mumbai, he said, on which he met young Indians like a carpenter called Girish. It was the dreams of men like Girish that he wished to fulfil, he said, acknowledging inadvertently that the dreams of thousands of Indians like poor old Girish had remained unfulfilled for too long because of bad government policies. Sadly, he offered no hint of what his policies would be to rectify past mistakes by Congress prime ministers, nearly all of whom were from his family.

It was against this bleak backdrop that Narendra Modi suddenly appeared in national politics like a shining comet in a very dark sky. At a time when India seemed to be led by a leader who was not so much a leader as a servant of a tired political dynasty, Modi began to sound and behave like a real leader. He was only a chief minister then but made speeches on Independence Day in 2013 that sounded more prime ministerial than poor old Dr Manmohan Singh's from the Red Fort. While Dr Singh delivered in his robotic manner of public speaking a speech that was the opposite of inspirational, Modi talked of India daring to dream big.

He talked of the importance of India learning to aspire to become a country in which there was real prosperity instead of just the tawdry aspiration to 'alleviate' poverty. He seemed so filled with ideas and leadership qualities that Indians across the country began to see him as not just a leader but a messiah. This book examines whether he delivered on the promises he made in his first term as Prime Minister. His having won a second term in 2019 with a bigger mandate than he got five years earlier indicates that he delivered on at least some of them in the eyes of India's voters but is he the messiah so many hoped he would be?

This book does not answer that question; it asks it. It is for you to decide if Modi is the leader India longs for and it is for India's voters to decide if there continues to be reason for them to invest their hopes in Narendra Modi. This book is an attempt to tell the story of Modi's first term as it unfolded.

1

'Har, Har Modi'

THEY said it would be Narendra Modi's expiry date. The day that the results of the general election came: May 23, 2019. Every one of his political opponents believed this and almost everyone I knew believed this too. So when the exit polls came two days before the actual results and nearly all of them predicted that he would become Prime Minister again a tangible gloom descended over Delhi. Opposition politicians gathered in Delhi's hot, dusty streets to march in formation to the Election Commission to protest against what they claimed was a massive electoral fraud in which EVMs (electronic voting machines) that had been used had been tampered with. They knew that this was impossible. They knew that just months earlier when the states of Rajasthan, Madhya Pradesh and Chhattisgarh voted out BJP governments they had happily accepted the verdict. They knew that the Election Commission had acted with impartiality and diligence in its duties but when it seemed as if Modi was definitely becoming Prime Minister again they were ready to blame democracy itself for this.

What had gone wrong with their predictions? What had gone wrong with the narrative they had created and in which they thought most Indian voters believed? In this narrative Modi was painted as a corrupt leader who had destroyed the economy and torn to shreds the political fabric of India. In this narrative the general election that was meant to mark his 'expiry' was not an ordinary election, it was a battle for what they called the 'soul of India'. Modi had in their view wrenched India's very soul out of her in the five years he was Prime Minister. Were the lynchings of Muslims not proof of this? Was the unhappiness of farmers not proof of this? And what about those Dalit youths who were tied to a car and beaten with iron rods in that town of Una in Gujarat for the 'crime' of skinning a dead cow. Were these things not enough to put India's voters off Modi? How could such a litany of ugly stories not have persuaded ordinary Indians that they would be making a terrible mistake if they voted for Modi again?

Later everyone said that they had always known Narendra Modi would be given a second term. Later there were those who said they had always known that he would get more than 300 seats. Later there were pundits who said that the opposition parties had run a useless campaign. Later I found myself wondering how it was that I had not known Modi would win a full majority on his own. I should have known there was a Modi wave so strong that it would beat all the usual reasons why incumbent prime ministers lose. On my travels during the campaign I interviewed more than a hundred people in towns and villages that were thousands of kilometres apart and almost everyone I talked to said they would be voting for Modi. But it was only late on the evening of May 23 that I remembered this after a long, frenetic day of rushing from one TV studio to another in Noida to comment on a result that, if truth be told, I had not expected. Like almost everyone I knew I did not believe it was possible for Modi to win nearly every seat in northern and western India as he had in 2014. And so like everyone else I predicted that he would get around 250 seats and become Prime Minister again but with the support of allies in the National Democratic Alliance (NDA).

I should have known better. There had been signs that this would happen. One of the last places I visited before the campaign ended was the village of Jayapur that was in Modi's constituency and that became famous after he adopted it and promised to make it a model village. It is an hour's drive from Benares and I went back there because I had gone two years earlier when the first signs of development or 'vikas' were just becoming evident. To get to Jayapur on that first visit I drove through a squalid semi-urban cluster of villages that seemed to be drowning in filth. What made their squalor more obvious was that signs of modernity had appeared. So although the shops that teetered on the brink of open drains continued to look like hovels, they held up boards advertising cell phones and computers. Once in a while in the middle of this wasteland of hideous urbanization I would notice a reminder of an older, more beautiful time when the landscape in this part of northern India was of mango groves and green fields and the occasional whitewashed temple.

Images of that older India that I remembered from my childhood had almost disappeared behind ugly villages with their drains clogged with blue and green plastic bags. So Jayapur even two years earlier had looked different. There was a neat little covered bus stop on the edge of an open field in which stood solar panels. Opposite this field on the other side of a road covered in broken stones was a shiny new bank with an ATM. A young girl with blow-dried hair stood near the ATM. She told me that the road was under construction, so if I wanted to go inside the village she would show me a path through some fields. I had just had a surgery to fix a torn meniscus in my left knee and decided that it would be unwise to accept her offer. So instead I just chatted to her about the changes that had happened since Modi adopted the village.

When I went back on a blistering hot April day in 2019 the road was ready. And beside the bank I saw when I was last here I noticed that another one had opened. I also noticed a new girls' school. The new tarmac road led deep into the village but I had to get off it onto a dirt trail to reach the house of the sarpanch. He sat on a plastic chair in the courtyard of a two-storey house that had clothes hanging to dry in an upper veranda. Women peered down from behind the clothes. The sarpanch was a lean, middle-aged man with a gaunt face and grey hair. He said his name was Sri Narain Patel. I said I was a reporter from Delhi and was here to find out about the election and about how the village had changed after Modi adopted it.

'Who do you write for?'

'*Amar Ujala*. Does it come here?'

'Yes. Please mention my name in your story.'

'Of course. How big is the village? How many people live here?'

'There are 535 houses,' he said, 'about 3,200 people altogether. As for the changes since Modi adopted the village. There has been nothing but changes. We now have two banks – Union Bank and Syndicate Bank – and there is a post office. We have electricity for 22 hours a day and get piped water in our homes for six hours a day. We have toilets in every home. There is a khadi udyog where 350 women work, earning Rs 200 a day.

And there are centres in the village that teach computer courses and train people in tailoring. But the journey of "vikas" has no end so what we want now is to have "pucca" roads inside the village. In the rains the village streets become very muddy.'

'So Modi will win again for sure?'

'There is no question about it. Ask anyone in the village.'

So I did. I talked to the village teacher and some village elders who sat under a large banyan tree on rope beds. When I asked about Modi they said, 'Har, har Modi. Ghar, ghar Modi.' Praise be to Modi, he is praised in every house. A man called Arvindji, a teacher, said that before Modi adopted the village there was no such thing as government help of any kind that they had ever seen. So the transformation was something that they could hardly believe. A man who said he worked as a chowkidar in Benares said that Modi had made him proud to be a chowkidar. Others in this group of village intellectuals analysed the political situation as being one in which the only choice was to vote for Modi.

When I asked if Rahul Gandhi was someone they could see becoming Prime Minister after the election they laughed. Then Arvindji said, 'Rahul Gandhi seems to have lost his mental balance. He doesn't even know how to speak politely...he seems to say anything that comes to his mouth.' When I asked what exactly he meant by this he said that it was wrong for anyone to call the Prime Minister of India a thief. 'It seems as if nobody taught him any manners. How can you talk like this about someone who works day and night for the country? He isn't working for his family but for the country.' It was in Jayapur that I first heard rural people mention 'parivarvaad' (hereditary democracy) as a curse. They said it had to be stopped because it was keeping good people from being in public life. Nobody gets a chance, they said, unless they come from some big family.

Was this why they did not think of Rahul Gandhi as a candidate for India's next Prime Minister? It was one of the reasons, they said. So how did political pundits in Delhi not notice what people really thought of the man who had the arrogance to believe that Modi's time was up and that it was his time now. The main slogan of his campaign was 'Ab hoga NYAY'. The acronym was for a minimum income guarantee programme (Nyuntam Aay Yojana) that he declared would be a 'surgical strike' on poverty. The word nyay means justice in Hindi and so it was a play on this acronym. When it was announced political pundits in the highest ranks of Indian political punditry declared that this was a 'game changer' and that Rahul Gandhi was a man of hidden genius.

His face was splashed on the covers of major political magazines and this fooled foreign correspondents. Nobody got the mood of this election more wrong than major international newspapers. My own son, Aatish, who has paid little attention to anything I have said since he was 15, wrote a cover story for *Time* magazine that called Modi 'India's Divider in Chief.' I had tried my best to persuade him that there was real change going on quietly in rural India and that this could work in Modi's favour but he was adamant to see Modi only as a man who had divided Hindus and Muslims. *Time* magazine is taken very seriously by Indian politicians so Modi himself said in one of the many interviews he gave during this long, long election campaign that the writer of this article was a Pakistani and was serving their agenda. Aatish is not Pakistani but the flaw in his article was that he saw Modi entirely through the ugly prism of the lynchings of Muslims that had so marred his first term as Prime Minister.

That evening when I got back to Benares I went to the Assi Ghat, where I had stayed when I was in Benares in 2014 on the day that Modi came to file his nomination papers. I remembered that I had woken early that morning and climbed up into a sort of turret on the highest terrace of the Ganges View Hotel to watch the sun come up on the Ganga. I remembered that it was still dark and the empty ghat glowed dimly in the yellow lights that hung randomly here and there, swaying on grimy wires. The old sadhu with his monkey companion, a permanent resident of this ghat, slept under a red cloth and from distant temples came the sounds of muffled bells. The river was silent, still and had about it a dark, ominous quality.

Then dawn broke and everything changed. The morning light in Benares is so special that poets have tried to capture its magic in verse and writers in words but it is not till you actually see dawn break over the Ganga that you understand why this morning light is so special and so hard to describe. The light comes stealthily as if to give the spectator time to savour each magical change of colour. From my perch in my little turret I noted in my notebook that the first colour was dark grey, the colour of the steel that swords are made from. The second colour was of luminous grey pearls that turned slowly to the pink of mother-of-pearl and then suddenly it was morning. Everything changed. The ghat filled with noise and movement. Pilgrims stood half-naked on the edge of the river. Temple bells got louder and I climbed down from my perch to sit on the terrace and drink my first cup of tea.

As I sipped the thick, sweet desi chai I thought about the day ahead. How would Modi be received? Would people line the streets as the political pundits of Benares had been predicting? This was not my first visit to Benares that year. I had come before and spent many hours talking to students in Banaras Hindu University, political pundits and ordinary people. Everyone said

Modi would become Prime Minister and they looked forward to this for different reasons.

In Banaras Hindu University, in a dusty veranda filled with broken chairs and tables, students in the Sanskrit department told me they were deeply unhappy about reservations in educational institutions. They were, with one exception, from Brahmin families and as they talked their resentments and rage spilt into every conversation we had. Resentment over caste-based reservations, resentment over the bleakness of their prospects after leaving college. They were trying to keep Indian traditions and civilization alive by learning Sanskrit, they said, and their prospects for the future were bleak. What hope is there for us, they asked me over and over again, when the only jobs we can get are as priests? 'Modi will create new jobs for those who learn Sanskrit out of love for our ancient civilization. And he will end reservations.' The person most vocal about the need for new jobs was a professor of Sanskrit who was retiring the next day. He sat in a dark office filled with heavy furniture and ugly pictures and said pointing to the Brahmin student who brought me to him, 'What is his future? They tell us they want to keep Sanskrit alive but then they fail to provide jobs for those who spend years studying it.'

Returning to the Assi Ghat brought back other memories from the 2014 election. Memories of spending long, hot evenings in Papu's teashop on this ghat, talking to local intellectuals and politicians and learning from them how fed up they were with the way the country was being run. They believed that Modi's promise that he would bring 'parivartan' would ensure that he became Prime Minister.

So had Modi been true to the promises he made? Had he done well by Benares? The Assi Ghat had certainly changed since I was last here. Where there had once been shanties that housed pilgrims there now was a sort of terrace with pavilions and steps leading down to the river. It was here that Narendra Modi was to give an interview to *India Today* days after my visit to Benares. Other things had changed in this city that Hindus believe is older than time. The bunches of thick, dusty wires that hung over the narrow lanes in the old city and blotted out the light had been put underground in many places and some parts of the city looked cleaner. On earlier visits to this city there was almost not a street that you could walk down without feeling that you were walking on layers of excrement, both human and bovine.

In 2014 on the day that Modi came to file his nomination papers I remember rushing to the nearest Bata shop to buy myself a pair of closed shoes because walking without them meant taking the risk of picking up some form of skin disease from the filthy streets. On this visit my partner Ajit and a friend from Mumbai had come with me and both of them were pleasantly surprised to find Benares not nearly as filthy as I had told them it would be. But not everybody was pleased with the changes Modi had wrought as the MP from Benares. The Mahant families who had looked after the Vishwanath Mandir and its ancient traditions for centuries were furious that their crumbling old homes were being torn down to make way for a 'karidar' (corridor) that would lead down to the river from the temple.

On the evening of May 23 as I sat at home mulling over the magnificent mandate Modi had been given I found myself wondering how I had not noticed that it was only the Mahants, of all the people I interviewed in different parts of India, who said they would not be voting for Modi or Yogi. Why had I not noticed that most of India's voters would not have seen Rahul Gandhi as an alternative to Modi because he had sounded so much like an angry schoolboy during the campaign. The enduring images of him were of the manner in which he had mocked the way Modi spoke, mocked his foreign policy, mocked him for stealing money from the people and 'putting it in the pocket of Anil Ambani'. Of these images the one that remained engraved most vividly in my mind was of Rahul and his sister Priyanka entering Lucknow on the roof of an open truck, with Rahul holding a model of a Rafale fighter jet in his hands.

It was this deal to buy French fighter jets that Rahul had made the leitmotif of his campaign. It was this deal that caused him to yell 'Chowkidar chor hai' (the watchman is a thief) at every public meeting he addressed. Whoever advised him to try and use Rafale to defeat Modi in the election, as his father had been defeated by another arms deal to buy Bofors guns, advised him wrongly. In the Bofors deal there was evidence of bribes having been paid to high officials in the Government of India. With Rafale all that Rahul had was the hope that if he repeated the allegation often enough it would seem like the truth. The charge that Anil Ambani was given Rs 30,000 crore out of a deal whose total worth was around Rs 60,000 crore was in itself absurd. When Rahul Gandhi was asked about this in an interview he gave to the *Indian Express* all he had to say was, 'The benefit to Mr Anil Ambani from the offset contract and all the Rafale proceedings will be Rs 30,000 crore. There is enough documentation available that shows this.'

When the interviewer pointed out in his next question that the offsets did not add up to Rs 30,000 crore the Congress president went into a long diatribe about Anil Ambani having no 'locus standi' to make fighter jets, without answering where he had got the figure from. This was the only time he was questioned about the charge of corruption that he had made against Modi and he was unable to say more than that they had done the calculations and that there were procedural flaws in the deal. He ended his answer by saying something he said often in his campaign speeches, 'I've said to the PM let's have an open debate. You speak for 15 minutes, I'll speak for 15 minutes, let's see who is left standing. The PM won't be able to face the Indian public after a debate on Rafale.'

Had he and his advisors had their ear closer to the ground they would have noticed early on in the campaign that Modi's strongest point was his image of being completely incorruptible. So by attacking him where he was strongest Rahul Gandhi helped Modi. And because he made his charges with such arrogance and disdain he came across as an angry schoolboy instead of as a prospective Prime Minister. He behaved as if people should vote for him because he was entitled to rule India. He ran a bad campaign and Modi benefited enormously from this. But there is little doubt, in retrospect, that there was a wave that went unnoticed by almost everyone who covered this horribly long summer election. Almost the only person I met who said he had seen definite signs of a wave was M.J. Akbar, a minister in Modi's first term. We met by accident on a Vistara flight from Mumbai to Delhi a few weeks before the campaign ended. When we talked about the election he said, 'There is a wave but as I said in a lecture I gave in Mumbai yesterday the thing about a wave is that you don't know it's there till it hits the shore.'

Delhi is a city of political fairytales. It is as if a new one gets written every day and soon everyone starts believing it to be more than a fairytale. In the days before the results came the most popular fairytale was that Rahul Gandhi would become India's next Prime Minister. He believed in this almost more than anyone else did and gave interviews and press conferences in which he talked as if he was already Prime Minister and somehow convinced major political and business magazines that he was India's future leader. They wrote cover stories about his plans for the future and showed him striding purposefully forward or staring meaningfully into the camera. After the results came and Rahul had lost his own seat and got not even enough seats for his party for him to become leader of the opposition in the Lok Sabha they began to weave a new fairytale.

Once more everyone began to believe in it. The new fairytale was that Modi had won for two reasons. The first was that he had 'marketed' himself well and the second that Bharatiya Janata Party (BJP) president Amit Shah had created an election machine that was capable of doing anything. The implication being that he had learned how to manipulate the Election Commission and the entire 'machinery' of winning elections. The man who first told me this new fairytale in long exchanges on WhatsApp sent me lurid details that he said he had got from his friends 'on the ground'. This friend has lived in retirement on a farm in the hills for many, many years. And the only information he would have got 'from the ground' would have come from domestic staff, employees and defeated politicians but he believed implicitly that the 'two bearded men' (Modi and Amit Shah) were wizards at making votes disappear if they had not been cast for them.

In our exchanges on WhatsApp he told me of people who had come out of voting booths and rubbed the indelible ink off their fingers and gone back and voted again many times. He told me of EVM machines that had been altered to cast every vote only for the BJP and he told me of EVM machines that had quite simply disappeared. He sent me pictures of EVM machines lying in ponds. I had seen them before – they were from local elections in West Bengal – and when I pointed this out he sent me long articles written in leftist magazines that hated Modi. It was they who specialized in creating Delhi's political fairytales and in ensuring that they spread far and wide.

So in Mumbai I met a Delhi intellectual soon after Modi was sworn in for the second time as India's Prime Minister. I had met him during the campaign and he had convinced himself and tried to convince me that Modi would get between 220 and 250 seats. 'So you got the election all wrong,' I said when we met again.

'Well, nobody can take on the machinery that they have created,' he said, taking a large sip of red wine.

'What machinery?'

'You know what I am talking about,' he said, 'everyone knows that Amit Shah has built a machinery to win elections that can never fail.'

'So could he have managed to get someone other than Modi elected?'

'No. I am not saying that.'

'Why not? If there is such incredible machinery in place then it should be able to get anyone elected.'

'No. Of course it was Modi's election all the way. All I am saying is that the machinery is something that Congress quite simply does not have.'

'So could Amit Shah have used his machinery to get Rahul Gandhi elected?'

'No. I am not saying that.'

The only person I met in Delhi after the election results who seemed to have analysed what had happened correctly was Arun Jaitley. I had known Arun for more than 40 years. I met him first during the Emergency when he was released from jail. He was arrested along with other opposition leaders because

he was president of the Delhi University Students' Union and
a member of the student wing of the Jana Sangh, an earlier
incarnation of the BJP. I remember him from those days as being
very handsome and unusually passionate about public service.
We remained in touch in the years that went by and it did not
surprise me that Atal Bihari Vajpayee chose to make him a
minister in his Cabinet. It did not surprise me when the second
BJP Prime Minister chose to give him the important portfolios
of defence and finance. Sadly his time in Modi's government was
marred from almost day one by health problems. First, there
was bariatric surgery that caused an infection, then came kidney
problems that required a transplant and finally just before the
general election news came that he needed chemotherapy for a
malignant growth in his thigh.

The side-effects of chemotherapy were so debilitating that
he told the Prime Minister that he would not be able to accept
a position in his new government. It was a few days after this
announcement that Ajit and I went to see him. While waiting
to see him in an elegant sitting room that had wooden flooring
and fine Indian paintings on the wall I pointed to spaces from
which paintings had been taken down. Arun had announced
that he would be giving up the government house on Krishna
Menon Marg that he had been allotted as Finance Minister.
A remarkable thing in itself since most people never leave a
Lutyens bungalow once they get one. I know princes, movie
stars and millionaires who have been forcibly evicted from the
environs of Lutyens' Delhi. I also know senior political leaders
who, if they become chief minister of some state and move out
of Delhi, ensure that they retain their Lutyens bungalows by
forcing one of their children to stand for election.

While waiting to see Arun that evening I remembered that
I had asked him soon after Modi became Prime Minister if he
would make a grand gesture by giving up the official occupation

of Lutyens' Delhi. It is almost completely occupied by officials and politicians and taxpayers' money is used to pay for this privilege that is not given to elected representatives in any other democratic country. I remember that when I asked Arun if Modi would consider such a move he said, 'Not in his first term.' It was now the start of his second term and there were no signs of any of his ministers or MPs giving up this ultimate privilege. I was thinking these thoughts when an aide came to lead us to the room in which Arun sat.

He looked so frail and had lost so much weight since I last saw him just weeks earlier that I was taken aback. He must have noticed because the first thing he said was that the chemotherapy had made it hard for him to keep food down and this led to him feeling drained of all energy. Then the foodie in him surfaced and he said that the odd thing was that he managed to keep mangoes down quite easily and had taken to getting his cook to make 'rabdi' (a Punjabi sweet made of milk and sugar) for him with sugar-free sweetener and that this went down quite well. I think I said that I was shocked to see how much weight he had lost because the last time I had seen him was at a conference on terrorism that Rajat Sharma had organized after the Indian Air Force's cross-border strike on terrorist camps in Balakot in February 2019. He had been a speaker at this conference and looked so well that I was under the impression that he was fully on the mend. He said it was the chemotherapy that had done him in.

Then he changed the subject from his health to politics. I asked if he had expected the BJP to get more than 300 seats and he said he had. 'I said as much in interviews I gave to some of your younger colleagues.'

'I have to say that I didn't think that the BJP would get more than 250 seats on its own. I thought that it would get the seats it needed to form a government with the help of its allies.'

He said, 'This is because of the narrative that was prevalent in the circles in which you move. But what they have not noticed is that more than 40 per cent of Indians are now middle class and aspirational. By 2030 more than 50 per cent of Indians will be middle class. It is from this aspirational middle class that Modi gets his support.' He added that this was also the reason why parties led by hereditary politicians had done badly this time and why parties led by casteist chieftains had failed.

Ajit and I sat with Arun for about 20 minutes. But I noticed that talking was beginning to tire him and suggested to Ajit that we let him rest. On the way to the Oberoi Hotel for a CII dinner I said to Ajit that it was interesting that Arun had noticed from his sickbed what most journalists had not noticed from their travels in rural India. He had noticed that the Indian voter had changed.

In the ballroom of the Oberoi Hotel there were glittering lights and waiters in white uniforms bearing fine single malt whiskey from Scotland and glasses of red and white wine from India. Some carried trays of Indo-European snacks so there were little bits of pizza and quiche and spicy prawns and kebabs. There was the buzz of too many conversations and the crush of too many people. There were diplomats and journalists and some of the richest and most powerful Indian businessmen. It was one of those dinner parties in which there are so many conversations happening at the same time that they all become meaningless. So wiser guests had already migrated to the next room and sat down at tables covered in white tablecloths and laden with fine china and cutlery by the time we arrived.

I was going to suggest to Ajit that we find a place at one of the tables and eat something when I spotted T.N. Ninan. He is one of the finest financial journalists and I grabbed my chance to have a word with him about the state of the economy. He said ominously, 'Indian business is dead.'

'Why don't you write about this?' I asked.

'I have been writing about it,' he said, 'I've been writing about it for months.'

'So what does Modi need to do to bring back private investment?'

'He needs a really powerful Finance Minister, an economic czar,' he said and disappeared into the crush of guests. The next morning he sent me an article he had written four months earlier in which he had listed the names of major Indian companies that were either bankrupt or on the verge of going bankrupt.

Modi's biggest challenge at the start of his second tenure was to revive private investment so that he could find the money to finance the welfare schemes that had defined his first term. Private investment had dried up mostly because he inherited a banking sector that was in dire straits and because he had made the hunt for 'black money' a mission. Black money is a peculiarly Indian idea to describe money on which taxes have not been paid. Often it is because financing political parties is done entirely with black money so businessmen avoid paying taxes on money that they have to in any case give away to politicians as a sort of tax. At one time when tax rates could go up to 97 per cent under Indira Gandhi's socialism, a parallel black economy existed that was almost the size of the white economy. The end of the licence raj in the '90s and a gentler tax regime had brought down most of this black money but there was enough of it sloshing around in the system for Modi to be able to justify his obsession with it.

It was unfortunate that the obsession led him to forget other important aspects of the economy like the need to find new ways to deal with the very bad situation in state-owned banks. There were real reforms needed in labour laws and land acquisition that were pushed on to a back burner for the sake of this hunt for black money.

2

A Defunct Country

THE day after the results came I woke later than usual. So it was a little after 8 a.m. that I checked the messages on my phone. Among the requests from TV channels for 'time' that day was an avalanche of messages from friends. The import of these messages was that Modi had 'stolen' the election. He had done this, they said, by subverting every institution of democracy. He had the Election Commission and the Supreme Court in his pocket and had I not noticed how the intelligence agencies were forced to behave like 'caged parrots'. I tried pointing out that the expression for these agencies was an old one but no argument worked against people who believed that Modi was evil personified.

Nobody was more horrified that Modi had won a second term than the people among whom I had spent my childhood and most of my growing years. With the exception of my sister, Udaya, almost everyone I knew hated Modi. They had convinced themselves that there was not the smallest chance of him becoming Prime Minister again. So during the campaign I had many conversations with several close friends and cousins that went something like this:

'He is definitely going to lose.'

'How can you be so sure?'

'I always rely on what I hear from my servants and they tell me that he has become very unpopular because he hasn't delivered on his promise to give them jobs.'

'Have they not mentioned that their villages have new roads and that the welfare schemes are actually working?'

'Yes...but it's jobs that really matter and although they now have bank accounts, they were expecting to receive that Rs 15 lakh he promised and it hasn't come.'

'You know that he never actually said this...he said Indian money that is believed to have been taken out of this country and stashed in foreign bank accounts is so huge that if it was brought back we could probably give every Indian Rs 15 lakh in their accounts.'

'Stop defending him for God's sake. He is a monster. Have you not been horrified by the lynchings? You've written about them in your columns, so come on, let's admit that the atmosphere he has created is horrible.'

'I have written against the lynchings but have you not noticed that there have been no major riots?'

'I never thought that I would ever be having a conversation like this with you. I am truly appalled at what has happened to you.'

These conversations were with people with whom I spent my childhood and my youth. They are not bad people, just people whose India has always been a tiny world of extreme privilege. A world in which everyone went to boarding school in Dehradun. A world in which summer holidays were always spent in Kashmir or Simla. A world of cantonments and gymkhana clubs, a world in which access was always easy to the highest echelons of political power. In this tiny circuit of privilege, middle-class Indians rarely appeared and poor Indians belonged in another country. Not everyone in this circle was rich but everyone was privileged and everyone spoke English. Not everyone was a supporter of the Imperial Dynasty whose scion was now Congress president but everyone hated Modi because he belonged so clearly to an India that they hoped would never break through the cocoon of privilege in which they had spent their lives. It was these people who Modi labelled as the 'Khan Market gang' in one of the interviews he gave during the campaign. He said he had never been able to win them over in the five years he had been Prime Minister and indicated that he could not care less.

The irony is that they would have liked very much to understand Modi and his popularity better. In the middle of the 2019 election campaign, in the first week of March, there was an *India Today* conclave in Delhi at which most guests belonged to the 'Khan Market gang'. For the two days of the conclave there were sessions on a range of subjects from nationalism and jihadist terrorism to cinema and Brexit. Among the speakers were British politician Boris Johnson and Bollywood stars like Ranveer Singh and Kangana Ranaut.

The star of the conclave was Modi. The air strike on terrorist camps in Balakot had just taken place and it was during the conclave that the Indian Air Force pilot captured by Pakistan returned to India, so the mood was exultantly nationalistic and Modi was everyone's hero. People from his hated 'Khan Market gang' queued up for hours in their jewels and evening clothes to hear him speak at the last session of the conclave. In the vast hall of the Taj Palace where this session took place there was no standing room and everyone listened to him with adulation bordering on wonder.

So Modi may not have been completely correct in his assessment that the 'Khan Market gang' hated him. But there was little doubt that most of the people in this gathering would have found it hard to have a full conversation with Modi about anything. Not just for linguistic reasons but because in their privileged little world the concerns were very different from the things that concerned Modi. It was the last time I was to meet him before the election ended. A small group of us were taken for a private meeting with him. We posed for pictures in formal rows in two different sections. In the more exalted section were TV Today chairman Aroon Purie and his family and Ajit and I were in the lesser section but positioned to stand directly behind the Prime Minister. Before the photographer took our picture Modi walked down the line greeting everyone. He greeted Ajit warmly but I got a cold namaste. I was considered a 'bhakt' or devotee of Modi among my friends but he appeared to think I had been too critical of some of his policies.

This was true. I had been critical of many things that happened on his watch. I thought demonetization was voodoo economics and wrote this in my column. I thought the lynchings of Muslims on suspicion that they ate beef was beyond barbaric. But I was also fully aware that the country Modi took charge of in 2014 had failed in almost every sense and needed change desperately. Having seen countries like Thailand and Indonesia move from India's level of development in the '70s into the middle income category it appalled me that India was unable to provide such basic things as clean drinking water to most of her people. I believed that this was because Congress prime ministers (nearly all from the Dynasty) had not understood the need for 'poor people' to have such things as clean water, electricity or a sanitary environment. From their privileged vantage point poor people had only themselves to blame for choosing to live in squalor. Poverty was so incomprehensible to them that Rahul Gandhi had just before the election in 2014 described it as 'a state of mind'.

In the circle of privileged Indians that surrounded him this was thought of as a clever remark and not a statement of policy. So if someone had said that the tools that could help people escape the horror of poverty were decent schools, halfway decent healthcare and roads it would have mystified them. When the political princelings who made up Rahul Gandhi's inner circle travelled to the constituencies they had inherited from Daddy or Mummy they went in air-conditioned SUVs. In these SUVs usually sat in the very back a help who was in charge of supplies of cold, bottled water, clean food and anything else that might be needed on these journeys into the 'real' India. So it is not that they did not know that the public services that exist in rural India are unusable but that they could not have cared less about this. They never needed to use them. Tokenism was the defining hallmark of Nehruvian socialism and in no area was this more true than in the provision of basic public services to ordinary Indians. Everything built for ordinary Indians was to just about meet the basic needs of tokenism.

The monsoon was late. So June turned into a terrible month for much of India. Reports of drought came from every state that relied on the rains to plant their next crops. In Chennai people stayed up all night to queue up for the two plastic pots of water they would get from the tankers that arrived just before dawn. From rural India came images on TV of small children walking miles to collect a small pot of water for the whole family. Modi had already announced that water would be at the top of his list of priorities in his second term and a special ministry had been set up called Jal Shakti. The secretary in charge of this mission was a friend called Parameswaran Iyer, who was directly responsible for the success of the Swachh Bharat programme in Modi's first term.

We had taken to meeting for breakfast regularly for about two years and so we met in the first week of June for breakfast in the India International Centre. Param is a tall, thin man with fine features who at our breakfasts always orders an Indian 'masala' omelette which he eats as if he has not even tasted it because his concentration is so much on what he is talking about. His passion for helping bring about a sanitation revolution in India made him give up a job with the World Bank in Washington and return to India when Modi announced from the ramparts of the Red Fort on August 15, 2014 that he wanted to end the ancient Indian practice of open defecation that caused terrible diseases to spread and stunted the growth of children. You will read more about the Swachh Bharat Mission in a later chapter.

On the morning that I met Param Iyer for breakfast our discussion was entirely to do with water. He talked of the Israeli model and about how much we needed to learn from countries that had managed to solve their water problems better than we had. That morning all he could tell me about the new water mission was that it was going to be more complicated than Swachh Bharat but that he was looking forward to it. He left promising to keep me posted about the progress of this new mission.

While waiting for my next meeting in the veranda of the India International Centre I watched a dust storm sweep through the garden and wondered if this was a sign that the monsoon was coming. I hoped that it would be in Mumbai by the time I got back in the second week of June. But it did not come. And it did not come in the third week either. What did come was terrible news from Bihar. By the time of the third week of his second term in office while Modi was leading celebrations for Yoga Day (June 21) in Ranchi, TV screens across India began to fill up with horrible images of dead children, covered in grimy white sheets, lying on stretchers in the filthy corridors of a government hospital in Muzaffarpur. In the wards of this hospital, crowded three and four to a bed, lay many more small children who, despite the oxygen masks on their faces and the saline drips stuck in their tiny arms, seemed barely alive. Their mothers, skinny women with large sad eyes staring out of gaunt faces, sat on the floor beside them hoping for the best. But by the time famous TV reporters from Delhi descended in droves and relayed across the country pictures of rotting garbage in the corridors and hospital waste piled outside the children's ward it was clear that most children suffering from Acute Encephalitis Syndrome would not survive. In the end nearly a hundred died.

In a better hospital they may have lived. But the images beamed across India made absolutely clear that this hospital, the Sri Krishna Medical College and Hospital, which was meant to be a teaching hospital, was itself the victim of criminal negligence. Where there should have been drinking water there were broken taps in rusty basins. Where there should have been clean corridors there were open drains and garbage and where there should have been hospital gardens there were junkyards filled with dangerous waste. And in the hospital's backyard were discovered the remains of human beings that had just been thrown there to rot. Some of these remains had been cremated but most had not.

The first session of the new Lok Sabha had just begun when this hospital of horrors made headlines. Modi sent his Health Minister, Harsh Vardhan, to Bihar to see for himself what had caused so many children to die. When the minister arrived he was nearly beaten up by desperate parents. So when the Chief Minister of Bihar, Nitish Kumar, made his visit, shamed into it because of public pressure, he avoided meeting victims. His cavalcade of white SUVs swept into the hospital and then swept out minutes later. The visit made no difference. Children continued to die. Reporters continued to arrive and the more diligent of them went to the villages in which the children had lived and discovered that none of Modi's fine welfare programmes had reached there and the villagers' low caste was as much a cause of their horrific poverty as was the absence of government help.

Nitish Kumar was an ally of Modi. But their relationship had been fraught with tensions. He was Chief Minister of Bihar in alliance with the BJP till 2013 when Modi was declared the BJP's prime ministerial candidate. He resigned in what seemed like a fit of sulks. Beneath his 'humble' exterior beat the heart of a deeply ambitious man whose ambitions had been fanned by fawning 'secular' journalists who lost no chance to speak in glowing terms of his supposed good governance in Bihar. So he dreamed of being Prime Minister. And why not? He was so exalted by a particular section of the Indian media that my old friend Imran Khan, nurturing prime ministerial dreams himself, invited him to Pakistan for consultations on building his own welfare state.

For me personally Nitish was no hero. On my travels in Bihar I had seen that nothing seemed to change except for the worse. I remember especially a long drive from Patna to a distant village called Dharmashati Gandaman in the district of Saran. This was just before the Bihar election in 2015 and my reason for going was that it was in this village school that 23 children had died of poisonous cooking oil on July 16, 2013. The school cook had complained to the headmistress, Meena Kumari, that the oil smelled funny and she was told to shut up and cook. When the children ate their midday meal they complained that the food tasted awful and they were told to shut up and eat it. Half an hour later they started to complain of acute pain in their stomachs and began to die. Sixteen died in the school and the rest in a nearby hospital. Among the dead were the cook's own two children. Nitish Kumar was Chief Minister at the time and the media never really took him to task for allowing such an awful tragedy to happen on his watch.

So why had Modi not noticed in his first term as Prime Minister that healthcare was in terrible shape? When the horrors of the hospital in Muzaffarpur were revealed a lot of people asked this question. They also asked why the Prime Minister had not ensured that the states in which there were BJP governments led by example. The only explanation I could come up with was that Modi was so involved in trying to improve sanitation standards across the country that he had been unable to give healthcare the attention it deserved. In Gujarat he had made a huge difference as Chief Minister. I remember travelling in rural parts of that state in 2006 and being impressed that even small primary health centres in remote Adivasi villages were clean and had doctors and patients. So it was not as if Modi did not know what needed to be done.

The villages in which the dead children had lived were so primitive that they revealed how little change had happened under Nitish Kumar. The children who got sick had lived mostly in windowless hovels of thatch and mud. Their parents were too poor to give them even one nutritious meal a day so they were too malnourished to survive a serious illness. What made things worse for Modi was that the BJP was once more in a coalition government with Nitish Kumar. It harmed Modi's personal image that while the children were dying the BJP Deputy Chief Minister of Bihar, Sushil Modi, was spotted dining with a large group of party legislators in a five-star hotel in Patna. Bihar's Health Minister, also a BJP man, exhibited sickening insensitivity by asking reporters the score of an ongoing cricket match when they went to ask him about the dying children.

What happened in Bihar was so horrific that the media mostly ignored the President's speech to the first joint session of the new Lok Sabha. He painted a wonderful picture of the 'new India' that Modi planned to build in his second term. An India in which everyone had a 'pucca' home with electricity, gas and a toilet. The speech seemed to mock Muzaffarpur's dead children. It was not an auspicious beginning to Modi's second term as Prime Minister. It was not auspicious either that the monsoon was delayed by nearly a month and cities like Mumbai and Chennai were among the cities that the government admitted were running out of water.

Then came news from Mumbai that the Chief Minister had not paid his water bills and that none of his ministers had either. And since this Chief Minister was not just from the BJP but a Rashtriya Swayamsevak Sangh (RSS) man from Nagpur, where the organization has its headquarters, the damage was greater. It did not help that while Maharashtra was reeling under one of the worst droughts in its history the Chief Minister's wife, wearing heavy make-up and dressed in skimpy, glitzy skirts, was posting pictures on Instagram of a musical tour she was on in the United States.

To add to the general sense that the start of Modi's second term was inauspicious came news from Jharkhand of a lynching. A Muslim youth called Tabrez Ansari was caught by the people of the village of Seraikela Kharsawan, tied to a post, and beaten for hours on the suspicion that he was a thief. In the videos, believed to be authentic, the faces of the killers were carefully excluded but their voices were audible and they were forcing him to say 'Jai Sri Ram' and 'Jai Hanuman' while they beat him. The videos went viral on social media. They showed close-ups of the victim's face so that the terror in his eyes was clearly visible and his exhausted pleas for mercy audible. The people were proud of what they did and uploaded the videos to show what they assumed was their valour and their loyalty to Hindutva.

After beating him for hours they handed him to the police who, instead of taking him to hospital, chose to arrest him on suspicion of theft. He may have survived if they had taken him to hospital in time. They did not for five days. It was only when he started showing signs of succumbing to the serious head injury he had sustained while being beaten by the mob did they finally take him to hospital. He was already dead. What made the story worse was that his family, when they heard that he was in jail, had tried to see him and were chased away by the police on the grounds that he was a thief and if they made too much fuss they could be arrested as well.

Modi's second term did not begin auspiciously. In Mumbai till the last week of June there was no sign of the monsoon. In the humid, white misery of long days we waited for rain. Every day there would come a little hope when clouds built up and now and then there was a little rain. It was not monsoon rain but showers brought on by a cyclone called Vayu that had some weeks earlier threatened to hit Gujarat but had then wandered off across the Arabian Sea without making landfall. I met businessmen who admitted that they were less worried about the monsoon than they were about the chances that the Budget would once more indicate that Modi was less interested in reforms like privatization and boosting private investment than he was about proving that he was a povertarian whose only interest was in uplifting the poor.

We talked in the living rooms of high apartments and in cosy restaurants in five-star hotels. And everyone I talked to said the same thing. He needed to sell failed public sector companies. He needed to privatize public sector banks that had been involved in corrupt practices and giving loans to the wrong people. He needed to overcome his obsession with black money and he needed to simplify the only real economic reform he made in his first term: the Goods and Services Tax (GST).

* * *

India was in a state of terminal decay long before Modi became Prime Minister in that summer of 2014. On election travels that year I saw rural schools that were exactly as they had always been since I first started covering elections in 1977. There were the same badly constructed rooms with unpainted walls and dirt floors. Barefoot children in unwashed uniforms sat on the dirt floors and did lessons from grubby, shared textbooks. For the teacher, if there was one, there was a wooden chair and table. One teacher taught every subject from Hindi and history to geography and arithmetic. Learning was so far removed from the purpose of these schools that they served mostly as day-care centres. Children from very poor families came in the mornings, often without even eating a morsel of stale bread or drinking a glass of milkless tea. They waited until the midday meal was served and then went home. Often this meal would be their only meal of the day.

On those travels in 2014 the only real change I noticed since I first travelled in Bihar and Uttar Pradesh more than 40 years ago was the advent of technology. I did not see a single village in which people did not have cell phones and from the roofs of even half-built hovels stuck out cable television dishes. I also noticed that private schools with names like Holy Angels Girls School and International English School had sprouted like a rash. They were usually two-room tenements without playgrounds. But the difference between them and the state schools was that they had teachers who actually seemed to be teaching. Teachers in these private schools were paid much less than government school teachers.

In all the years that I have been a journalist I have not met a single Indian official who sends his children to schools built for the 'common man'.

In Sonia Gandhi's constituency, Rae Bareli, I went to a village called Saini on a dirt road. Rakesh Kumar, who worked as a driver in Delhi, brought me here because this is where he had spent his growing years and this was where his brother and mother still lived. As we bumped along the dirt road he pointed to a small patch of land covered in yellow mustard flowers.

'That's our farm,' he said, 'my brother looks after it. We don't make any money from it but his family manages to somehow live off what they grow.'

'Does he also look after your mother?'

'Yes. But he makes so little from farming that I send money every month from Delhi.'

'How much do you make?'

'It depends on how many jobs I get from the agency. But I make a good living and my wife also works so we have enough to send my mother some money back every month.'

The village was small. It had a cluster of small houses, a tiny square and a temple under a big neem tree. Plastic chairs and a rope bed were brought for us and I began to ask the usual questions. Is there a school? Yes, but the building is in a very bad state so the children have to do their lessons outside. What about a hospital? It is a few kilometres away, they said, but since there is no pucca road we have to carry people there and sometimes pregnant women start going into labour on the way. Everyone in the village had cell phones and there were many homes that had television so technology had brought a whiff of modernity. But not enough to improve public services.

We went to the village school. It had rained and dirty water made a huge puddle in the school's small playground. It was on the edge of this, on soggy ground, that small children sat. The teacher was a small, skinny woman who had pulled her sari up above her ankles to avoid the slushy ground on which she stood. When I asked her why the school was in such bad shape she said, 'The government has not sent any maintenance money for a year.' It was an old story. From the school we drove down muddy roads to the primary health centre. It consisted of four small rooms linked by a corridor that reeked of urine and dirty clothes. But there was a doctor on duty which in itself was something of a miracle. I had seen rural hospitals where trees grew out of the broken roofs of wards in which medicines rotted.

Rural hospitals are sometimes built only so that some politician can make money by giving construction contracts to a friend or a relation. Hygiene is not a word that exists in the lexicon of those charged with looking after these facilities. So if you are a poor Indian villager and get sick it is safer to stay at home and hope for the best. Some surveys estimate that more than 80 per cent of Indians use private healthcare. In these private hospitals and clinics it is often quacks and half-baked doctors that people turn to but a doctor of sorts is better than no doctor at all.

In the India that Modi inherited the 'common man' was deprived of the basic tools for survival in the 21st century. Then there was the squalor to contend with. The idea of urban planning was considered too elitist by the socialists who took charge of India after the British left so they ruined even what there was. I was born three years after the Raj ended and my childhood memories are of beautiful towns and cities. My father was a soldier and so we travelled across India. Every two or three years he was posted to a new army station. This was less than ten years after the Raj ended so these army stations remained British. Officers dressed up in the evenings to go to the mess. And there was always a club in which army wives played tombola in vast halls with high ceilings that had once been ballrooms and we children had our birthday parties. The remarkable thing about these British cantonments was that they were spotlessly clean and so orderly that even trees lining the streets had their trunks regularly painted. I remember that in these cantonments of my childhood grownups talked of the 'civilian' parts of the city as being somehow beneath us.

We sometimes took rickshaws into the decaying bazaars of beautiful old cities like Lucknow and Agra and I remember noticing even as a child that they were filthy, crowded and chaotic. Municipal governance may have been deficient but these were towns that with minimum effort could have been preserved. They were allowed instead to decay. Later when I became a journalist I often wondered why the Nehru-Gandhi dynasty, which knew what beautiful old towns in Europe looked like just by being kept clean and orderly, never did anything to preserve India's towns. There came a lesser breed of 'socialist' political leaders who did even more damage by allowing urbanization to go ahead in haphazard fashion. What little planning there was usually had corruption as its motivation.

Private companies in search of new markets have done more to bring the 21st century to rural Indians than governments. Shops selling cell phones and computers are a common sight in filthy bazaars. On their roofs are advertisements that compete to sell better cell phone services, refrigerators, air conditioners and computers. And as if to remind travellers of a past that has not gone away, there also exist old-fashioned shops selling lentils and spices in open sacks and rice and wheat in large metal cans. Other reminders of the old India are narrow, low-ceilinged tailors shops standing beside grocery shops that sell everything from biscuits and wafers to hair oil.

In 2013 when Modi first indicated that he wanted to spread his wings beyond Gujarat this is what most of India looked like. So it should have surprised nobody that when he talked about the need for 'parivartan' and 'vikas' it resonated with millions of Indians across barriers of caste and creed. The only people it surprised were those who had never seen what Gandhiji's 'real India' looked like except from the safe distance of an aeroplane. What caused India to end up looking like a vast slum was that its planning was entrusted to bureaucrats and planners who sat in offices in Delhi in which not even a whiff of the 'real India' managed to penetrate.

The first time I noticed this was when Rajiv Gandhi was Prime Minister. He was given a mandate that was bigger than for any other Prime Minister ever. Had he known what to do with this mandate he could have transformed India. But he had never lived in a home that was not that of the Prime Minister of India and the only job he ever held was as a pilot in Indian Airlines, so governance was something he knew nothing about. What he discovered after becoming Prime Minister was that Indian bureaucrats could ruin the best laid plans and that the one word they hated more than any other was change. Not only were they unaware of the everyday problems of ordinary Indians, they could not have cared less about them. Rajiv's solution was to surround himself with 'experts'. Of these experts the man he trusted more than any other was Sam Pitroda.

The very same man who helped Modi become Prime Minister in 2019 by making one of the most insensitive remarks ever made. When a reporter asked him about the pogrom against the Sikhs in 1984 he said 'hua toh hua'. It happened so what? Rahul Gandhi made it clear immediately afterwards that he was appalled by this remark. But the damage was done and it was incalculable. In the years that Sonia Gandhi tried to prevent Modi from becoming a national political leader the one charge she made against him repeatedly was that he was responsible for the communal riots in 2002. She famously called him a 'merchant of death'. So for one of her son's close advisors to dismiss India's only actual pogrom as if it were of no consequence did immeasurable harm to the supposedly 'secular' credentials of the Dynasty.

At the time when I first met Sam he was Rajiv Gandhi's knight in shining armour tasked with bringing about a telecommunications revolution in rural India where telephones almost always could only be found in the homes of rich landlords. He had an office in the Akbar Hotel in Delhi. This former five-star hotel retains the quiet elegance it was designed to have when it was built as a five-star hotel. It fell upon bad times, as most government hotels have, because it was run by officials who saw it mostly as a facility for their private use and entertainment.

Most government hotels make no profit even today and some like the Centaur Hotel near Delhi airport have been allowed to fall to complete ruin. It is a scandal but most Indian journalists remain socialist so very few ask why the government should be running hotels in the first place. In any case it was in the Akbar Hotel that Pitroda had his headquarters and it was from here that he set about building his rural telecommunications network. Sadly the little public phone booths he set up became irrelevant almost as soon as they were built because of the arrival of cell phones.

In those halcyon days when I first met him in his office of sunlight and glass walls he had the status of a god. I remember talking to him that afternoon about how desolate most of India looked and he thought I meant that it did not have enough green cover. That was not at all what I meant but his eyes lit up as he suggested that he would tell the Prime Minister to set up a 'greening' mission. He was already in charge of other 'missions' to deal with a range of public services from telecommunications to drinking water. No single person should have been given such a diverse portfolio, especially not someone who had lived most of his adult life in the United States. But that was how things happened in India in the time when prime ministers always came from a particular class and caste.

Modi was India's first Prime Minister who was not just from a poor family but who was low of caste. His first mistake after becoming Prime Minister for the first time was to not tell people that he had inherited a country in which the economy was not the only thing that was in bad shape. Everything was. When I met him a year after he became Prime Minister for the only private conversation I had with him, he said he had made a mistake by not ordering a white paper on the state of the economy. He still had not noticed that he needed a white paper on a hundred other things. Almost every public service in India was in a state of terminal decay.

3

First Term, First Days

THERE were two groups of Indians who hated Modi from day one of his first term as Prime Minister. One can loosely be put into a category that the media soon began to call leftist-liberals and Modi's supporters on social media called 'sickulars'. In this basket were writers, journalists, poets, politicians and retired bureaucrats who had been powerful in Nehruvian socialist times. In the second basket were mostly people that I had grown up with and who Modi later came to call the 'Khan Market gang'. I always thought of this lot as India's traditional ruling elite because the truth is that we ran India through the good offices of those who sulked in the other basket. Most of us knew the Dynasty from having run into them over the years in Delhi's drawing rooms, so if we wanted something done it could usually be done. The only language my friends knew well was English, so they did not understand Modi's speeches or how his mind worked.

When he went to Parliament for the first time and touched his forehead to the floor in obeisance to the 'temple of democracy' a friend said, 'Surely kissing the floor is something that he has borrowed from the Pope. Such a Christian thing to do, wouldn't you say?'

'He did not kiss the ground,' I said wearily, having had this conversation with another friend, 'he bowed his head down like we do in temples and gurudwaras.'

'Well, he looked pretty absurd doing whatever he did…and what about how he burst into tears when he was addressing his MPs in Central Hall. Is that how a Prime Minister should behave?'

'He got emotional…he was talking about his mother. He comes from a poor family and has grown up seeing his mother suffer because of poverty.'

'Oh, so what? I still believe that he has no business to be Prime Minister.'

'But you believe in democracy?'

'Of course.'

'So he has become Prime Minister because of the will of the people of India. Is that not how democracy works?'

'The people…what do the people know about anything? Wasn't it Churchill who once said that the best argument against democracy is a five-minute conversation with the average voter…'

'Maybe. But wasn't it Churchill who also said that democracy is the worst form of government except for all the others?'

The friend I had this conversation with shall remain nameless. His name does not matter anyway because there were so many conversations of this kind that took place in the drawing rooms of Delhi in those early days of Modi's first tenure. He silenced some of these critics with his first speech in

Central Hall where he said, 'It is the power of our Constitution that a poor person belonging to a poor and deprived family is standing here today. This is the power of our Constitution and hallmark of our democratic elections that a common citizen can also reach this height.'

The first minister in Modi's Cabinet whom I met for what I hoped would be a meaningful conversation was Smriti Irani. She had been made Minister of Human Resource Development (HRD), which was the name Rajiv Gandhi had given to what used to be the Education Ministry. I went to meet her because I was passionately interested in finding a way to influence 'parivartan' in what I saw as a system that was broken from top to bottom. I knew Smriti slightly from her days in Mumbai as an actress. Now that she was in charge of a ministry that needed almost more reform than any other I decided to go and meet her. Not so much to have a truly meaningful conversation about the changes needed but to see if she understood at all the importance of the task ahead of her. The Indian education system had failed at every level to provide Indian children with the tools they needed to face a world in which literacy had come to mean computer literacy. Most government schools were so bad that if after leaving school a child could fill a job application correctly in any language it would be surprising.

The crisis had brewed for decades. Congress prime ministers since the time of Nehru had failed to understand that we had a system of education that was neither Indian nor useful to the vast majority of Indian children. This was because Nehru left unchanged the colonial system of mass education created by the British. He added to it tiny frills like the Indian Institutes of Technology and some new universities – all institutions of higher learning and so useful only to educated, high-caste children. Not useful at all for children born of low-caste, illiterate parents crippled by hideous poverty.

Schools are administered by state governments, so this is an excuse Nehru's supporters give to defend his mysterious decision not to have invested in universal primary education. It is a poor defence. Most state governments were run by his party when he was Prime Minister and he liked writing long letters to his chief ministers telling them what to do in even small matters. So, had he wanted to create a system of mass education that allowed children who could not afford private schools to achieve more than basic literacy, he could have done. Most Indian children emerge from government schools to this day without being able to read a story book or count to a hundred. For Indian children who come from rich, privileged families there are excellent private schools but they teach using English as the language of instruction, so they churn out little brown facsimiles of English or American schoolchildren.

Having myself gone to an expensive private boarding school I can say with all honesty that I had not read a single book written by an Indian writer in an Indian language. We read Tagore, Nehru and Gandhi in English and although there were token attempts to teach Hindi and Sanskrit they really were just token. After becoming a journalist I learned both Hindi and Urdu and became finally aware of the magnificence of writing and poetry in these languages. Sanskrit remains a mystery to me to this day. The colonial process that the British sought to create in the hope of producing armies of clerks to run their empire continues well after their departure. Optimists like me hoped this would change when Modi became Prime Minister because in so many ways his victory represented a class revolution. He was India's first truly subaltern Prime Minister.

It was with thoughts of this kind in my head that I went to meet Smriti that afternoon. On the way there I comforted myself with the thought that if highly educated ministers in earlier governments had made such a mess, how much worse could Modi's semi-educated education minister be? He did not get much of an education himself, so how would he know that what makes India lag behind much poorer countries is the failure of successive governments to understand the importance of education? India always comes in the bottom section of international human development indices and the fundamental reason is our failure to build good schools and colleges for the average Indian child.

Smriti Irani's ministerial office was in one of the ugly Soviet-style buildings that sprawl at the feet of Raisina Hill. They are so indistinguishable from one another that even if I go a hundred times to some ministry office I usually fail to remember which Bhawan to go to. This time as usual I flashed my press card in a smelly reception area and shoved my handbag into an X-ray machine. Then I climbed a flight of grimy, grey steps and entered a corridor decorated with potted plants, at the end of which was an ante-room in which a lady told me, 'You might have to wait a little; the minister is already in a meeting.'

This gave me time to ponder over what I should concentrate on asking her in what I thought then would be the first of many meetings. I was hoping that I would be able to persuade the new minister of HRD that she would be doing India a real service if she gave us an education policy that ended the licence raj in education. Ajit runs two engineering colleges in Maharashtra and has often joked about how government control over the education system is so all-embracing that technically a mother cannot tutor her child in science or mathematics without taking permission from the AICTE (All India Council of Technical

Education). I knew from friends who had tried to build private schools and colleges that getting all the permissions needed defeated the most ardent educationists.

Technically, the HRD ministry's only job is to regulate educational standards but the reality is that its officials have such enormous powers that they can even decide what teachers should be paid in private schools and colleges. And what courses they should teach. Under the aegis of the government Sonia Gandhi ran with Dr Manmohan Singh as her proxy, more damage was done to school education by an absurd Right to Education law which did nothing to improve government schools but gave officials much more power to interfere in private schools.

They came under officialdom's jackboot after being ordered to reserve a quota for children from 'economically weak' families. Just before Modi came to power I visited one of Delhi's best private schools to find out how these quotas for 'economically weak' children were working. Senior teachers had gathered in the lady principal's office. Tea arrived and biscuits. The teachers looked at each other to see who would go first and how much they were prepared to trust me. Finally, it was the principal who said, 'The quotas are not working.'

Then suddenly everyone was talking.

'We have the quotas in place and if we don't fill the seats then we can be fined and even closed down. But children whose parents are illiterate need special tuitions to keep up with those who come from educated families. We cannot charge for extra tuitions, so the children don't keep up.'

'But isn't it a good idea to have children from different backgrounds studying together?' I asked the question with genuine curiosity because on paper it seemed like a good idea for everyone from all strata of society to be able to allow their children to mingle and learn from each other. The teachers said this only worked in theory.

'Yes and no,' one of them said, sipping her tea. 'Yes, because this makes it possible for privileged children to see how less privileged children live, but it has its problems. Economically weak children develop all sorts of complexes when they see how their classmates drive away in fancy foreign cars while they have to walk home or take the bus.'

'So what is the solution? Isn't it a good idea to give underprivileged children the possibility of better education?'

'Yes. And we have suggested that the way forward is to ensure that every private school in the country takes under its wing a neighbourhood government school and improves standards in it.'

This was one solution. Another possibly better solution would have been to insist that every Indian child went to the school that was closest to his home. If the children of officials and rich Indians were forced to do this there is no doubt that the schools would improve. I remembered an interview with Kapil Sibal, who had devised for Sonia Gandhi the law that gave Indian children the right to education. I remembered that we had talked in his drawing room and that the walls had been covered in paintings by famous Indian artists. Kapil had been a rich and successful lawyer before becoming a politician and had retained the ability to argue his case well. So with that half-smile that always seemed to linger on his face he had given me a glowing picture of how the Right to Education law would change the face of Indian education. I remember asking him how many poor Indian parents would be able to afford going to court to demand this right and I remember him saying that the point really was that they now had the right to demand good education for their children. It was from this that had come those quotas in the best private schools for underprivileged children. It was because of this misguided law that government absolved itself of the responsibility to improve state schools.

I was still lost in thoughts of this kind when a businessman I knew well from Mumbai emerged from the minister's office. I wondered what had made him one of Smriti's first visitors since he had absolutely no known interest in education. When I was ushered into the presence of the minister I found her seated voluminously in a bright silk sari amid boxes of files. This was her first government job and she seemed thoroughly pleased with herself and with the servile manner in which her aides fawned over her. When they left and we were alone together she started complaining about a 'disobedient' vice-chancellor. This was the vice-chancellor of Delhi University who had introduced a course that involved undergraduate students spending an extra year in university as part of their education. Dinesh Singh's idea, he told me later, was to give them a fuller education outside their immediate disciplines. But some students affiliated to the BJP's student wing, the Akhil Bharatiya Vidyarthi Parishad (ABVP), did not like spending this extra year in college, so they complained to the minister.

She was incensed that the vice-chancellor was making decisions without consulting the ministry and showed me all sorts of files to prove that he had 'gone rogue'. Then she started to gossip about Madhu Kishwar having tweeted against her appointment. Madhu Kishwar understood academia and had tweeted about it being a mistake for Modi to have given charge of improving education to a minister who was semi-educated. 'The Prime Minister is not pleased about this tweet,' Smriti said with a coquettish smile. She seemed to imply that she had special access to the Prime

Minister. To many it was puzzling just why she was made a Cabinet minister without her having had any administrative experience. By the time she had vented her ire against rogue vice-chancellors and Madhu Kishwar there was little time left to discuss anything. So all I managed to suggest was that she disband the University Grants Commission (UGC) and allow universities to raise their own resources, appoint their own professors and decide their own courses. She paid not the slightest attention to what I said.

In my column soon after this encounter with Modi's minister of HRD I wrote, 'The new minister of HRD has the chance to do for higher education what Dr Manmohan Singh did for Indian industry in the Nineties: abolish the licence raj. When she makes her new education policy, she needs to begin by stating that she wants 1,500 new universities to be built over the next five years and anyone who wants to build them will need no licences. The UGC can be restricted to setting standards for accreditation.' What made me write this was that it was that time in the summer when college admissions happen and that year the shortage of colleges was so acute that what they called the 'cut-off' point was nearly 100 per cent in some Delhi University colleges.

This meant that only students who had passed out of school with nearly 100 per cent marks could apply. Kapil Sibal once told me that India needed at least 1,500 new universities to meet the demand. After that he did nothing about building them or allowing private investors to build them mostly because of the licence raj that controlled higher education. Smriti could have begun the process of dismantling it but she seemed to have no idea of the urgency required or of anything else that she needed to do.

Soon she was on the warpath not just with the vice-chancellor of Delhi University but with students in Jawaharlal Nehru University (JNU) and then finally found herself in deep trouble when a Dalit student, Rohith Vemula, killed himself because Hyderabad University expelled him and stopped his fellowship of Rs 25,000 within months of her becoming minister. His fellowship was stopped in July 2015 because under the banner of a Dalit body called Ambedkar Students Association he protested against the death penalty for Yakub Memon, who was convicted for involvement in the 1993 Mumbai bombings. More than 250 people were killed in a terrorist attack that was linked to Pakistani military intelligence. His brother Tiger Memon, the mastermind of this plot, continues to live under the protection of the Pakistani government.

As minister of HRD Smriti Irani should have stayed away from meddling in the affairs of a distant southern university but she did not. She was blamed for Vemula's tragic suicide because a letter written by ABVP students complaining about his activities was forwarded to her and it was at her behest, or so it was said, that his fellowship was stopped and he was forbidden from attending classes or living in the hostel. Vemula tried to make ends meet and somehow complete his studies but failed, so on January 17, 2016, he hanged himself, blaming the 'system' for his death.

His suicide note said, 'The value of a man was reduced to his immediate identity and nearest possibility. To vote. To a number. To a thing. Never was a man treated as a mind. As a glorious thing made up of stardust. In very field, in studies, in streets, in politics, and in dying and living.

'I am writing this kind of letter for the first time. My first time of a final letter. Forgive me if I fail to make sense. Maybe

I was wrong, all the while, in understanding the world. In understanding love, pain, life, death. There was no urgency. But I always was rushing. Desperate to start a life. All the while, some people, for them, life itself is a curse...If there is anything at all I believe, I believe that I can travel to the stars. And know about other worlds.'

Vemula's suicide became a symbol of Smriti Irani's petty meddling in university affairs without ever looking at the grander scheme of things. It also sounded her death knell as minister of HRD. By July of 2016 she was transferred to the Ministry of Textiles. I never got another chance to talk to her about the things she could have done to improve Indian education. But the next time I met her was at a dinner party, where she wore a splendid sari of handloom Benarsi brocade instead of the colourful, factory-produced saris she wore before. And when the 2019 election came around she became its biggest star by defeating Rahul Gandhi in the Dynasty's pocket borough of Amethi. This victory proved her skills as a politician but somehow these skills never got reflected in her role in government. She was a disaster as minister of HRD and almost as much of a disaster when she was moved to the Ministry of Information and Broadcasting.

One fine morning I was taking my dog to the vet in Mumbai when I got a call from Sreenivasan Jain of NDTV asking me what I thought about Ms Irani's new order on 'fake news'. I admitted that I was stuck in a traffic jam with a sick dog in the car and so had not paid attention to what was happening. He said the Ministry of Information and Broadcasting had warned journalists that their accreditation would be withdrawn if they published 'fake news'. And who is going to decide what that is, I asked, and he said that is exactly the point. By the time I got home the order had been hastily withdrawn on the instructions of the Prime Minister's Office and Ms Irani's tenure in this ministry came quickly to an end.

What puzzled me was why the Prime Minister, who was more connected to the digital world than any other Indian politician, had not seen it fit to end the existence of this ministry altogether. It had been irrelevant ever since social media came into being, and with Internet now spreading rapidly into rural India, only those completely desperate for something to watch would be turning to Doordarshan for information. But somehow the ministry continued to exist as if the world had not changed at all from those early days of India's Independence when we copied this ministry from our role model, the Soviet Union. During that brief period between 1975 and 1977 when Indira Gandhi became a dictator, the ministry had played an important role. It was given charge of press censorship and performed this duty with such ruthless efficiency that it became the main source of fake news in India. In newspaper offices we wrote what we were told to and if we tried to write anything worthwhile our stories would come back from the ministry with a red line cancelling them. I tried to circumvent the censors by writing stories that technically came under the category of 'human interest' but found that even a series of articles I wrote on the state of hospitals in Delhi drew the ire of censors.

In those 'dark days', as they came to be known, the media was small enough for censorship to work. There were no private TV channels and only a handful of national newspapers that were mostly in English and so of little consequence except to the tiny elite that controlled India. When Ms Irani became minister of Information and Broadcasting in 2017 there were more than 350 private TV channels, more than 450 million Indians using the Internet and nearly every Indian had a cell phone. So her attempt at threatening journalists was foolish. But her failures in government were forgotten when she defeated Rahul Gandhi. When she took her oath in Parliament as the new MP from Amethi there was thunderous applause and in the media they began to call her the Kingslayer. *Game of Thrones* had just ended its final season as the 2019 election campaign ended.

4

Still Early Days

WHEN I woke up on the morning of July 1, 2019, the monsoon clouds outside my window in Mumbai were so dense that I hesitated to go to my gym that was just a short drive away. As a gym fiend I decided to take my chances. But this short ride that morning felt as if I was driving through a deluge. The monsoon was delayed through the whole month of June. There was almost no rain in the city or in most of Maharashtra. Then suddenly in those four days before the first budget of Modi's second term it rained so much in Mumbai that the city fell apart. Walls crumbled in the slums, killing people. A little girl that morning was trapped under debris. They could hear her cries for water and help, NDTV said on the news I watched on the treadmill, and then no more was heard of her. Schools closed and the government announced that it was best to stay home for the next 48 hours. The weather office said that the rain the city received in those four days was as much as it usually does in the whole month of June. It was not unusual for Mumbai to drown in this season of rain. It happened every year but what I noticed was that the BJP government had not brought the promised 'parivartan' needed in municipal governance.

This was another area in which real change could have happened under Modi. Cities like Mumbai, Delhi and Kolkata are now so huge that the only way to govern them properly would be for them to have elected mayors with the powers to govern that mayors of huge metropolises should have. Why did this not happen? Was it because Modi had not thought of the importance of change in this area? Was it because the Chief Minister of Maharashtra was reluctant to surrender control of a city that worked like an ATM for the rest of the state? Whatever the reason it did not happen and I found myself mulling why as waves of torrential rain swept through the city for days.

It halted briefly on the evening that the celebrated author Amish Tripathi was launching his new book *Raavan: Enemy of Aryavrata*, so Ajit and I drove through rain-washed streets to the launch in the Crossword bookshop. Amish's books sell more than those of almost any other Indian writer. He has mastered the art of taking tales from Indian mythology and history and making them come alive like nobody has been able to do before. So it did not surprise me that the bookshop was crowded with his fans who had braved the rain to get there. What surprised me was that most of his fans were very young. Ajit and I were almost the only elders in a sea of young people. They were all English-speaking and middle-class and would have come from homes in which grandmothers no longer sat children down in the evenings to tell them stories about ancient kings and gods. But when there was a quiz about Amish's earlier books about Shiva and Parvati and Ram and Sita a forest of hands went up.

Everyone knew the answers. Was it the atmosphere of Hindutva that Modi had brought with him?

Ajit and I first met Amish at one of the annual conferences the India Foundation organized in Goa. These conferences drew together writers, journalists, artists, dancers, musicians, social activists and politicians in the hope that there could be built a lobby of thinkers who were not leftist and 'secular'. It was something that needed to be done because India's public square had been dominated since Independence by leftists who only ever used the word 'Hindu' in a pejorative manner. They exalted their idea of secularism to such heights that anyone who said that it was time to acknowledge that Indian thinkers did not need to espouse western secularism because there had always been a separation between religion and the state in Indian civilization was instantly labelled fascist. Or, even more damning in an Indian context, communal. Translated, that word means anti-Muslim. The denigration of the Hindu idea of religion was so successful a project that Indians hardly remembered that behind the idols and the flowers and the elaborate rituals in Hindu temples lay possibly the most modern idea of religion in the world.

The fundamental principle of the Sanatan Dharma is that everyone has a right to their own way of worship, their own gods and their own faith. Since there was no book, no son of God and no Prophet with the 'last message' from God, religious tolerance is woven deep into the fabric of Indian society. It was disappointing for me personally that the India Foundation did not succeed in doing more than holding its annual conferences and that, as the years went by, these gatherings came to be infiltrated by narrow-minded bigots and nationalists of rabid disposition.

I listened to Amish explain to his young audience, on that rainy Mumbai evening, that there was no black and white in Indian thought, so not even Raavan was a complete villain. He was an erudite, accomplished Brahmin who was destroyed by his own ego. I found myself wishing that more people like Amish had been given charge of promoting the Hindu project. Sadly when Ram Madhav, a founder of the India Foundation, became more occupied with his duties as a senior general secretary in the BJP, the India Foundation sort of lost its way and the influence it could have had waned. An example of this was its inability to make important changes in the curriculum of Indian schools.

Some years ago Ajit had invited Amish to be the chief guest at the graduation ceremony of one of the colleges he runs. Amish asked the gathered students how many had studied mathematics and every hand went up. These were engineering students, Ajit told me, so this was inevitable, but when Amish asked them how many had heard of the great Indian mathematical genius Bhaskaracharya, only one hand went up.

A few days after the launch of Amish's new book, Ajit and I went to Delhi. Modi was about to present the first Budget of his second tenure and both of us wanted to be there. Ajit went off, as he usually does, to sit and analyse the Budget with a group of businessmen who are brought together by CII and who comment on it as it unfolds. I watched from home. The Finance Minister, Nirmala Sitharaman, had experience as a spokesperson for the BJP that had trained her to deliver speeches articulately and in comprehensible English. This she did with the presentation of her first Budget. But those who commented on it later on various TV channels said they were disappointed that it had not shown signs of dramatic reforms.

Swaminathan S. Anklesaria Aiyar, whose views on the economy I respect, had this to say on the front page of the *Economic Times* the next day: 'Finance Minister Nirmala Sitharaman's first budget was unexciting and incremental, rather than radical, providing no fiscal boost to accelerate GDP growth to the 8 per cent target for Modi government 2.0.' This and other comments by people who know more about analysing Budgets than I do reminded me that the big disappointment of Modi's first term in office was that he had not made the kind of reforms that would have liberated the Indian economy from the clutches of the state.

When Arun Jaitley presented the first Budget after Modi became Prime Minister, Modi's supporters in big business – and there were many – had hoped for dramatic reforms of the kind Margaret Thatcher and Ronald Reagan had made to withdraw government interference in business and commerce. This was because candidate Modi promised, during his first campaign, that he would make India a country in which it would be easy to do business. So this was not an unrealistic thing to hope for. They hoped for changes in labour laws that would make it easier to sack people. In most Indian states, government permission is required to sack someone who works in an establishment that employs more than a hundred people. So instead of creating new permanent jobs, companies and big industries prefer to employ people on contract.

Land acquisition had become a real problem because of a law passed in the last months of the Sonia-Manmohan government. It legally guaranteed to give farmers more than double the value for their land and this made land acquisition impossible even for vital projects. Arun Jaitley, who was Minister of Defence as well in those first months of Modi's government, said that it had become impossible to acquire land even for defence purposes. Modi tried to make land acquisition and purchase easier through an ordinance but the Congress Party immediately started making a racket about how he was 'anti-poor' and so attempts to reform the land acquisition law were abandoned. Other reforms to move India's bumbling socialist economy towards becoming more market-friendly were not pursued either. So timid was this first Budget that Jaitley presented that economists and businessmen listened to it with deepening and visible dismay.

I saw their faces drop as Jaitley delivered a Budget speech that showed no signs at all of a new direction. What astounded everybody was that he did not even get rid of the regressive and damaging retroactive tax that Pranab Mukherjee had brought in as Finance Minister in the previous government. It had driven away major foreign investors. It was so absurd a tax that technically it allowed for taxes to be imposed retroactively as far back as the East India Company. Not ridding India of this tax was such an obvious mistake that Jaitley's immediate predecessor in Sonia's government, P. Chidambaram, said with barely concealed glee in an interview to Barkha Dutt, 'If we had a full majority, we would definitely have got rid of the retroactive tax.' Pranab Mukherjee was kicked upstairs to Rashtrapati Bhavan soon after he introduced this tax and Chidambaram brought in as Finance Minister to rectify the damage done by it but it was too late by then.

Disappointment with this first Budget did not affect Modi's personal popularity. It reached dizzying heights after his first speech in the Lok Sabha. Ajit and I watched it with a group of friends from business and journalism, and by the time he finished speaking we were in agreement that 'this man can really bring about the change India desperately needs'. As someone who has been a critic of the Congress Party since the time of Indira Gandhi, it pleased me personally that the Lok Sabha itself looked completely changed. The mighty Congress Party that had dominated the house almost forever was now reduced to a ragtag little huddle of MPs. In the front row of this ragtag crew sat Sonia Gandhi with a scowl on her face that deepened as she watched Modi enter the House as Prime Minister and sit where she was used to seeing members of her own family or her chosen prime ministers sit. She made a valiant effort to turn her scowl into a weak smile when he greeted her with a namaste.

When he began to speak I thought I saw the scowl deepen into an ugly frown. I disliked Sonia's political and economic ideas but also had a personal reason to dislike her for what she had done to Ajit's dream of building a model of sustainable Indian urbanization in the form of a hill city called Lavasa near Pune. Sonia ordered it closed down because it was said Ajit had built structures that were at an elevation of over 1,000 metres from sea level, which meant that he needed permission from the central government. For this, Sonia's Environment Minister, Jairam Ramesh, in his first missive ordered the city to be demolished. This was done without anyone from the government visiting Lavasa. Had they actually visited it, they would have noticed that only one structure, the entrance gate, was at an elevation of more than 1,000 metres. Every other structure was in conformity with the Maharashtra government's policy for building hill stations in the Western Ghats. The policy was designed to attract tourism and create new channels of employment.

Lavasa would have been the size of Paris when completed if it had not been suddenly halted by Sonia for vindictive reasons. Some saw it as her revenge against Nationalist Congress Party (NCP) chief Sharad Pawar, whose money she seemed to believe was invested in the city. Sonia may have been in alliance with Pawar in the governments she stitched together in 2004 and 2009 but she never forgave him for raising the issue of her foreignness. This had led to his leaving the Congress Party and forming his own political outfit in 1999. In journalistic circles, people said it was because of me that she had closed Lavasa down. There is no way of knowing what her real reason was for doing what she did, but high officials in her government confirmed that there were 'orders from above' that caused Lavasa to attract Sonia's ire.

Just before the order to demolish Lavasa came, Sonia's best friend, Suman Dubey, had come to stay with his brother-in-law Arun Shourie, who was Lavasa's first and most distinguished citizen. Suman had taken lots of pictures, which he may have shown Sonia. Was this what made her order the first planned Indian city since Chandigarh to be demolished? It's hard to tell, but when in the Lok Sabha that afternoon I watched her frown and saw the twitch in her eyes that indicated irritation, it gave me great pleasure.

What gave me more pleasure was to hear Modi outline a new direction for India. He said it was no longer enough to 'alleviate poverty'. It must be destroyed as an 'enemy of the people of India'. As someone who has always believed that India was poor only because of bad economic policies, I was thrilled to hear him say this. In my journal of June 11 I wrote these words: 'It was his first speech in Parliament or at least in the Lok Sabha and he made possibly the best speech he has ever made. Best not just for its eloquence but for the manner in which he outlined a new direction for India in which poverty was not just something that needed alleviation or antyodaya but something that needed to be destroyed as the enemy of India's people. This was so clear a departure from the romantic "inclusive" nonsense that we have heard for ten years that it took my breath away.'

To me nothing was more typical of the kind of policies that Sonia's government followed than MGNREGA. Originally its full name when it was started in 2006 was the National Rural Employment Guarantee Act. At some point 'Mahatma Gandhi' was attached to its name, possibly to give it more credibility. It was a scheme devised by Sonia's favourite NGOs, which formed a powerful kitchen cabinet that took decisions that should only have been taken by the Cabinet. Sonia's National Advisory Council was extra-constitutional but because the media had always been reverential when it came to India's imperial Dynasty, nobody made a fuss. My problem with it was that to guarantee a family a hundred days of work a year meant that it was really a guarantee to keep them mired in poverty forever. Nobody earning Rs 12,000 a year in those days could hope to do more than get some minimum relief to 'alleviate' their poverty.

In its initial incarnation it involved an expenditure of more than Rs 40,000 crore of taxpayers' money, which in my view could have been much better spent on building schools, hospitals and roads that rural Indians so badly needed. So it delighted me that afternoon during Modi's first speech in the Lok Sabha when he said he had no intention of getting rid of MGNREGA because he did not want people to forget that after ruling India for nearly 70 years the only jobs that the Congress Party had been able to create was to get people to dig ditches.

* * *

In September 2014 we followed Modi to New York. Ajit had work at the United Nations and I wanted to see how Modi would fare on his first foreign trip as Prime Minister. We arrived a day before Modi. It was a beautiful September day with blue skies and the scent of autumn in the air and I would have loved to just loaf around one of my favourite cities in the world, so it annoyed me to have to spend it cloistered in a hall in The Pierre hotel, attending an *India Today* conclave. There was no avoiding this because a dazzling array of economists and political analysts were there to discuss the future of India under Modi.

Jagdish Bhagwati and Arvind Panagariya, who had both supported Modi openly, were there and all manner of BJP leaders big and small from India, including Ram Madhav, who was in charge of arranging which journalists would be allowed to meet Modi. I pleaded with him to let me do an interview for the *Indian Express* and was told politely that no Indian journalists were being allowed interviews with the Prime Minister while he was in the United States. Many journalists had followed Modi here. Ram Madhav explained that this was a time which the Prime Minister had kept for meeting foreign journalists.

In between sessions at this conclave Ajit and I were on our way to have a cup of coffee when we spotted Jairam Ramesh looking even more like a tabla player than usual. He wore Indian clothes but, as if because he was in a foreign country, seemed to have blow-dried his long white hair. He was the man Sonia had chosen to do the hatchet job on Lavasa. Ajit pointed to him and said, 'And here is the man Sonia Gandhi chose to destroy the Indian economy.' He smiled and said he was only following orders, or words to that effect.

I did not bother to stay for his session not just because of the harm he had done but because I could not imagine that he would have anything new to say. Also I thought it would be more worth my while to go and check what was happening at the Palace Hotel, where Modi was staying. It had been taken over entirely by the Indian government. Officials buzzed around busily and Indian journalists flooded the media centre. If there were any foreign journalists there, they remained unseen.

The American media was totally uninterested in Modi. When he arrived the next day there was hardly a mention in the New York newspapers. He attracted attention only when he went to a concert in Central Park where Hugh Jackman introduced him to the crowd as India's new Prime Minister. Modi, for reasons known only to him or his speechwriters, decided to say, 'May the force be with you.' This odd remark found its way on to *The Daily Show*, with host Jon Stewart saying with a huge grin on his face that it was nice to know that in India people took *Star Wars* seriously.

The first thing on Modi's itinerary was a visit to the 9/11 memorial. Us hacks woke at dawn to gather at the Palace Hotel for the shuttle that took us to what used to be called Ground Zero. The last time I had been here was within months of 9/11 when all that was left of the Twin Towers was a vast crater. I remembered a wall of heart-breaking messages from those whose loved ones were so senselessly killed in the name of Islam. I was happy to see that now, 13 years later, there were gardens and fountains and a memorial of grey granite on which the names of the dead were engraved. There was something deeply moving about those names written in stone. So we walked in silence as we read them to ourselves and sometimes softly aloud. Then we waited for an hour in small groups for Modi to arrive.

The group of reporters I stood among were mostly from Delhi and to a man (and woman) hated Modi. They interpreted his visit to the memorial as a special insult to Muslims. I did not see how they made this leap of analysis since almost no Indian

Muslim till that time had shown any support for the worldwide jihad but I said nothing. Since I had openly supported Modi in my column I was already a pariah. Modi arrived wearing a white kurta-pyjama with a shawl draped over one shoulder. When my little group spotted him they immediately started to gossip in sneery tones about his clothes.

'Very Gandhian in white today.'

'Look closely at his shawl. It is a pashmina if not a shahtoosh.'

'Or something by some big western designer.'

'Who knew that he had such a fondness for clothes.'

'And watches.'

'Yes…and his glasses look as if they could be Cartier.' Modi's shawl looked inexpensive to me and I knew that his watch was Indian and his glasses were made in a shop in Ahmedabad.

What surprised me was that none of these policemen of political fashion had ever talked about Sonia Gandhi's collection of shahtoosh shawls. She had more than a hundred (according to stories spread by Kashmiri shawlwallahs) in every imaginable colour. She wore them proudly until her estranged sister-in-law Maneka pointed out that shahtoosh was banned by the Indian government because of the ibex having become an endangered species. If the fashion police in my fraternity had noticed that Sonia's shahtoosh shawls had suddenly disappeared, they did not comment on this.

When Modi walked past us that morning in New York I took a close look at the shawl to confirm that it was neither an expensive Kashmiri one nor particularly attractive. When he saw us he acknowledged our presence with a glance in our direction but made no effort to either smile or talk to us. He walked solemnly past us into the 9/11 memorial, stayed there for a while, and then walked solemnly out. The only time he smiled was when he spotted a small group of Indians who

cheered behind a barricade. They had driven all the way from
Boston, they said, just to get a glimpse of India's new Prime
Minister.

The next day came the highlight of the visit to New York.
Indians of the diaspora had waited for Modi to come to the
United States for a long time. For years he had been denied
a visa by the American government at the instance of human
rights groups which had untruthfully made the case that he was
the first Indian leader to preside over a massacre. These Indians
of the diaspora were said to have held meetings in his support
with an empty chair waiting for him. So his arrival in New
York after his spectacular election victory was something they
wanted to celebrate in a way that nobody would ever forget.

They booked Madison Square Garden to welcome him.
This enormous stadium has the capacity to seat 20,000 people
and is usually only booked for rock stars and major sporting
events. The celebration for Modi was something that America's
Indian community had waited so long for that they managed
to sell all their tickets in what seemed like hours. By the time
we tried to get some there were none available. Ajit somehow
wangled passes for his friend Sam Bhada and me through a
quota reserved for CII. Sam and Ajit went to school together
in Mumbai but he has been a New Yorker for many years. He
came with me reluctantly because he was no supporter of Modi.

We arrived early and found endless queues both outside and
inside. Sam and I had passes of a humbler kind, so we sat so far
from the stage we almost needed binoculars to see what was
happening. Ajit managed to get a seat closer to the stage in the
CII enclosure. In the hour that we waited for Modi to arrive we
were treated to a carnival of Indian popular culture. There were
Bollywood songs and dancing girls, classical Indian dances and
patriotic and religious songs. The moment Modi arrived, the

vast hall exploded with shouts of 'Vande Mataram' and 'Bharat Mata Ki Jai'. And then shouts of 'Modi, Modi, Modi'. I saw more enthusiasm in that vast hall than I had seen at any of his election rallies, and he seemed deeply moved.

Modi made a long and eloquent speech about his dreams for India. The line I wrote down in my journal was: 'Aap logon ne mujhe bahut pyaar diya hai. Main yeh karz chukaoonga aapke sapnon ka Bharat bana kar.' (You people have given me so much love. I will repay it by building the India of your dreams.) At the end of his speech I noticed that Sam was truly moved. 'I am going to save my ticket as a souvenir,' he mumbled as we left. When we got outside I noticed that there was a crowd and a commotion. At the centre of it was Rajdeep Sardesai, who had been one of the TV journalists responsible for creating the impression that the violence in Gujarat in 2002 was the first of its kind. Apparently the problem started when Rajdeep started asking these Indians from America what they thought of Modi. There was a hint of bias in his questions, so the crowd became incensed and there were fisticuffs.

In that moment on that day in Madison Square Garden, Modi was a god. To say anything against him was blasphemy. Indians from the diaspora, tired of being ashamed of the shabby country they came from, really believed for that moment that he would change things enough for them to start being proud of India. I talked to some of those who came that day to this Modi carnival and they said that they wanted simple things to change like the harassment they were subjected to from the instant they landed at an Indian airport. 'The officials start harassing you at immigration and then at customs. Then, all the time you are in India, some official or the other harasses you for something or the other.'

'He will change these things.'

'He will clean up the filthy cities.'

'He will get rid of poverty in the villages.'

'He will modernize India and bring it into the 21st century.'

'He will make India a country in which it is easy to do business.'

'If India changes we will be able to retire at home.'

They had reason to hope. Weeks earlier Modi had made his first address to the nation from the ramparts of the Red Fort and announced the abolition of the Planning Commission. For me this was the most significant thing he had said since becoming Prime Minister. The Planning Commission represented for me the worst aspects of Nehruvian socialism because it was the shiny symbol of an era when most Indians lived in that terrible darkness that comes with illiteracy and extreme poverty and so they left it to a small group of bureaucrats to plan their future for them from an office in Delhi. This centralized planning reached such absurd levels that even decisions like where to build public toilets and primary health centres were made in Yojana Bhawan or the House of Planning.

In the musty, smelly corridors of this House of Planning, noted down by hand in dusty files, lay the future of India. So it was not surprising that most of these plans did not materialize on the ground or that most of rural India remained bereft of such basic human needs as water and primary healthcare. Since most of India remained illiterate long after the era of Nehru and his daughter had passed into history, this idea of centrally planning the future of a vast and diverse country remained unquestioned. The media in those times was a feeble, impoverished and irrelevant entity, so had there even been opinion-makers who could have exposed the flaws of central planning it did not happen. So to hear Modi announce the instant demise of the Planning Commission came as music to my ears.

It was in this speech that he also talked of the importance of sanitation and how his government planned to deal with it through the Swachh Bharat programme. He said it might shock some people that a Prime Minister should talk of building toilets in an Independence Day speech but he came from a poor family and so understood the need for the poor to have some dignity and this would come from living in cleaner surroundings. 'I, therefore, have decided to launch a "Clean India" campaign from the 2nd October this year and carry it forward in four years. I want to make a beginning today itself. All schools in the country should have separate toilets for girls. Only then will our daughters not be compelled to leave school midway.' He urged Indians in this speech to resolve to keep their surroundings clean as their way of participating in the programme to make India less filthy. Not since Mahatma Gandhi had an Indian leader dared point out that most Indian towns and villages were truly, deplorably unsanitary.

But what impressed me most about this speech was the announcement about the Planning Commission. I remember writing in my column after the speech that this could be the first Indian Prime Minister who was not a socialist and who was not encumbered by the rules written in stone for Congress leaders by Jawaharlal Nehru. They were rules emulated carefully from what he saw as the Soviet Union's great march into modernity and equality. The truth about what was really happening in Stalin's Soviet Union was not revealed till much after Nehru died.

Ajit and I followed Modi from New York to Washington. We drove and as we travelled through America's landscape of orderly towns and cities and carefully arranged forests, we stopped along the highway at facilities that sold food and groceries and marvelled at the choice for lunch between fast food and fine dining. We pondered over how magnificent India could be if we could build a cleaner, greener, more orderly country. Like the Indians of the diaspora, we too were infected by the hope that Modi could really take India in a new direction.

This hope was magnified in Washington. President Barack Obama received Modi with more honour than expected for a leader who till just the other day had been treated as a pariah. Most of his events at the White House were closed to Indian journalists, so we gathered at the Willard Hotel, where a media centre had been set up. Here, over spicy Indian snacks and desi chai, we gossiped about our new Prime Minister's ability to fast for nine days twice a year. Even the most hostile members of the pack conceded that this was a remarkable feat.

'It must be something that he learned from the sadhus he met when he disappeared into the Himalayas for those two years.'

'They say there is a Baba who lives in a cave somewhere near Rishikesh who is his Guru. They say it was he who told him to go back to the real world because asceticism was not what he was born for.'

Modi's meetings began at dawn and went on all day and at no stage did he seem tired or inattentive. There may have been more detailed and sympathetic reportage of his visit if he had not broken with the tradition of allowing reporters to travel with him. Since everyone had travelled to New York and Washington on their own steam and without official support, we were kept out of Modi's meetings. But I managed to get invited, courtesy Ajit, to the meeting he had with American businessmen. He made a speech in Hindi at this gathering and promised that under him India would roll out a red carpet for investors instead of red tape. To strengthen his case he reminded them that he was a Gujarati and, as they probably knew, it was said that Gujaratis had money running in their veins instead of blood. Some of the most important American businessmen were there and listened carefully. I ran into Frank Wisner, whom I had known when he was ambassador to India, and he said that the visit had been successful on every level.

It was a moment when everything seemed possible. Modi was Superman and God rolled into one for that moment.

5

Domestic Affairs

AFTER we returned to India, the euphoria of the American visit soon dissipated. This was because on the home front there were few signs of real change. The first people to notice that things were not changing fast enough for India to really take a new road were businessmen. In Mumbai, where I live for a part of every month, I began to notice a gloom start to descend by the end of Modi's first few months in office. Decades of living under the jackboot of an economic dictatorship have taught businessmen to never speak openly about the government. But in whispers they did talk in the salons and forums of India's commercial capital. They said that most of the changes to make it easier to do business in India were cosmetic. Some complained that the Prime Minister's Office had closed its doors to businessmen and that this made it difficult for them to take their grievances to him. When I mentioned this to a BJP leader in Delhi he said, 'He is not going to meet businessmen. They should get used to this.'

Cosmetic efforts to show that India was open for business continued meanwhile and in Mumbai in February 2016 a 'Make in India' week was organized. A magnificent temporary convention centre was built in Bandra where in high-ceilinged exhibition halls products that were already being made in India, from JCB machines to consumer goods, were put on display. Every major businessman came to hear the Prime Minister speak. The Chief Minister of Maharashtra announced that huge investments in the city were imminent. He behaved as if Mumbai had already become a second Singapore. He convinced nobody. In the audience businessmen gossiped among themselves about how nothing was happening on the ground. I spent my time eavesdropping on conversations that went something like this:

'There are no new projects happening.'

'The Companies Act remains so restrictive that to say it has become easier to do business in India is rubbish.'

'Not even the small things have changed...you come into Mumbai airport and the harassment begins at immigration even for Indians. I got stopped for several minutes because I had misplaced my boarding pass. This has become compulsory, now that they have stopped immigration forms for Indian citizens.'

'Try importing something into India and you will see that the regulations remain as complicated.'

They said that Modi talked a lot about India becoming a country that would welcome private and foreign investment but that it was only talk. The ministers he had put in charge of economic ministries were actually doing almost nothing to make a difference. I attended a session in which Arun Jaitley was interviewed by the Indian-American journalist Fareed Zakaria. Fareed asked him what he was going to do about the crisis in public sector banks. Had he considered privatization? Arun said that this was something they would be thinking about at a later date. As things turned out later, it was actually something that they should have been thinking about already because most banks in the public sector were in terrible shape.

Between sessions, Ajit and I managed to have a quiet lunch with Arun. Ajit wanted to talk to him about how Lavasa could be saved from going bankrupt because of the damage done to the project by Sonia. There were high officials from the Finance Ministry with him at this lunch and he told them how Jayanthi Natarajan had come to see him and told him that the project was closed down on the orders of Sonia Gandhi. And how she had been told that as the Minister of Environment appointed by Sonia she must be sure that two projects should never be revived. One was Lavasa and the other was Anil Agarwal's bauxite refinery in Lanjigarh in Odisha. While we were talking, the Chief Minister of Maharashtra walked in and Arun said to him, 'We must help Ajit. He was deliberately targeted by the last government.'

Ajit and I left this lunch feeling really hopeful that something would happen that would help him save what for him was a project into which he had invested not just his money but his heart and soul. He dreamed of making it a city that would become a centre of art, culture, education and tourism. He dreamed that it would become India's model for sustainable urbanization and all he needed from the Maharashtra government was moral support and a public acknowledgement that it was built in total accordance with environmental guidelines. This never came. Ajit tried many, many times to meet the Chief Minister after this lunch but somehow he never had the time. People said it was because when he was Leader of the Opposition in the Maharashtra legislature he had opposed the project and did not know with what face he could now support it. He seemed not to care that the city was already half built and that it had the potential to create more than 1,00,000 jobs if it went ahead.

Already it had transformed the economy of the area that earlier had no economy at all except of the most primitive kind. Villagers burned the already sparse vegetation on denuded hills to frighten animals into coming out in the open. They would then kill them for food and after curing their hides travel six hours to Pune to sell them for meagre sums of money. Ajit built a road that reduced the distance to half an hour. It should have been in the interest of Maharashtra to save the project but the Chief Minister appeared not to think so. It could have been Modi's model 'smart city' because all the water was reused and it was designed such that residents could walk almost anywhere. But somehow nobody cared enough about Lavasa to save it, so despite Ajit's best efforts he was unable to prevent it from going bankrupt.

At a wedding in Delhi, on a balmy pre-winter evening, soon after returning from the United States, I met a businessman who had been such an ardent supporter of Modi that he gave up his business for three years to dedicate all his time to creating a digital platform to reflect Modi's political ideas. Now, mere months after Modi became Prime Minister, he seemed despondent. When I asked him why he said, 'Let me answer that in the words of Peter Drucker...there is nothing quite so useless as doing with great efficiency something that should not be done at all.' When I asked if Modi was doing all the wrong things instead of the right ones, he said he was.

As someone who had openly supported Modi I found it hard not to be dismayed by the slowness with which reform was happening. Why was there no attempt to at least sell public sector companies like Air India that swallowed vast resources that could be spent so much better? Why were projects that had been closed down in the name of the environment by Sonia Gandhi not being helped? Why was a massive Nokia factory in Tamil Nadu allowed to close? Why were foreign companies like Vodafone still being forced to fight court cases against horrendous taxes? Having witnessed the effect that the end of the licence raj had had in the '90s and the transformation that had happened in India because of this one economic reform, I found myself waiting for something similar to take place. It did not.

Instead of liberalizing the economy, as people like me thought he would, Modi appeared to become completely obsessed with finding what he called 'black money'. So obsessed that even on his travels in foreign lands, and there were many in those first few months, he would talk about 'black money'. He did not notice that 'black money' was so peculiarly an Indian concept that in other countries very few people understood what it meant. Money laundering and tax evasion they would have understood better but Modi never made the connection.

He would have known from having been Chief Minister of Gujarat for over 12 years that all elections in India were funded by what he called black money. He would have noticed that most small businesses thrive on black money because paying taxes is so complicated that without the help of a chartered accountant it is not even possible to file tax returns. Small businessmen quite simply cannot afford the luxury of paying a chartered accountant for his services. He would also have noticed that the most corrupt officials are those who work in the income tax department, and yet in those first few months after becoming Prime Minister all he seemed to do was hunt for black money.

In a column that appeared in the *Indian Express* on November 30, 2014, a note of disappointment had already crept in. I wrote, 'The Finance Minister promises to end tax terrorism but in the next breath orders tax inspectors to go forth in search of black money. Vodafone has been given temporary relief by the courts but the retroactive tax remains valid. And although we hear that the government has grandiose plans to improve the decrepit transport systems, power stations and ports it inherited, it continues to refuse to pay those who build them. The infrastructure industry is owed more than Rs 1.5 lakh crore in government dues and this has crippled major companies. No amount of efficiency in announcing new projects will make a difference unless old dues are cleared.'

Someone in the Prime Minister's Office appeared to have noticed because when I next met Modi he said, 'Are you angry with me?' I met him at a glittering gala dinner that India TV chairman Rajat Sharma had organized to celebrate 21 years of his show *Aap Ki Adaalat*. No liquor was served but a feast was arranged for more than 500 people. Among the array of VVIPs were the Prime Minister, the President, several chief ministers and big Bollywood stars like Salman Khan and Shah Rukh Khan. So, other than this snippet of a conversation, it was not possible to discuss anything else with the Prime Minister. I did manage to say that I wanted to come and see him and he said, 'You are most welcome.' But the distance he kept between himself and the Delhi media was so great that most people had no idea whom to even call to seek an appointment.

I ended up calling a lady called Kavita who had once summoned me to meet him when he was Chief Minister of Gujarat. She said she had stopped working in his media department when he became Prime Minister but would call someone who would know whom to call to arrange a meeting with him. Days later I got a call from the Prime Minister's Office asking me to come to '7RCR' the next day. This was the abbreviation used for the Prime Minister's residence, located on 7 Race Course Road, until the road's name was changed to something more Indian and less memorable.

Thrilled that I had been granted an interview I sat down and listed questions that I would ask him. I thought long and hard about them and prepared a list because I knew from the time I met him in Ahmedabad a year earlier that when he gave people time he left it to them to decide how long they should have. At that time, when he had summoned me because of a piece I wrote on the fears of Lutyens' Delhi, we had talked for more than an hour without a single aide's or a telephone call's interruption. In the end it was I who ran out of conversation and said I needed permission to leave as I had a flight to catch.

So it was a huge disappointment to arrive at 7RCR and discover that I was among a group of ten other journalists that included Nalini Singh. Her brother Arun Shourie had turned against Modi already because of not having been made a Cabinet Minister. So sure was he that he would become Finance Minister that he had given a cheerful little interview to Barkha Dutt before the Cabinet was announced in which he virtually said that he would be. When his name was not even on the list of ministers, he became bitter about it. He started speaking against Modi to everyone he met. It was mere weeks after Modi came to power that he invited me to his home in West End for coffee. It was as if he sat in a visible pall of gloom. After some minor chitchat about the excellent quality of the coffee he always served and about Lavasa that had still not recovered from the demolition notice, he said that he was 'disappointed' with my column.

After pondering over his words, as he is wont to do, he said, lowering his already whispery voice, that Modi was never going to do anything by way of reform. I reminded him that many years earlier he was one of the first people who had told me that Modi would become Prime Minister one day. He ignored the interruption and went on to say that in his view all that Modi was going to do was initiate some showpiece projects like the bullet train. He is never going to make the administrative, economic and political reforms that we need so badly, I remember him saying.

So it was something of a puzzle that Shourie's sister was invited for this private audience with Modi. Others in this small group of journalists that I knew were Kanchan Gupta, Kaveree Bamzai, Neerja Chowdhury and R. Jagannathan. I had not been at 7RCR for more than ten years. I used to be on quite good terms with Dr Manmohan Singh when he was Finance Minister in P.V. Narasimha Rao's government but fell out of favour with him once his boss became Sonia Gandhi. So I was never invited for his meetings with the press. As I looked around that morning it surprised me that the only thing that had changed in 7RCR since I was last there to interview Atal Bihari Vajpayee was that the security systems had become more sophisticated. And there was an air-conditioned reception area where we deposited our cell phones. For the rest there were the same neat, municipal-style gardens and rooms modelled on the interiors of lesser hotels. Instead of grand Kashmiri carpets and paintings by fine Indian artists, there were rooms so bland in their wall-to-wall sameness that there was a depressing quality about them.

Rajat Sharma, who knew Modi better than any other journalist, said that Modi was such a loner that he came home late at night and spent the few hours before he slept in digital mode, cruising around in cyberspace. He said he was fascinated by digitization and could spend hours online, examining the sort of things that went on there. When I asked if he did not have friends he could call for a chat or family members he liked confiding in, Rajat said, 'I think the only two people he might call if he has spare time are Arun Jaitley and Amit Shah.' It is always worrying when a leader has no friends and especially worrying in Modi's case.

This was December 5, 2014, just six months since he had become Prime Minister, and already it was being whispered in Delhi's corridors of power that he had a strange inability to interact normally with human beings. I had heard this from a minister who worked closely with him. And from an economist who had worked for earlier governments and who was very well respected I heard an even more worrying titbit. 'I met him,' he said, 'and tried to engage him on economic reforms but it was pointless. He thinks he knows everything.'

Thoughts of this kind went through my head that morning as we waited for the Prime Minister to arrive. We waited in a little oval room that had a wall of glass through which we saw verdant lawns and pots lined up as if they were on parade. We chatted among ourselves. None of us took notes but I wrote down a few things when I got home:

'Most (of the gathered journalists) were typical Delhi hacks of the kind that think they have full knowledge of everything but come from publications nobody has heard of...Before he (the PM) arrived they talked with certainty about chit funds and said they knew that [allegedly] Sahara concealed Mulayam's money, Saradha Mamata's and a Punjabi fund concealed Badal money. Kanchan said that even if Subroto Roy (of Sahara) managed to collect the money to make bail there would be nobody to pay it back to because 90 per cent of the listed investors did not exist.

'When the PM walked in we all stood up and the awe we felt was tangible. He sensed this and seemed amused by it. "Swagat hai aapka," he said and sat down. He wore (a) beige kurta and waistcoat and a very well made pair of desi juttis. He looked slimmer than I remembered him from NYC and as if he had just come from a gym and sauna.

'He said he was seeing small groups of journalists regularly now and that these meetings were off the record but we could ask him anything. We did. On his foreign visits (he said): I wanted to establish a personal equation with major leaders. Abe is the only one I knew well from before. Now I know most of them. On travels in the region: this is where real diplomacy has to be. I have just sent five planeloads of water to Male because their water plant burned down. On Pakistan: the handshake in Kathmandu with Nawaz was just courtesy.'

After he said this one of us should have asked about Hafiz Saeed having just held a huge rally in Lahore with the support of the Sharif brothers. But there were too many questions for anyone to be able to ask a follow-up. Most of the questions were about banal administrative things because when journalists meet a Prime Minister in a group they rarely ask real questions. I asked what was the worst legacy issue he had inherited and he said that it was 'avishvas'. He explained that there was a lack of trust between government departments, between ministers and officials, and between people and the government.

I also managed to ask him about reforms and why they were moving so slowly and he said, 'I read your column about too much centralization in the Ministry of Human Resource Development and what I would like to say to that is there is no possibility of centralization in a country like India.' I am not sure what he meant since the University Grants Commission and the AICTE were virtually running a licence raj in the field of higher education.

The most memorable thing he said in the hour we spent with him was that it was wrong for Subroto Roy, who headed the once mighty Sahara group, to have spent two years in jail for alleged economic offences. Roy, who had once had the most powerful politicians in India eating out of his hand, had been denied bail by a Supreme Court judge because he had been arrogant enough to not turn up for hearings. The charges against him were obscure and bail was set for such an outrageous amount that he had spent his two years in jail trying to raise enough money by selling his properties abroad that included the Plaza Hotel in New York and the Dorchester Hotel in London. He had bought these at the height of India's economic boom when it had seemed like good times would last forever.

It was a time of such exuberance in Indian business circles that the Tata group had bought Jaguar in England, Lakshmi Mittal had bought the mighty French conglomerate Arcelor and renamed it Arcelor Mittal, and Anil Agarwal had become the biggest metal trader in the world. For this he was punished in India by Rahul Gandhi, who decided that a group of Gond Adivasi tribes had the right to claim the entire Niyamgiri range of hills in Odisha on the specious grounds that for them it was their God. The hills are believed to contain the richest bauxite deposits left anywhere and Anil Agarwal set up a refinery at the foot of the hills, calculating that if transportation costs were reduced the price of aluminium internationally could be halved. After spending more than Rs

11,000 crore on building the refinery he was unable to run it because bauxite mining was banned in the Niyamgiri Hills at the behest of Rahul Gandhi.

This was one of the major projects closed by the Sonia-Manmohan government for vaguely defined environmental reasons. One of the things that businessmen hoped would happen after Modi became Prime Minister was that stalled projects of this kind would be given a new lease of life. That morning when we had this private audience with Modi I would have liked to ask him why he had not moved faster in the direction of making India a country in which it would become easier to do business. But I got no chance because instead of an interview what we had with him was a mini press conference. I would have liked to ask other questions like why the lifestyle of his officials showed no signs of change. There were rumours that the Prime Minister was keeping a close watch on corrupt practices but the most corrupt practice of all, which was that taxpayers were paying to keep them living in vast colonial bungalows in Lutyens' Delhi, was left untouched.

Later at some social event I asked Arun Jaitley about this and he said, 'We can't make that kind of change so quickly. It could happen next time we win.' So the officials who worked in the government of a man who called himself the pradhan sevak or prime servant of the people of India continued to live like princes. Land in Lutyens' Delhi is probably the most expensive in India. So, other than the remnants of old families who descended from the contractors who helped Edwin Lutyens build the city of New Delhi, the only people who can afford to live in this part of the city are billionaires. But even they occupy no more than a couple of streets. The rest of this prime real estate is occupied by high officials and elected representatives of some of the poorest people in the world. Behind high walls and high security these humble elected representatives luxuriate in vast bungalows set in acres of lawn at a cost of more than Rs 1.5 lakh crore to the people of India.

By the end of Modi's first six months in office two things became clear. He was not going to make the sort of economic reforms that would reduce the powers of the state. He was not even going to sell public sector companies in which it was completely clear that officials had no business to be like Air India and the Ashoka Hotel. Air India was a bottomless pit. And selling it would have been the first indication that Modi was a true believer in free markets and the dictum that government should not be in the business of doing business. Government hotels had mostly been run into the ground by the time Modi became Prime Minister but there was still the Ashoka Hotel sitting like a sandstone eyesore just behind the Prime Minister's official residence.

It had proved decades earlier that it could not compete with privately run hotels like the Taj and the Oberoi and that if it benefited anyone it was officials. It was here that they came to organize the weddings of their children, with taxpayers subsidizing these private festivities. And it was here that they came to wine and dine with their friends and family. It was also here that our elected representatives stayed at almost no cost until a Lutyens bungalow became available to them or a vast apartment that, if they paid market rents for it, would cost them more than Rs 2 lakh a month. I knew this because of having just rented my own apartment off Aurangzeb Road to a company owned by Modi's close friend Gautam Adani. There were also vast tracts of very expensive land in Lutyens' Delhi that belonged to the ministries of defence and railways that could have been exploited commercially to release funds for development in rural India. But Modi did nothing about this. In

2014 the only real reform he made was to abolish the Planning Commission. Or at least give it a new name.

The other thing that became clear by the end of 2014 was that the Hindutva fanatics in Modi's team were going to be allowed to fully exercise their right to free speech. So a sadhvi whom he had made a junior minister became notorious for calling Muslims names. She did this by playing with the words 'Ramzaade' and 'Haramzaade'. Hindus, she said, were the children of Ram and those who were not Hindu were bastards or 'haramzaade'. Other ministers said equally offensive things. Then there was an ugly incident caught on video of an MP from the Shiv Sena, an ally in Modi's government, trying, it seemed, during the month of Ramzan to force a fasting Muslim waiter to eat a chapatti that he did not think was cooked well enough. This was in the Maharashtra Sadan in Delhi and Modi's enemies in the media – of whom there were many – turned the event into front page news.

What was as worrying as the hate speech by Modi's ministers was that RSS activists started a movement called 'Ghar Wapsi' that invited back into the Hindu fold those Muslims and Christians who were happy to give up their faith in order to 'return home'. When along with these activities also came the usual RSS attempts to treat cow's urine as a panacea for all diseases and an elixir of good health, it began increasingly to seem as if Modi had handed his massive mandate to his alma mater. It was called so because it was under the aegis of the RSS that he had acquired whatever education he had managed to. He left school at a young age to help his father run his railway teashop. Financial difficulties outweighed the pleas by his teachers that he be allowed to complete his education because he was intelligent and good at his studies. When he became a full-time worker in the RSS office in Ahmedabad, it was a man he considered his mentor who noticed that between completing his menial chores Modi liked reading and writing. It was he who encouraged him to complete his education through correspondence courses.

In those first six months of Modi's first term as Prime Minister it was not so much the rise of Hindutva vigilantism that was the problem as the absence of real economic reforms. He had the mandate to bring about the changes that would have created jobs and ended the moribund state that Sonia-Manmohan had left the private sector in. Even Modi's most ardent admirers were beginning to get worried about his seeming reluctance to use his first hundred days to bring about serious economic changes. With his gift of eloquence he could have easily persuaded even the most rabid socialists in India that there had to be a change in economic direction so that jobs could be created by private investors. For this to happen what was needed was changes in labour laws that restricted employment and changes that would restrict the degree of official interference in the private sector.

He could have done this easily because he did not have the restrictions of abandoning the socialist path that had forced P.V. Narasimha Rao to end the licence raj stealthily instead of openly. Had Narasimha Rao been able to explain why it had become necessary to end the licence raj, he would have had more support than he got for his reforms and may even have managed to win the general election he lost in 1996. But he could not have reformed openly because Sonia Gandhi's shadow loomed large over him. As the daughter-in-law of the Prime Minister who had amended the Constitution to insert the words 'socialist' and 'secular' in the description of the Indian Republic, she would never have let him move away from socialism. Narendra Modi did not have these constraints.

* * *

By July 5, 2019, when Modi presented the first Budget of his second term as Prime Minister, it should have been clear that he was not going to take any dramatic steps to demolish the economic dictatorship that had kept most Indians mired in horrendous poverty for decades. It should have been clear that he was no Deng Xiaoping who would say that he could not care less if the cat was black or white as long as it caught mice. It was after Deng dumped Maoist economics into the garbage bin that China had begun to race ahead of India in the '70s. Until then China had lagged so far behind India in economic terms that Indian bureaucrats loved boasting about India's achievements in the forums of the world. They loved talking of the democratic way to lift people out of poverty.

What became clear after Modi's first Budget of his second term was that not only was he no Deng, he was not even P.V. Narasimha Rao, whose Budget in 1991 began the process of the dismantling of India's infamous licence raj. It was because of that first Budget that by the end of the '90s India began the process of creating a middle class. Until then there was a ruling class of a tiny handful of Indians and there were 'the masses'. In the ruling class existed educated, upper-class Indians who were from the higher castes, educated and lived relatively comfortable lives. For the vast majority of Indians there was poverty, illiteracy and deprivation. So Narasimha Rao can be credited with playing the role of India's Deng. But because ten years of Sonia Gandhi's rule had taken India back to socialism, there was a real need for Modi to do something dramatic in the first Budget of his second term. Everyone hoped he would.

As I mentioned in an earlier chapter, I watched the proceedings of this Budget from home. I understand very little about numbers, so it is only later when people who understand them better start explaining them that I can see if there has been a broad change of direction. So, coffee in hand, I sat before my TV screen at home in Delhi and watched Nirmala Sitharaman arrive outside Parliament House. Closely behind her followed an elderly couple who were identified by TV reporters as the Finance Minister's parents.

I knew Nirmala from the days when she was a BJP spokesperson. We met regularly in TV studios to discuss the political issues of the day. I had always been impressed by her ability to articulate clearly her position on even the most difficult subjects. She had about her a prim, professorial manner and always wore beautiful south Indians silk saris.

She kept up this tradition on Budget day and wore a red and gold silk sari that matched the red silk folder, which is called a 'bahi' in Hindi and which contained the Budget. When reporters asked why there was no briefcase this time she said it was time to move away from western habits. The folder she brought the Budget in was made by her aunt and blessed in a famous Mumbai temple before she put the documents in it. These details were reported in the next day's newspapers, as were comments from analysts and economists who mostly said that the Budget was a terrible disappointment.

Aroon Purie, in the July 22, 2019 issue of his magazine, *India Today*, said this: 'In business schools, they tell visionary companies to have a BHAG (pronounced bee-hag; Big Hairy Audacious Goal) or, in new-age terminology, a moonshot. Prime Minister Narendra Modi is a great one for this. He had one in the latest Budget too – to double India's GDP to $5trillion by the end of his second term in 2024. It's easy enough to set a grand target, but whether India can get there is open to question, looking at the ground reality. The economy must grow at 8 per cent over the next five years to get there; what it managed was a five-year low of 6.8 per cent.

'The Budget last week was not a good start. It was a damp squib, in fact, with no "big reform" signals in spite of a resounding electoral victory. There was some declaration of intent: to spend Rs 100 lakh crore over the next five years on infrastructure and connectivity through a government push towards "one nation, one grid". The disinvestment target of Rs 1 lakh crore is also a good beginning, though current market conditions are not conducive to disinvestment.'

On the cover of the magazine was a picture of Modi in a hot air balloon. In this picture he wore a saffron-coloured kurta and on the basket of the balloon written on a saffron banner were the words 'MISSION ECONOMY'. Beside the balloon and also in large letters was written: 'THE 5 TRILLION DOLLAR QUESTION'. Aroon's words, and the words in other articles in this issue of the magazine, resonated with me because I happened to read them while driving on the Mumbai-Goa highway that had been under construction for at least ten years. The landscape I drove through did not resemble a country with dreams of becoming a $5 trillion economy in five years so much as a ravaged wasteland of a country that had not even been able to build such basic things as roads and bridges that survived a season of rain.

Through blinding monsoon rain I noticed that the road had huge ditches which formed muddy puddles of water. Some were vast and posed an imminent danger to drivers. The countryside was bleak wherever it had been touched by human endeavour. There were townships, many half-built, that were no more than clusters of tall, utilitarian buildings built so carelessly that they seemed not to have paid any attention to beauty or design. There were villages with little hovel-like houses that were as ugly in a lesser way. And there were craggy cliffs of mud and stone, which was what remained of the hills that had been torn down to build the highway. But then we drove into the Karnala bird sanctuary and it was hard not to gasp at the stunning beauty of the jungles that spread upwards towards more hills covered in trees. The rains had turned rice fields beyond the sanctuary into peridot carpets that shone in the dull topaz water in which they lay.

I found myself wondering as always why a country so spectacularly endowed with nature's gifts still looked far from being even a halfway developed country. But then I remembered the speech Modi himself had made in Varanasi a day after the Budget was presented in which he told BJP workers that the goal of making India a $5 trillion economy was no pipedream. He said that when he became Prime Minister India's economy had only reached $1 trillion after 70 years of being an independent nation. In the five years of his rule he had managed to speed up economic development so much that he had doubled the size of the economy in one term. So why would he not be able to achieve the goal he had set for himself? Do not listen to pessimists, he added, there is a professional breed of people who spend their time spreading negativity. He meant the media but did not say so. And I found myself wondering if he knew that thousands of high-income Indians had left India for good and had settled in places like Dubai and Singapore. According to data compiled by Ruchir Sharma of Morgan Stanley, 23,000 dollar millionaires had left India since 2014.

Modi's weakest point in his first term was his inability to put what his Finance Minister in the second term called the 'animal spirits' back into the economy. She said this at a CII dinner on Budget night. She seemed to sense that the gathering of some of India's richest businessmen was disappointed and said, pursing her thin lips tightly, that she had done whatever she could to make it easier to do business. It is now up to you, she said, to put the animal spirits in by investing. Private investment and new jobs had almost dried up in Modi's first term. So why did he win again? And with a mandate bigger than the one he first got. I was brooding over these questions one morning, two weeks after the Budget, when an interview with Rahul Gandhi popped up on my Instagram account.

It was just a clip of the interview he had given on May 13, 2019, in a small market town in Punjab called Khanna. The interview was to journalists from a channel called News Nation and he sounded cocky and cheerful. He said that Modi had given to the people of India only pain in the past five years, which was why within ten days (the election results came on May 23) he would lose. He explained why. He said that all that Modi had given the people of India was demonetization and the Gabbar Singh Tax. This was his way of mocking GST (the Goods and Services Tax), which was the only real economic reform that Modi had brought. Gabbar Singh was the dacoit in the famous Bollywood film *Sholay* and Rahul Gandhi implied that Modi had used the tax to loot ordinary Indians. He clarified exactly what he meant by adding that Modi had given Rs 30,000 crore to 'his friend' Anil Ambani but had not given ordinary people the Rs 15 lakh he had promised in his last election campaign.

In this same interview he said, as he had said many times in campaign speeches and other interviews, that Modi had insulted his family. He hates my family so he can do this but I come from the Congress Party and so I will always return his hate with love, he said.

Most of his speeches during the campaign sounded exactly as confused and arrogant as this interview, so one reason why Modi won again so handsomely was that, of the two, he seemed like the better man. Compared to Rahul Gandhi he was the more credible leader.

6

The Suit

WHEN was it that I first noticed that the euphoria of those first weeks of Modi's first term was beginning to wane? Perhaps it was on that gloomy, grey morning in January 2015. I was sitting in my car outside a veterinary hospital in Gurgaon reading my newspapers while my dog, Rani, was being given a drip inside. She was very sick and did not make it in the end and it was this that was causing the morning to seem so gloomy.

My reason for reading the day's newspapers while I waited was to take my mind off what might happen to Rani. I found that the words swam before my eyes and I could not really concentrate on reading and it was then that I saw the first pictures of 'the suit'. The pictures were of Modi in a dark suit and were prominently displayed on the front pages of most Delhi newspapers. Modi smiled happily in what seemed like an ordinary pinstriped suit. Then I looked more closely and saw that the pinstripes were enlarged in big red bubbles with fat arrows pointing to the letters that vertically spelt 'Narendra Damodardas Modi'. The suit became a big national story by the next day. So big that it almost became a bigger story than Barack Obama coming to India as chief guest for the Republic Day parade. Modi's detractors, and there were many from day one, mocked his vanity and his lack of taste. And I found myself wondering if I had misjudged Modi altogether. If he had the spiritual side that I believed he did, where did vanity fit in?

My reason for openly supporting Modi was not just because he was the choice of the Indian people, but because having grown up in Lutyens' Delhi and having understood well the corrupt, entitled nature of our political class it pleased me to see Modi rise to the top. Since India became an independent nation, political power at its highest echelons was controlled by people who were mostly upper caste, privileged and cocooned in an India that had nothing to do with the real India. A handful of token Dalit and Adivasi leaders were encouraged to pierce through this cocoon, but in all the years of my childhood and youth political, military, bureaucratic and social power lay in the hands of people like me – people who were born to privilege.

My grandfather was one of the contractors who worked with Edwin Lutyens to build New Delhi and it was in this most privileged of enclaves that I spent much of my childhood and life. In the days of my childhood it was not the centre of political power that it is today but it was always an enclave of privilege. We who grew up in its streets filled with flowering trees and soft breezes had no idea that most Indians did not live like we did. We knew India was a poor country because we had domestic staff who came from poor, rural places and we knew from cousins who lived in foreign lands that there were countries in which beggars in rags did not clamber about you at traffic lights. We spoke English as our first language, went to English boarding schools, read only English literature and appreciated western civilization so much that we never found it in ourselves to explore our own. It was a very colonized, blinkered world we lived in.

My childhood memories are of people who came from princely and feudal families and who lived in large houses in Lutyens' Delhi. We sneered at the first businessmen who came among us because even if they were rich they seemed common. It was in the time that Rajiv Gandhi was Prime Minister that I first saw a denizen of a famous business family move into a house on what used to be called Ratendon Road and is now Amrita Shergill Marg. The family was much richer than we were, so we liked going to their home for wine-soaked garden parties that we could not afford but we sneered at their taste. It did not take them long to acquire 'taste' as we saw it. It did not take long for Amrita Shergill Marg to become an enclave of India's richest businessmen. It is today one of only two or three roads in the city that Lutyens built that is not occupied entirely by official residences.

Power has shifted into the hands of a new political elite. It is because I consider this a good thing that I welcomed Modi's rise to the pinnacle of political power. Another reason is that I despise hereditary democracy and the courtiers and sycophants it has spawned, making a mockery of democracy. I have been witness to the rise of hereditary democracy because I took my first steps in journalism when it began. I got my first job in Indian journalism a month before Mrs Gandhi used the Emergency to hand the reins of her government and the Congress Party to her younger son, Sanjay.

It was in the summer of 1975. I remember vividly that hot summer morning when my mother woke me to tell me, in a voice filled with alarm and excitement, that she had heard on the radio that India was now under a state of internal Emergency. She balanced a bulky transistor radio in her hands and turned it towards me so I could better hear Mrs Gandhi's thin, girlish voice announcing it. Her speech was being played over and over again. It was very early in the morning but I remember white, hot sunlight was pouring in through the curtains of my bedroom window. I must get to the office, I remember telling my mother, before gulping down a glass of tea and racing off.

In the reporters' room of *The Statesman* there was both exhilaration, because journalists love being witness to history, and fear, because nobody was sure if the newspaper would be able to continue employing us if press censorship and the Emergency lasted for years. I was living with my parents but I needed my job. Jobs in journalism were so difficult to get that it had taken me more than a year after coming back to India to get my first job. One reason why I had gone to England to work as a trainee reporter in the first place was that I had not been able to find a job in India. I wrote only in English in those days and there were only a handful of newspapers and magazines to choose from. Would I get another job ever again, I remember thinking gloomily as we drank endless cups of tea and chatted about the editor's decision to defy censorship and print blank spaces on the front page of the paper where stories about the arrest of the opposition leaders had been censored.

The Indian media was a small, harmless creature in 1975 and it was easy to impose censorship. After declaring her Emergency all that Mrs Gandhi needed to do by way of censorship on that first night was to turn off the power supply to Bahadur Shah

Zafar Marg, where most newspapers had their offices. *The Statesman* and *Hindustan Times* escaped this move because their offices were in Connaught Place. There were no private TV channels and no social media, so censorship was easy to impose in totality. We could not report what was happening but we could see, so it soon became evident that the man who was ensuring that censorship was total was Sanjay Gandhi. We also discovered that he was virtually ruling India on his mother's behalf. This came as a shock to me personally because I knew Sanjay socially and knew that he was a man without political ideas. Now he was Mrs Gandhi's heir. More important than any Cabinet minister. And the Congress Party was such a tame creature by then that its president Dev Kant Barooah's most famous response to the declaration of the Emergency was to announce that 'India is Indira and Indira is India.'

By the time Modi became Prime Minister the highest echelons of political power were fully occupied by a small elite group of 'socialist' leaders. They called themselves socialist but lived like princes and made pots of money for themselves and their families while speaking all the time about the importance of 'socialism' and 'secularism' for India. The highest bureaucrats supported them fully and corruption had seeped into the very soul of India. High officials became as mysteriously rich, despite their low salaries, as political leaders did while the vast majority of Indians struggled to survive in horrible poverty.

Modi had my support because he seemed to represent an India that had long been denied a say in the running of the country. There had been BJP leaders before him and even a BJP Prime Minister who survived a full term. But Atal Bihari Vajpayee was a learned Brahmin who mingled easily in the exalted realms of Delhi where it was hard for those who were not high-born to find standing room. It had been this way from even before India won Independence from the British. Those who led the freedom movement were nearly all English-speaking, middle-class and well-educated people. Many of them studied in fine western universities and were Indian only in name.

This was especially true of the civil service that at Independence consisted entirely of high-born Indians who were so westernized that very few spoke Indian languages. They had contempt for political leaders who came from rougher, more rural families and the deepest respect for India's first Prime Minister, Jawaharlal Nehru, whom they saw as not just high-born and patrician but almost British. So the process of colonization continued long after the British left.

When Modi became Prime Minister he was advised by analysts of elitist disposition to try and become like Vajpayee, meaning by this that he should continue with the Nehruvian political culture that Atalji made no effort to change. They did not realize that Modi represented something else altogether. Not only was he low of caste but came from a very poor family from a small town in Gujarat that nobody had heard of till he became Chief Minister. He had the rough edges of a man who had risen from the ranks and a romantic back story. He ran away from home in his teens when his family married him off against his wishes. Nobody knew where he went. He vanished for two years and then returned home with no belongings other than a cloth bag in which he had a change of clothes and a few rupees.

He soon left home again and found his way to Ahmedabad, where he survived by doing menial jobs in the RSS office and enrolled for a correspondence course with Delhi University. It was not the sort of education that opened doors in Lutyens' Delhi. So hardly anyone outside the BJP knew of him in the days when he lived for several years in a small room behind the party office. He shared this room with another RSS worker called Govindacharya.

Modi was not the sort of BJP worker expected to rise to dizzying heights within the party, and if he was chosen by Lal Krishna Advani to travel with him on his famous 'rath yatra' to Ayodhya in September-October 1990 it was to act as a general gofer and odd-job man. It was when the 'rath yatra' reached Delhi that I saw him for the first time. He stood on one side of Advani and on the other side was Pramod Mahajan, whom I knew as an important leader from Maharashtra. I paid no attention to the bearded man on the other side because there was too much else to pay attention to.

The Toyota van on whose open top Advani and his two charioteers rode had been dressed up to look like an ancient chariot of the kind the god-king Rama may have used. Ahead of the 'chariot' pranced a parade of painted and costumed people who donned clothes and hairstyles copied from ancient Hindu statues. Most of those in the parade were bare-chested and carried fake weapons of the antique kind. Some had painted their skins blue to look like the god Krishna, and some in shades of saffron and monkey masks resembled the god Hanuman. It was a carnival so weird and wondrous that few people noticed the bearded man standing on the chariot beside Advani.

The grand finale of Advani's chariot ride from the Somnath temple in Gujarat to Ayodhya was the demolition of the Babri Masjid that stood at the site believed to be the birthplace of Rama two years later on December 6, 1992. Through it all Modi remained no more than an obscure BJP worker living in his small room in the BJP's main Delhi office, 11 Ashoka Road. I remember the room because I sometimes went there to meet his roommate Govindacharya. I remember that it had almost no furniture other than two narrow beds and two small tables and that it resembled the servants' quarters in the bungalows of Lutyens' Delhi. Had I any inkling at all that the man who shared this room with Govindacharya (then considered by journalists to be the RSS resident intellectual) was going to one day become India's Prime Minister I would have paid more attention to the room and him.

As things turned out I did not have a real conversation with Modi until more than ten years later when he had become notorious for having allegedly organized the massacre of Muslims in Gujarat in 2002 as the Chief Minister of the state. Shekhar Gupta, editor of the *Indian Express* at the time, asked me to go to Gujarat a year after the violence to report on the aftermath. So I took a night train from Mumbai's Bandra railway station to Godhra, where I was to meet a photographer. We drove through villages that had seen the worst violence and then on to Ahmedabad, where I hoped to meet the man who had now become notorious for his alleged role in the 'pogrom'.

What I remember from that night journey to Godhra was that I was sickened by how filthy Bandra railway station was. Bandra is where the shining stars of Bollywood live in fine bungalows that face the sea. Bandra is where famous cosmetic surgeons have their clinics to which stars come discreetly at night to have their faces repaired with Botox and fillers. Bandra is famous for its fine restaurants and shopping arcades, so the railway station – a fine old British building from the outside – came as a shock. While waiting for the train to Godhra I noticed that the platform smelled like a latrine but a lot of public places in India reek of urine and human excrement, so I paid no attention till I noticed that beside the track was a long line of defecators. They came in a steady stream from the slums that sat on the edge of the railway station. Open defecation until Modi became Prime Minister was normal in India.

What horrified me was that they were defecating on a piece of public land that appeared to be layered entirely with human faeces. Stray dogs and barefoot children wandered among the defecators. For their part the defecators behaved as if it were perfectly normal for evenings in Bandra to be spent this way. The train was late, so I had a whole hour to gawp at the defecators. They were all men and children and they chatted to each other as if they were at a social event. The sound of Hindi movie songs came from the slum. Indians who lived in slums in this pre-Modi era had no option but to use railway tracks as latrines. What shocked me was that this should be happening in Bandra.

When I got to Ahmedabad at the end of a long, painful journey filled with terrible stories of violence I called Modi's office and was given an appointment immediately. But when I got to his office he did not ask me in. When he saw me standing in the doorway he looked up from the desk he sat behind and gave me a cold, long stare. Then he said, 'You have known me from the time when I worked in Delhi. Right? So how could you believe that I organized the violence?' That was the end of my first interview with Modi.

I did not meet him again till years later, when he had won his third term as Chief Minister of Gujarat and set his eyes firmly on becoming Prime Minister. By then in the eyes of most Indians he had been absolved. So the man I met for this second interview already had a prime ministerial air about him. He had a new office in a new building. It was Spartan and neat, with tiny pots of Chinese bamboo as decoration and so little else that it looked more like a meditation cave than a politician's office. It worried me a bit that from the moment I entered this new building I saw monitors with Modi's face on them everywhere. This indicated vanity but once I was inside his office I forgot them.

He told me that he had asked for me to come to Ahmedabad because he liked the article I had written in my *Express* column about how the dwellers of Lutyens' Delhi were quaking at the thought of him becoming Prime Minister. 'It's true that I never belonged to Delhi even though I worked and lived there for years,' he said. He told me that he had never wanted to be a politician. His inclinations, he said, had always been spiritual, which was why he had run away when his parents forced marriage and domesticity upon him.

He talked of how India had become a country that was consumed by despair. This needed to change, he said, and there needed to be a new direction so that young Indians could learn to hope once more. In that hour I spent with him I got the impression of a man who seemed completely dedicated to transforming India and its corrupt, elitist political culture. So when those pictures of him in that suit appeared I was taken aback. It indicated the sort of vanity that destroys politicians, especially those who dedicate themselves to 'really doing something'. He wore it for a banquet in Rashtrapati Bhawan in honour of President Obama and his wife, and the other surprising thing was that he graced Sonia Gandhi with a seat at the high table right next to Michelle Obama.

Modi was so fooled by the euphoria of his first months in office that he seemed not to notice that Sonia and her son had never accepted him as Prime Minister. Not even on the day the results of the general election came, on May 16, 2014, and it became obvious that he had helped the BJP form its first majority government in Delhi did Sonia seem to show that she accepted Modi as India's future Prime Minister. When it became clear that the Congress Party had been reduced to the lowest point in its long history, Sonia and Rahul Gandhi made a joint appearance at the party's headquarters to concede defeat. She scowled as she congratulated the 'new government' but did this without mentioning Modi's name. Had Modi not noticed this? Had he not noticed that she might interpret her placement at the high table at the banquet for the Obamas as a sign of weakness?

It soon became obvious that this was exactly how she had interpreted it. Within weeks of the Republic Day celebrations the Congress Party began its attacks on Modi. Rahul Gandhi's first reaction to the election results was to disappear. Later we learned that he spent several weeks in early 2015 on a secret vacation at an undisclosed meditation retreat in Thailand. He came back a new man. When he appeared in the Lok Sabha for the first time after his holiday he used Modi's suit to mock him for running a 'suit-boot ki sarkar'. A government for people who could afford to wear suits and boots.

This remark not only seemed to terrify Modi, it made him retreat from the new economic road he was taking and flee back on to the socialist road that Sonia Gandhi had set. It was not a road that had prosperity as its goal but only the 'alleviation' of poverty. In the '90s, a process of economic reform had started to dismantle the vast infrastructure of statist charity, and the money saved was used to build rural roads and other things vital to development. But once Sonia Gandhi put her stamp on the government she remote-controlled for a decade, she reversed this process and went back to the old idea of throwing crumbs off the high table to India's desperately poor people while their 'socialist' representatives continued to live like colonial potentates. Candidate Modi made it clear that he wanted to change this. During the election campaign he talked in his public speeches about creating a new Indian dream of prosperity and economic change. He said often that he saw no reason at all for India to have remained a poor country. But no sooner did the 'suit-boot' jibe come than he changed course and started to bang on about how his government worked only for the poor.

He could have responded to the jibe by throwing it right back in Rahul Gandhi's face by saying something like, 'I dream of an India in which every Indian will be able to afford suits and boots.' Instead, his confidence seemed to crumble completely. The whole mood of the government changed. Or was this only what people like me thought happened? Was Modi always going to take only the road long travelled by Congress prime ministers? Was he in his heart of hearts as keen on government controlling the main levers of economic power as they had been?

I remembered that in Davos that year, weeks before Rahul made his 'suit-boot' jibe, I had a disturbing conversation with an official from the Finance Ministry at the India Evening. This event is a fixture at the World Economic Forum's annual meeting and in the more than 20 years that I have gone to Davos with Ajit I use it as a barometer of how the world is viewing India. In years when investors were flocking to our shores there would be nearly as many foreign businessmen in attendance as Indians. On this particular evening there were not as many as I had seen at the India Evenings of yore. But while cruising around through the scent of Indian spices and waiters bearing trays of wine I somehow ended up in conversation with this official. As I remember it he saw me and introduced himself and we struck up a conversation that I remember going like this:

'It's such a shame,' I said, 'that the retroactive tax has not yet been thrown into the garbage bin of bad laws.'

He bristled with indignation and said arrogantly, 'The Government of India should never give up any of its powers. It is a bad idea to do this.'

'But it's the reason why foreign investors began to flee...'

'So what?'

'Don't you want to send a signal that the Indian government can now be trusted not to retroactively tax foreign investors?'

'No. The Indian government must never give up any of its powers to do anything.'

This made me reel with shock and realize that this conversation was going nowhere. It was at this point that I spotted Arun Jaitley, his boss, and used this as an excuse to flee. Arun and I had known each other a long time, so I felt I could be frank with him. I took him aside and said that as a friend I wanted to advise him not to fall into the traps that his bureaucrats would lay for him. I am not sure he understood exactly what I meant but nodded his assent in the manner of indulging a schoolgirl.

In Davos that year he was at least a serious, credible minister of the new government. The others strutted about the congress centre like peacocks, but in the sessions they addressed they talked of things that were of interest only to Indians. Taxpayers' money seemed to have been wasted on sending them to this forum because they talked to Indians, for Indians and about

Indians at one of the most celebrated international annual meetings in the world. The only remarkable thing they achieved was to exhibit extreme arrogance.

One snowy evening I happened to be chatting to an Indian businessman in the lobby of the Central Sport Hotel, where most Indians stay, when a newly appointed minister, whom I knew well, arrived. He plonked himself down and started talking to the businessman, ignoring me with such deliberate offensiveness that I had no choice but to get up and leave. Until Modi made him a powerful minister he was unknown outside the municipal limits of Mumbai. Others there of similar ilk behaved with similar arrogance. Indian businessmen, before whom they had earlier gone on their knees to beg for money and favours, they now treated with disdain.

The businessmen noticed. Over evening drinks and dinner – and in Davos there are many every night – Indian industrialists with famous names gossiped about how Modi seemed to have put small men in positions of huge importance. They gossiped about how the new ministers had neither the technical qualifications to handle vital ministries nor the humility to seek the advice of those who did. These were businessmen who had supported Modi for years and invested generously in his election campaign, but who within six months were already disappointed with the slowness with which the new government was addressing serious 'legacy issues' like bankrupt banks and stalled projects.

Some, like Vedanta's aluminium refinery in the shadow of the Niyamgiri Hills in Odisha, were closed out of spite rather than for environmental reasons. The bureaucrat whose report formed the basis for the closure of this project himself admitted in an interview to the *Indian Express* that Vedanta had brought prosperity, schools, jobs and other things and that he would not have closed the plant down had it created 500 more jobs. This should have been easy enough to do for a company that was investing thousands of crores of rupees in a refinery, but somehow no fuss was made about the wrongful closure of a project that could have transformed the state. Not even when Sonia Gandhi's chosen Minister of Environment, Jayanthi Natarajan, said in the early months of 2015 that she had rejected environmental clearance to the Vedanta project in response to 'requests' from the Gandhis. Had this not happened it is possible that the desperately poor state could have been transformed by this one project into the world's centre of aluminium production.

It should have been a priority of the Modi government to get projects of this scale working again but somehow all they did was talk about reviving them. Lavasa was another such project. Modi had personally visited Lavasa when it was still running as a proper city and was so impressed with it he asked Ajit if he would build something similar in the special investment region of Dholera in Gujarat. That project never took off because it did not have the infrastructure or the funds to sustain it but when Modi as Prime Minister began his talk of building 'smart cities' I was personally convinced that he based this idea on Lavasa.

Ajit had more than one reason to hope that the Modi government would at least declare his city an infrastructure project so that he could find it easier to refinance it. His reasons were based on Arun Jaitley having said to the Chief Minister of Maharashtra in front of me that he must help Ajit because he had been targeted by the last government. Devendra Fadnavis was among the new political stars in Davos for the annual meeting in January 2015. And it so happened that he was on the same flight as us on our way home. He sat in the first row of Swissair's first-class cabin with the smug air of a potentate. Or more accurately with the air of a small man in a big job. Ajit went up to him and they had a long chat but, somehow, when we got back to Mumbai he never had time to even have a meeting with Ajit to discuss Lavasa.

Meanwhile, Ajit tried many times to meet the Prime Minister again with the idea of reviving a project that could have been a model for Modi's idea of building 'smart cities' for the 400 million Indians expected to embrace urbanization by 2030. Modi never replied to his letters. When I made some inquiries with a journalist considered closer to him than most, he said, 'I think he wants to keep away from businessmen.' Was it because of the suit-boot jibe? I think it was.

It made him alter his economic direction so completely that there was truth in the Congress charge that Modi was not a gamechanger but a namechanger. With messianic zeal he invested huge amounts of taxpayers' money in welfare schemes for rural India that were already in existence but that now had new names. Did he do this because he was losing confidence or because he had never fully understood the economic reforms that India needed?

One balmy Delhi evening Nirmala Sitharaman, not yet Minister of Defence but of Commerce, invited a group of us to her home to meet the famous economist Lawrence Summers. We sat in the garden around tables set in a horseshoe-shaped arrangement. She sat beside him at the tip of the horseshoe. In the gathering were businessmen, bureaucrats and people who the BJP considered academics. Everyone asked questions. And they were mostly dull questions that seemed to be asked for reasons of asking, so Summers said almost nothing of any consequence. When the meeting ended he headed towards the area of the garden where tea and snacks were laid out and I got a chance to slip in a question that I had dared not ask in front of those who seemed to know so much more about economics than I. Did he think that Modi was on the right track where economic reforms were concerned, I asked diffidently. His answer clarified for me something I had not seen till then. He said, 'Modi is not a liberalizer. He is a reformer.'

7

The Lynchings

THE euphoria of Modi winning a second term was still hanging over everything that happened in the month of June when from Jharkhand came images that showed Tabrez Ansari being slowly beaten to death. His killers, as had by now become the norm, made a video of the whole horrible event and uploaded it on social media. It was shown on TV channels across India many, many times. I forced myself to watch in some kind of desperate need to understand why ordinary people had yet again suddenly turned into killers. In the pictures I saw at first the man leading the mob was middle-aged, with greying hair, a protruding belly and skinny legs. Later I saw other videos of other men armed with solid wooden sticks. One of them was dressed in a yellow T-shirt and grey pants and carried a much stronger stick. He stood proudly right next to his terrified, shackled victim as if ready to strike another blow. Behind him stood a group of skinny young men. Some wore jeans and some were barefoot and in vests and short sarongs. They watched as if mesmerized by what was happening, as if they were not sure they were watching a real killing.

Tabrez was not caught stealing, skinning or transporting a cow. He was a thief, the police later said, and was trying to steal a motorcycle in the village of Dhatkidih when he was caught. Instead of handing him to the police the men who caught him shackled him to an electricity pole and began to beat him with sticks, forcing him to say 'Jai Shri Ram' and 'Jai Hanuman' every time they hit him. In the videos you saw him shout these slogans willingly and then look with pleading eyes at his tormentors for release. His cries grew fainter as the beating continued and his eyes got a look of deep fear. But they continued beating him for hours until he was nearly dead. Then they called the police.

Since he was still alive the police arrested him as a thief and kept him in custody for four days without allowing his family to see him. His uncle later told reporters that when they found out where he was being held they went every day with food and fresh clothes in the hope of being able to meet Tabrez but the police chased them away, saying they would also be arrested if they continued to come to the police station. It was only when he vomited and fell unconscious that the police finally took him to a hospital, where the doctors declared that he was brought dead. A post-mortem revealed that he died of head injuries.

Afterwards arrests were made in the village in which he was beaten. Afterwards the story of police negligence emerged. Afterwards newspapers printed pictures of Tabrez's young widow. In the pictures she wore a fancy green salwar-kameez with gilded edges and little gold flowers on her dupatta. She looked as if she was dressed to go to a wedding. The other women in the picture were dressed in normal everyday clothes. Afterwards we learnt that Tabrez had got married just two

months before he was killed. Afterwards the usual battle began
on social media between supporters of Modi and the people
they called 'sickularists' to show their contempt for secularism.
When I tweeted that I was horrified by the images of this new
lynching my timeline became clogged with angry tweets that
came with pictures of dead Hindu youths with bloodied faces
and broken limbs. 'Will you tweet about this, Mam? Why do
you never tweet about Hindus being lynched?' These were the
polite ones. The uglier ones charged me with being a Pakistani
and being anti-Hindu. There were as many tweets from Muslims
who said that Muslims are no longer safe in India.

Modi, who tweeted regularly, said nothing. Later in the
Rajya Sabha he made a speech condemning all acts of violence.
So when after the International Court of Justice ruled that
Kulbhushan Jadav, an alleged Indian spy sentenced to death in a
Pakistani jail, was entitled to a new trial and consular access and
he tweeted that justice had been done, he was mocked. Modi's
tweet said this: 'We welcome today's verdict in the @CIJ_ICJ.
Truth and justice have prevailed. Congratulations to the ICJ for
a verdict based on extensive study of facts. I am sure Kulbhushan
Jadhav will get justice. Our Government will always work for
the safety and welfare of every Indian.' This tweet was retweeted
by Muslims who asked if there would also be justice for Tabrez
Ansari. His lynching brought back memories of the lynchings
that had come to define Modi's first term.

* * *

When the first lynching happened in September 2015 it
came as a horrible shock because there was seeming and
unexpected harmony between Hindus and Muslims. Leftist
political parties and analysts who had predicted the 'end of

the idea of India' even before Modi became Prime Minister seemed disappointed that there had not been a communal conflagration immediately after he took office. They had done their best to spread the idea that it was imminent. Every little incident that seemed to indicate that Muslims, Dalits and Christians were in danger was magnified in the media. Most journalists continued to despise Modi, especially in the English media, and helped whip up an atmosphere of doom and imminent devastation.

Days after Modi became Prime Minister for the first time a group of Hindu fanatics on motorcycles killed a Muslim student in Pune. Maharashtra was then governed by a Congress chief minister but Modi was blamed. In Maharashtra Bhawan in Delhi a Shiv Sena MP was caught on camera trying to force food into the mouth of a Muslim waiter who was fasting for Ramzan. Again blame was laid at Modi's door. Three rationalists were killed, two before Modi became Prime Minister, and these incidents were also used to create the impression that Modi was responsible for the attacks on free speech in India.

A handful of churches were vandalized in Delhi. This was interpreted by usually intelligent, thoughtful analysts as a direct attack on the Christian community. It turned out the incidents were the work of vandals and robbers but they succeeded so well in spreading the word that Modi hated Christians that prominent members of the community, like the long retired police officer Julio Ribeiro, wrote long articles saying there was no room left for Christians in the Hindu Rashtra that Modi had created. That most of these charges were spurious became clear in the manner in which Christians were quickly forgotten as soon as that first lynching occurred in a village called Bishada on the edge of Delhi.

This village is so close to Delhi that it has been subsumed by unplanned, squalid urbanization. No longer is it a place of cow-dust and mud trails. Concrete roads lead to it from a new highway whose verges are decorated with bougainvillea. On the way to it you drive past new colonies of high-rise apartments that have come up in the past ten years and eaten away the villages and fields that once existed there. On the road that leads to Bishada there is a large state-owned power plant that gives employment to many of the young men who formed part of the mob of cow vigilantes who, late on the night of September 28, 2015, gathered in the narrow lane that leads to the house of the man who was to become the first Muslim killed for the sake of a cow in Modi's first term.

Mohammad Akhlaq and his brother lived next door to each other in a village dominated by Rajputs. Their father had been settled in the village by the Rajput community because they needed a man who knew how to fix iron farm tools. Nobody knew any of this on that night when he was beaten to death in the street in which he lived and his young son, Daanish, was left half dead with head injuries. All we knew was that his lynching had something to do with cows. All we knew was that he had lived with his family in relative comfort in a home whose furnishings indicated hopes for a better life. The mob looted it after killing him but even in the wreckage there were bits of colourfully painted furniture and clothes that showed signs of modest wealth.

Three years later, in the last months of Modi's first term, I went to Bishada to see what had happened to Akhlaq's killers. As soon as I entered the village I stopped at a shop that sold farm tools to ask where Akhlaq's house was. The young man at the counter scowled when I asked the question and said, 'I don't know anything.'

'I am just asking directions to the house.'

'Ask further up. I don't know anything. It happened far away from here. I wasn't there.'

Bishada is a big village, almost a town. What may once have been dirt roads are now paved and wider than normal village roads. It is a prosperous village in which most people seem middle-class. The houses I drove past were colourfully painted and every one of them had TV dishes on their roofs. Beyond the bazaar there were mostly houses on most sides of the road and nobody wandering around with whom I could speak, so I drove through the village to the end of the road, beyond which lay a large dry pond. My driver pointed out that this was the end of the village. I agreed and we turned back. We had just driven for a few minutes before I noticed a large open doorway, through which I spotted a group of men sitting on a rope bed. Beyond was a large farmyard in which a tractor stood and the living quarters that were basic but showed signs of rural prosperity.

When I introduced myself to the men who sat on the bed and told them why I was there, one of them said, 'They don't live here any more. But we had no problem with them. It was my grandfather who brought this Muslim family to the village because we needed someone who knew how to fix iron tools.'

'So what happened that night? Why was he killed?'

'We don't know who killed him...there were thousands of people who came from outside.'

'But what caused them to come?'

'There was a calf missing. We had looked for it all day and then that night some boys from the village saw the calf's head in the well and they got really upset and went to Akhlaq's house. They knew it was him.'

'How did they know this?'

'Would Hindus kill a cow? He was the only Muslim in the village. It had to be him.'

By now other men from the village had gathered around. One of them was a plump, short man with an angry manner. 'It was nothing,' he said. 'If you media people had not made such a big thing out of it our boys would not have had to spend months in jail.'

'Your boys?'

'My nephew was one of the boys they picked up because the media made such a noise about what happened. He was not even there when they killed him. The police picked him up from the house. He was asleep in bed.'

Then someone from among the gathering said, 'He deserved to be killed. You cannot hurt Hindu sentiments in India any more. And he had changed. He had started visiting his Masi (aunt) in Pakistan and he came back a completely changed man. He stopped saying "Ram, Ram" when we greeted him and he was always talking about the Koran. He started talking like a jihadi.'

'But why did he have to be killed for this?'

'Well, you cannot kill cows in India any more and get away with it. You must know that the meat they found in his fridge was tested in a laboratory and they found that it was beef.'

'He cannot have been a jihadi,' I said. 'His son is in the Indian Air Force. Even after his father was killed so brutally he said on TV that India was the best country in the world...saare jahan se achcha Hindustan hamara.'

This was not received well. People started muttering and getting up to leave. Someone said that the son was all right, it was the father they had problems with.

On my way out of the village I stopped to ask for directions to Akhlaq's house. A fat woman in a salwar-kameez who said she was a social worker led me to a narrow street and pointed to two brightly painted metal gates. Nobody has lived here since it happened, she said, adding that if I wanted to meet them I should go look for them in Noida. She had heard that they were given a fancy apartment there by the government.

On the night that the mob gathered outside this house with its brightly painted metal door, Mohammad Akhlaq and his family would have been completely oblivious of the hatred building up against them. Akhlaq and his family were preparing for bed when the mob came. They broke down the painted door and dragged Akhlaq and his younger son Daanish out into the street and beat Akhlaq to death. Daanish survived with severe head injuries. They would not have even known what their crime was because until then the ugliness being spread in the name of cows was subterranean.

News of this first lynching spread quickly to Delhi and it did not take long for TV reporters to arrive and interview Akhlaq's widow and young daughter. She was about to get married and among the wreckage of the ransacked little house lay her bridal clothes. The images of the ravaged house with its aspirations to middle-class prosperity were splashed on TV screens across India. There was a fridge and a television alongside the furniture in bright, happy colours. Somehow this made the lynching of Akhlaq more poignant than if he had lived with the simplicity of the average Indian villager.

Everyone expected that the Prime Minister would say something to indicate that he did not approve of what had happened. He said nothing. I saw him next at a conclave organized by *India Today* magazine to celebrate his campaign to build toilets in rural India. It was an event at which famous singers from Bollywood sang in a magnificent concert and all of them gave little speeches about the importance of sanitation.

Sonu Nigam told a story of how he had never seen toilet paper until he went on a tour outside India.

When the Prime Minister arrived he was greeted like a rock star by the socialites and rich businessmen who made up the audience. He spoke against a backdrop of enlarged images of toilet paper and toilets. They had been so elaborately enhanced that he seemed to be standing inside some digital fantasy of a spotless toilet amid enormous toilet rolls. He talked of the importance of sanitation and hygiene and how important this campaign was for India.

In the audience we talked about the horror of what had happened in the village of Bishada. I sat at a table where there were other journalists and all we could talk about was the Prime Minister showing not the smallest hint of empathy. Was this first lynching part of a political scheme? It is hard to say because civilized members of the BJP, like Ram Madhav, made it clear when I talked to them that they totally disapproved of this kind of violence. But nobody said this publicly.

When I met a senior RSS leader some days after Akhlaq was killed he said, 'Well, at least the Hindus have learned to fight back now.' We met in an ugly new building that was an institute run by the RSS. It had halls and classrooms and in these classrooms were young people listening carefully to lectures by men who seemed to be RSS propagandists. The RSS leader took diligent notes as I spoke and said very little by way of interruption. When I finished talking he talked. He told me that he dreamed of an India that would find her rightful place in the world because a new kind of Indian was being created who would be patriotic and nationalistic and brave. Every time I tried to come back to the lynching he would change the subject. He told me that the RSS was running programmes to train a new kind of civil servant. This leader shall remain nameless because our conversation was private but I came away from the meeting disturbed by his total lack of basic humanity.

Days after the first lynching came the second. A Kashmiri truck driver travelling to Delhi stopped in Udhampur to refuel his truck. He was attacked under circumstances that were never fully clear except that there were rumours that his truck carried dead cows. The newspaper reports gave no details about why it was his particular truck that was targeted. Nor did they explain why the mob appeared to have come fully prepared with Molotov cocktails. They threw these into the truck. Zahid Ahmad Bhat, 24, was burned alive and died soon after. His young nephew, Zahid Rasool Bhat, 16, died of severe burn injuries in a Delhi hospital days later.

Kashmir, always on the edge, erupted in protests and anger began to build against the government of Mufti Mohammad Sayeed, who was in alliance with the BJP. The Chief Minister described what happened as a 'dastardly' crime. He said, 'One more precious life has been lost to the politics of hate and intolerance that is posing a grave challenge to the state and the country's plurality.' Jammu and Kashmir's former Chief Minister, Farooq Abdullah, said that it was probably time to acknowledge that Mohammad Ali Jinnah may have been right when he said that Hindus and Muslims could never live together.

The Prime Minister said not one word. His silence was seen by violent proponents of Hindutva as secret approval. The lynchings continued and turned into what began to seem like open season on Muslims. Cows no longer needed to be the excuse to attack them. You wearing clothes that identified you as Muslim was excuse enough. A young boy called Junaid who had just reached his 17th birthday was beaten to death on a train that ran from Mathura to Delhi. He lived in a suburb of the city and was travelling to Delhi's Sadar Bazaar to shop for Eid. His clothes identified him as Muslim. Later, travellers in the same train carriage told the police that they had seen a group of Hindu men taunting Junaid and his brothers for being 'beef eaters'. This was enough for them to start beating the Muslims up. Junaid was still alive when he was thrown off the train at the next station. His brother said afterwards that he had pleaded with people to help him get his brother to a hospital but nobody helped. Junaid died on the railway platform of a Delhi suburb.

For people like me it was hard to understand the sudden explosion of rage that seemed to have turned ordinary Hindus into killers. The only explanation I was able to come up with was that lower-middle-class Hindus across northern India are bred on a hatred of Muslims. Memories of Partition have not faded because many north Indian Hindus belong to families that came to India as refugees. And there is a narrow view of history that has created a deep sense of grievance against Muslims in general. These grievances go back to medieval times when Muslim conquerors came to India to loot its wealth and massacre people they considered infidels. Since there has been no attempt by any government to deal with this, these wounds from the past continue to fester. A certain kind of Hindu wants revenge and something about Modi becoming Prime Minister signalled to this kind of Hindu that it was now his time.

In that older, gentler India in which I had spent my childhood and youth, we knew about these things but were taught not to blame Muslims for what had happened. In the secular English boarding schools we went to, history books barely made reference to Partition, leave alone the brutality of Muslim conquerors. This was no accident. A deliberate sanitization of history textbooks was ordered in the time that Indira Gandhi was Prime Minister. The only historians allowed to write textbooks were those of leftist or Marxist persuasion and the books they wrote were full of erasures. Mughal emperors were glorified as great rulers and India's ancient pre-Islamic past was treated as if it had produced nothing of value. It was a cynical, dishonest writing of history and after Modi became Prime Minister I met more and more Hindus, of all classes, who began to articulate their anger at what had happened. It was as if this was an explosion that had been building up for a very long time.

My father's family were refugees from Pakistan and had initially chosen to stay on in that country when it was created. It was when violence against Hindus and Sikhs began that they were forced to leave. But the pain of what happened was so great that nobody talked about it much. Only after I became a journalist and met for the first time lower-middle-class Punjabis did I discover that there were millions of people who hated Muslims with a passion. But in secular times they learned to keep these sentiments to themselves. They expressed them only in the RSS drills that many of them attended. Something changed after Modi became Prime Minister. Strident new voices began to be heard, mostly on social media. Leading this army of digital Hindutva warriors were a small group of harridans who spoke in the shrillest voices of all. Muslims were taunted routinely about their religion in tweets that had a remarkable uniformity.

* * *

It was not till the middle of 2016, almost a year after the first lynching, that Modi said anything at all. This was after Hindu vigilantes in a small Gujarati town called Una attacked a group

of Dalits. Young boys found skinning a dead cow were tied
to the back of a moving car and beaten with iron rods. The
video of this new atrocity went viral on social media and it
may have been this that made Modi speak at last. He was at
the centenary celebrations of Gandhiji's Sabarmati Ashram in
Ahmedabad, so he used the Mahatma to make his point. He
said, 'Today I want to say a few words and express sadness on
some of the things going on. We are a land of non-violence. We
are the land of Mahatma Gandhi. Why do we forget that? No
one spoke about protecting cows more than Mahatma Gandhi
and Acharya Vinoba Bhave. Yes. It should be done. But killing
people in the name of gau bhakti is not acceptable. This is not
something Mahatma Gandhi would approve. As a society, there
is no place for violence.'

It was too mild a reprimand and came too late. The violence
continued. Now it was not just Muslims who were the victims
but Dalits as well. These are the two communities most involved
in the cattle and meat trade and usually it is the poorest among
them that take on the unpleasant business of slaughtering and
skinning cows. So the hysteria that spread across India in the
name of saving cows affected them the most. Dalit intellectuals
tried to speak up about the damage that the beef hysteria was
doing them. They wrote articles in English newspapers pointing
out that the reason why Dalits ate beef was that it was the
only meat they could afford to eat. They went on television
chat shows to say this and tried to assert themselves in other
forums but beef seemed suddenly to become the most sinful of
all things to eat in India. In restaurants famous for their steaks,
anything that had the word 'beef' in it disappeared off the
menu. Businesses dealing in meat products closed.

Within a year of Modi becoming Prime Minister, the
celebrated cattle fair held annually in the first days of winter

on the edge of a beautiful lake in the Rajasthani pilgrim town of Pushkar reported a drop in animal sales of 97 per cent. Nobody seemed to be buying and selling cattle any more because it became too dangerous to transport cows. Vigilante gangs roamed the highways and proudly gave interviews to TV reporters in which they said that their intention was not to kill the people they caught but to beat them badly enough so that they became crippled for the rest of their lives. Sometimes if they died from the beating then too bad for them. They said this proudly as if they had achieved some new height of valour. The men who gave these interviews wore huge red tilaks on their foreheads and saffron scarves around their necks to show that they belonged to vigilante gangs. Some claimed affiliations with the RSS and its spawns.

The RSS disowned these links but its sympathizers on social media took to trolling anyone who criticized the activities of the vigilantes. Trolling took the form of questions. Why did you not write about the RSS worker beaten to death in Kerala? Why do you never write about Hindus beaten to death by cattle smugglers? Why are you so anti-Hindu? On my Twitter timeline I was inundated with questions of this kind when I wrote in my column that the videotaped beating to death of an old dairy farmer called Pehlu Khan was too awful to describe. He and his sons had gone to a cattle market in Jaipur and bought two cows for which they had documents for transportation and receipts. When they were taking them home they were stopped by vigilantes in an ugly highway town called Behror, dragged out of their truck and beaten so badly that Pehlu Khan died of his injuries.

This was in April 2017 and for me personally it became the moment when I began to seriously question my support of Modi. In a column that appeared in the *Indian Express* on

April 9, 2017, this is what I wrote: 'It is horrible to watch a man being beaten to death. And yet I forced myself to watch the video of Pehlu Khan's lynching more than once. Not from cheap voyeurism but because I found it hard to understand why this was happening at all. The young men who kicked him and beat him with iron rods did not look like fanatics. They looked like modern young Indians. They wore tight jeans and fancy shirts that indicated an interest in fashion. They seemed educated and middle-class and, for me, this made their savagery more horrible. More disturbing. They took obvious pleasure in what they were doing and made it clear that their intention was not to harm Khan and his sons but to kill them. They videotaped the lynching and posted it on social media, so the Prime Minister would have seen it and the Chief Minister of Rajasthan. Why did they say nothing to indicate that they were sickened by what they saw?

'In Parliament, a senior minister first denied that anything had happened at all and then bizarrely added that the House must be careful not to give the impression that Parliament approved of cow slaughter. The Home Minister of Rajasthan went one awful step further and said in so many words that both sides were to blame for what happened. Both sides? Both sides? A man was beaten to death in a manner that reminded everyone of earlier barbaric times when there was no rule of law. And there is another side? That this comes from the man who has the responsibility to enforce the law in Rajasthan is not just worrying but terrifying.'

Almost exactly a year earlier I had been granted an audience with Narendra Modi. I had gone to present him with a copy of my book *India's Broken Tryst* that had just been published. It was only because of this that I was granted an audience. It was the first private conversation I had with him after he became

Prime Minister. We met in that same room with glass walls looking on to manicured lawns in which I had last met him with a group of journalists more than a year earlier. He looked serene, well groomed and had about him an aura of power that I had not noticed in the days before he became Prime Minister. There was also a new coldness in his manner. He seemed to have forgotten how to smile and in his eyes was a messianic glitter as if talking to a mere mortal required effort.

As always, our conversation was uninterrupted by aides or phones. We talked about a lot of things, perhaps because this was not an official interview. He told me that he was unable to understand how to deal with the media, making it clear that the media had always treated him unfairly. When he was Chief Minister, he said, a journalist had criticized him for wearing designer glasses and expensive watches. He was hurt by the criticism. So he sent him to the shop in Ahmedabad where he had bought his glasses for many years so that he could see that they cost no more than a few hundred rupees. And shown him that he wore a simple Indian watch. He even sent him to the tailor who had stitched his clothes for years. He did this, he said, in the hope that the journalist would write that he had been wrong about these things. He never did.

Our conversation wandered about a bit. So we moved from his personal grievances against the media to the economy. I got the impression that he was worried that it seemed to be moving more slowly than he had expected and that foreign investors were not lining up at India's gates with bags bursting with money. With a really gloomy expression on his face he told me that he had made a mistake by not ordering a white paper on the state of the economy he had inherited. Things were much, much worse than he had believed. He did not say this in so many words but sort of admitted that he had papered over the extent of damage to the economy in the hope that investors would come from foreign lands to support his Make in India programme. I said that they might come in larger numbers if they saw signs of real reforms. As an example I reminded him that he had once said that government had no business to be in business and yet he had not even tried to sell Air India. He said he wanted to but felt he needed to improve public sector companies so that they could be sold without the government making huge losses.

He did most of the talking but at some point I managed to ask him why he had spoken so rarely against the lynchings. He said, 'The thing is that something terrible happens almost every day in this country, so if I started to talk about these things I would do almost nothing else.' It was a disheartening response. But I continued to support him in my column because I still believed that he was capable of changing India's economic direction in a way that would bring real prosperity. Not long before our meeting he had said while addressing Indians on a visit to France that he wanted India to become a country in which young people did not have to leave for other lands to make a living. I supported him also because I believed that most Delhi journalists, later known as 'the Lutyens cabal', had been less than fair to him. They had allowed Sonia Gandhi and her son to get away with every stupidity but had been trying to prove from the day Modi became Prime Minister that he was a monster who was bent on destroying the 'idea of India'.

The majority of Modi's critics were frauds and hypocrites who were intellectually dishonest. They had the loudest voices in the public square and raised them to attack him for being against the Christian community within weeks of him becoming Prime

Minister. Once the lynchings of Muslims began, the supposed atrocities against Christians were quickly forgotten. And the new cry was that it was Muslims who were being targeted.

Writers, historians, poets, artists and journalists returned their awards to the government after Akhlaq was killed. Most of them were in their eighties and nineties and had not been in the public eye for a while. Many of them had never hesitated to exhibit their loyalties to Marxist parties and to the Congress Party. These were all 'intellectuals' who had never taken a stand against the manner in which Sonia Gandhi ruled India for ten years without accountability. They never took a public stand when she turned the Congress Party into a family firm. This diminishment of the party of India's freedom movement was barely written about. Nor did these intellectuals speak up when Sonia belittled the office of the Prime Minister of India by appointing two prime ministers whose jobs depended on her. P.V. Narasimha Rao showed signs of defiance, so when he died Sonia did not allow his body to lie in state in the Congress Party's headquarters in Delhi, as was the custom. The intellectuals who returned their awards said nothing. They said nothing when Rahul Gandhi called a press conference to declare that he would have thrown into the rubbish bin an ordinance the Prime Minister had issued that would have made it possible for allies like Lalu Prasad Yadav to remain in electoral politics. Dr Manmohan Singh accepted this humiliation in the same spirit that he had accepted other humiliations. Silently.

So when Modi complained about the media's unfairness to him he had a point. At a personal level I continued to support him because having always lived in Lutyens' Delhi and consorted with the ruling class it made me happy that someone who did not belong to this English-speaking, colonized elite group had become Prime Minister. I continued to support him because I believed that this colonial elite class, to which I myself belonged, had not done well by India. We had continued to treat India as a colony in much the same way as the British had. Just as they had built for themselves summer resorts in the hills to escape the brutal heat of Indian summers and cantonments in our cities in which only they lived and clubs in which 'dogs and Indians' were forbidden, we had built our own India within India.

We could not have cared less about the dreadful public services that the government built for the natives because we had our own private schools. No bureaucrat or politician sent his children to government schools. Neither did we or our minions in government use civil hospitals. So we did not care that they were hellholes where stray dogs and cats wandered in the wards and new-born babies could be eaten by rats. As long as the roads where we lived were fine, we did not care if roads were built anywhere else. And if our children did not get into the foreign service or the administrative service to perpetuate our colonial ways, we were happy to let them work for foreign firms or even in foreign lands.

We built a private India Club into which the real India rarely entered, except in the form of mosquitoes which brought dreadful diseases like dengue and malaria to remind us of the cesspool that lay outside. And there were the flies which were a terrible nuisance at our garden parties and in our drawing rooms before air-conditioning solved at least this indoor problem. When the roots of democracy grew deeper and stronger and brought to Parliament semi-literate peasant politicians, we allowed them into our charmed circle so we could mock them privately. We loved peasant leaders like Lalu Prasad Yadav and

Mulayam Singh Yadav because they confirmed to us that on our
benign watch real democracy had reached India's grassroots.
Modi was another thing altogether. A phenomenon we did not
understand at all, and something that threatened our charmed
way of life. I, who was sick of the corrupt, colonial elite among
whom I had spent most of my life, welcomed the idea of a man
who might give ordinary Indians the chance to live a halfway
decent sort of life. Sadly, once he became Prime Minister, he
seemed to forget this promise of 'parivartan'.

8

Demonetization

THE rains had come by the time I got back to Mumbai after Modi 2.0 presented its first Budget. The wet, grey days added to the gloom that had settled like a shroud over India's commercial capital. I met nobody who had anything good to say about the Budget. I talked to traders, stockbrokers, shopkeepers and big businessmen and in one voice they said that they had given up all hope that Modi would ever bring the reforms that were so desperately needed if India were ever to take a new economic direction. A Budget can make a big difference, they said, because it sends a signal about the direction that the economy will be taking. They reminded me about the Budget that Dr Manmohan Singh had presented in 1991 that had signalled the end of the licence raj. I remembered it well. And I remembered that it was because of that Budget that India now had a middle class that was believed to consist of more than 300 million people.

In the India of my childhood there was us at the top and the poor at the bottom. It was a time when government factories produced everything. They made Modern bread that was white and tasted of wax. They made Mother Dairy milk for which we queued at kiosks in bazaars that sold shoddy, second-rate consumer goods that were also made in government factories. The lumpy telephones we used also came from government factories and connections were so hard to get that it took years before ordinary people could get a connection. I remembered pleading with friends who were bureaucrats or politicians to help me get a gas and telephone connection when I moved into my own flat. I got a telephone under a special category reserved for journalists and a gas connection through a friend who was an MP. I put my name on a waiting list to get my first Ambassador car and I think it took more than a year before it arrived. It was so badly made that in winter everything inside it froze and in summer the engine overheated. I was amazed when I finally got my first Maruti car and discovered that these problems did not exist.

It was that Budget in 1991 that began the process of India entering an age in which entrepreneurs began to produce high-quality goods and create jobs of a kind India had never seen before. Slowly government withdrew from the service industry and entrepreneurs created some of the finest airlines in the world. Hotels comparable to the best ones around the globe came up, and in Khan Market – despised by Narendra Modi – when I went shopping I bought excellent goods made in India.

India changed completely after that Budget in 1991 and because Modi had promised a new direction there was real hope that after the massive mandate he got in 2019 he would bring about real reforms. When instead of this Nirmala Sitharaman raised corporate taxes so high that they went up to more than 40 per cent my business friends in Mumbai lost all hope. Modi seemed not to know how bad things were, they said sadly, or perhaps he had left everything so much in the hands of bureaucrats that it was they who were to blame. Bureaucrats hate big business, they said, and I remembered a conversation I had once had with a high official in one of Delhi's mighty Bhawans in which he said, 'I may not have made much money in my life. But I have seen the richest men in India come and beg before me on their knees.' Modi seemed to believe that he had transformed the Indian economy but the truth was that the only real 'reform' he had brought was demonetization.

This happened on November 8, 2016. Ajit and I were watching the astounding results of the American election after dinner that night. Donald Trump won and like everyone else we were stunned. I think I was saying something like it was as if Vijay Mallya, India's most flamboyant businessman, were to become prime minister. And Ajit said something like Trump may not make such a bad president if he lowered taxes. Suddenly Modi appeared on our television screen to announce that from midnight that day he was making more than 85 per cent of Indian currency illegal tender. I remember that after the shock of hearing this the first thing I said to Ajit was, 'Clever move... he has bankrupted every political party just before elections are due in UP.' I am not sure what Ajit's response was but remember that I suddenly realized that I had no money to buy even basic groceries the next day. All I had were high-value notes in my handbag and in my safe. I think we went back to discussing the impact of Trump becoming president immediately afterwards because this seemed like the more momentous event.

The next morning when I found out that Modi had held his ministers captive in the Cabinet room until he could make his announcement on national television I began to worry. I remembered the expression on his face when he declared that 'from the midnight of November 8 Rs 1,000 and Rs 500 notes will no longer be legal tender'. It was this that worried me. There was that same messianic glint in his eyes that I had first noticed when I went to give him a copy of my book four months earlier. It was as if he did what he did because he thought of himself as belonging to a category of beings that was higher than mere mortals. As if he had taken the decision to suddenly throw a nuclear bomb into the Indian economy merely as an exhibition of his personal power. Just because he had the power to do it.

By the next day every political leader in India was hysterical with rage. Modi knew as well as they did that most of their money was stored in cash because it was 'black money'. Businessmen who finance political parties often keep donations away from the prying eyes of tax inspectors simply because they cannot donate large amounts to a political party without attracting unwanted attention. Most political leaders prefer to collect money in this way for the same reason.

As someone who has had the dubious pleasure of being a fly on the wall inside the homes of big political leaders at election time I have seen with my own eyes those cupboards filled with high-value notes. I have seen prospective candidates and party workers line up for their share and what they get as their share is always in cash. Even relatively honest political leaders collect black money for elections because the money that they are allowed to spend by the Election Commission is never enough. Modi would have known this better than anyone having been Chief Minister for over 12 years. He would have known that the people most affected by his dramatic midnight manoeuvre would be political parties and their financiers. In the next few days nearly every major political leader had appeared on a public platform to rant and rave against Modi's move.

Mamata Banerjee flew in to Delhi the very next day to join forces with Rahul Gandhi and Delhi Chief Minister Arvind Kejriwal at a rally to oppose Modi's move. In her shrill voice and with that hysteria that is so much part of her persona she raged against how she would not tolerate the harm that was being done to the 'common man'. Rahul went one step further and declared that Modi was stealing money from the poor to give his 'rich industrialist friends'. These leaders were so incensed with what had happened that they sat in protest outside the Reserve Bank of India for a whole day. But they calmed down when they realized that ordinary Indians did not think Modi had done a bad thing. For a few days there were long queues outside banks in which rich and poor Indians stood with old notes to exchange for new. For a few days there were hysterics in the media about what Dr Manmohan Singh called the 'monumental mismanagement' of demonetization and then the hysterics died down.

Modi himself seemed a little nervous about what he had done and when he defended his decision in public speeches he said over and over again that he had done this only because he believed that it was the best way to bring black money out of its hidey holes and into the coffers of banks. Later, when I talked to friends who understand economics better than I do I discovered that it was a gesture almost of insanity because it would seriously affect the Indian economy since most of it was in what is called the 'unorganized sector'. Later I discovered from people who understand the economic thinking of the Sangh Parivar better than I do that the RSS is full of 'economists' who believe in gestures of this kind. They did not hesitate to publicly applaud Modi for what he had done.

Some weeks after this melodramatic economic reform I travelled to Uttar Pradesh. Aatish was here from New York and wanted to take a look at what was likely to happen in the state election that was due in a few months. We drove to Lucknow on the magnificent new highway that then Chief Minister Akhilesh Yadav had inaugurated just weeks earlier. The driver who was taking us on this trip was a man called Rakesh, who came from rural Rae Bareli and wanted me to see how little had happened in his village by way of development. This despite Rae Bareli being the constituency Sonia Gandhi had inherited from her mother-in-law. It had been Indira Gandhi's constituency for a very long time.

Driving to Lucknow would have meant stopping somewhere on the way for one night in the days before there was the highway from Delhi to Agra. And now because of this new one it took us just over six hours. The drive had a surreal quality about it because of the contrast between the very modern, access-controlled, highway on which we travelled and the dismal villages we spotted below us. Where urbanization had not yet come the countryside looked green and the villages romantic and picturesque but wherever villages had become small towns there was squalor and wretched poverty. It was as if the highway was built to prevent travellers from seeing what the real Uttar Pradesh was really like.

When we got to Lucknow we got in touch with someone who worked for my old friend Suleiman, the Raja of Mahmudabad. On a long ago visit I remembered having a most delicious dinner in the Qaiser Bagh palace and then going with Suleiman on a nocturnal tour of the city. As an important Shia prince he had extraordinary access to the Imambaras, so we were able to see their vast halls lit at night with enormous chandeliers that spread light that was the colour of emeralds and rubies. This was in the '70s before Suleiman married a girl from my school, Vijay, whose father, Jagat Mehta, was Foreign Secretary during that brief period when Mrs Gandhi was ousted from power and the Janata Party ruled. Suleiman's political loyalties lay with the Congress Party but he had been treated very badly by them and by the Indian justice system.

His father had left for Pakistan after Partition, so his vast estates in Lucknow and Nainital were declared enemy properties by the Indian state and confiscated. This happened despite Suleiman and his mother never having been anything but Indian. He spent years fighting cases to reclaim the properties that he believed were rightfully his and won his case in the Supreme Court but somehow politics and political lawyers in both the Congress and the BJP always managed to get in the way. So although he continued to live in a portion of the lovely Qaiser Bagh palace, where Wajid Ali Shah, the last Nawab of Oudh, had once lived, his own palace in Mahmudabad was crumbling as he was forced to live in genteel poverty.

There was nobody from the Mahmudabad family in Lucknow this time but Ali, Suleiman's older son, had put a trusted retainer at our disposal. He was our guide as we visited the big Imambara and then the little one. Dusk was falling and they looked more magnificent in its pale grey light. The neglect of these wonderful old monuments was less visible as the light slowly faded. There was a lovely, old square which must once have been the centre of the city that the Nawabs of Oudh built but its beauty was marred by mounds of rotting flowers and fruit.

Mayawati, the Dalit Chief Minister of Uttar Pradesh who had been in power till the socialists came back, had spent thousands of crores of rupees on building huge, hideous sandstone parks. In these stood giant statues of her and her mentor, Kanshi Ram, as symbols of Dalit pride. It was never clear if she intended these vast monuments to be modelled on Rashtrapati Bhawan to lure tourists. If it was tourists she wanted, she would have done better to just clean up old Lucknow that remained a beautiful, medieval city. Night had fallen by the time we wandered into the old city in search of 'ittar' (Indian scent) that Aatish wanted to buy for a friend in New York. We walked down narrow lanes, lined with garbage, that led to an ittar shop that glittered like a shining jewel in the filthy street. All its lights were on and they danced off the elaborate glass bottles that contained the ittar.

The man who sold us the scents made from roses, jasmine and musk was a poet manqué and recited verses from his poems and those of more famous poets as he pasted little labels on the small glass bottles of scent that we bought. I asked him if he had been affected by Modi's single economic reform and he said, 'Notebandi has ruined many people. Small businesses were very badly hit and may never recover.'

Our guide said, 'My son got dengue fever and had to be admitted to hospital. He needed a blood transfusion because the platelets in his blood had dropped dangerously. I cannot tell you with what difficulty I managed to raise the Rs 2 lakh the hospital wanted in advance for his treatment.'

'There are many stories like this that you will hear in Lucknow,' the seller of scents said.

Laden with our small bottles of scent we walked across the filthy street to the kebab shop where Ali had said we would get the finest Tunde kebabs in Lucknow. It sat on the edge of an open drain in which I thought I saw congealed blood, offal and other waste. This put me off the idea of eating kebabs no matter how good they might be, but not Aatish. He ate enough for both of us, standing on the edge of the drain because the shop was crowded with customers eating small tin platefuls of soft, gooey kebabs. On the wall of the restaurant was a greasy, faded picture of Mr Tunde himself. It was said that he had invented the recipe for this particularly soft kebab because he wanted something soft enough for his own ageing teeth.

The next morning we drove out of the city towards Rae Bareli. Rakesh, whose home we were going to visit, said he did not know Lucknow's roads at all but knew how to get to his village once we got out of Lucknow. We used the GPS on Aatish's phone to find our way out of Lucknow. We went past the spotless, salubrious environs of the cantonment where I had spent many of my childhood years during my father's postings here. On the edges of the city we drove through squalid bazaars whose little shops advertised cell phones and computers. For the hundredth time I found myself marvelling at how most of the 'parivartan' (Modi's favourite promise) in India had happened because of technology and despite government policy. Did Modi understand that India had been impoverished by bad economic policies? Did he understand that this was India's real economic problem and not 'black money'?

On the way to Rae Bareli we went past little urban villages in which long queues of tired men, and women with babies in their arms, shuffled slowly outside ATM machines. We stopped to ask if there was enough money in them and heard a litany of complaints from people who said that they had come back every day for many days before being able to get small amounts of money out of the machines. Modi had announced his grand scheme to 'unearth black money' without noticing that the new notes of Rs 2,000 and Rs 500 that he had ordered did not fit into the ATM machines. Surely this was something that he should have thought of before his totalitarian abolition of nearly all of India's currency? Surely before disrupting the lives of millions of Indians he should have at least worked out these vital details?

If the lynchings made me wonder about his political ideas, demonetization made me seriously worry about his economic acumen. Were the rumours true that he was so sure of himself that he did not even consult his own economists before making decisions as disruptive as demonetization? There were whispers of this kind on Delhi's political grapevine even before he made his big move and they got really loud after November 8. The bureaucrats who worked for him were the source of some of these rumours. Most continued to revere him. I met one very high official who described him as 'God's gift to India', but there were some who were secretly leaking information about how he listened to nobody. This kind of information was lapped up by my friends in the media who had predicted that he would be a 'disaster' long before he became Prime Minister.

On this drive to Rae Bareli as we drove past those queues outside ATM machines and saw few signs of real 'parivartan' or 'achchhe din' (good days), I began to seriously worry about my support of Modi. Had I misjudged him completely? What I had begun to wonder about by the last months of 2016 was why he had no friends or even acquaintances close enough to be able to tell him the truth. What also worried me was that in his desperate defence of demonetization the messianic look in his eyes seemed to have got more messianic. In these speeches he talked of his currency abolition as a 'yagya', a sacred fire, to purify the Indian economy. Had he not noticed that it was not corrupt officials being burned by the fire but ordinary Indians, some of whom had lost years of hard work for having kept part of their money under their beds instead of in banks?

It was a beautiful, mild, north Indian winter morning. Soft sunlight put gold highlights on the fields of yellow mustard flowers we drove past and made gilded shadows dance off the dusty trees that lined the road. The only 'parivartan' I noticed from when I had last been here during the Uttar Pradesh election five years ago was that the road was much better. Akhilesh Yadav of the Samajwadi Party had invested a lot of his political and economic capital in building roads and this was evident. Before we drove off the highway on to a little dirt road that led to Rakesh's village we stopped in a little roadside bazaar. It had a blue wooden barber's shop that was no bigger than a large vertical crate under a large banyan tree. And a line of small shops that sold food grain and vegetables. Outside these shops a group of farmers sat on their haunches. They wore tattered clothes and tired, careworn expressions on their faces. I stopped to talk to them about how demonetization had affected them. The word in Hindi, 'notebandi', had barely escaped my mouth when a chorus of voices drowned it.

'We have sold our crops at half prices because of notebandi.'

'We were getting Rs 15,000 for a quintal of potatoes and now if we can sell them for Rs 500 a quintal we will be lucky.'

'We know people who have been totally ruined by this notebandi.'

'So it was a bad idea for Modi to do this?'

'Well, maybe it will end corruption and black money one day but for now we are ruined.'

On the dirt road to his village Rakesh said that most people there were happy with demonetization even if they had suffered temporary inconveniences because they thought that it would end corruption. 'People are sick of having to pay a bribe for everything,' he said, 'so if corruption is truly wiped out then it will have been worth it.' At the entrance to his village he pointed to a small patch of flowering mustard and said, 'That is my family farm. My brother looks after it but we make no money from it because it makes barely enough to feed his family. So my wife and I both have to work in Delhi to support our mother.' He worked as a driver for a diplomat and when the diplomat was travelling abroad rented his services to people like me through a car rental service. His wife worked as a nanny for a family which lived in Gurgaon. Between them they earned close to Rs 50,000 a month and it was with this that they had managed to educate their two children.

Rakesh's village was a cluster of ramshackle houses on either side of a narrow dirt road. Chairs were produced for Aatish and me to sit in between the cluster of houses. Snacks and tea arrived and I began running through my usual questions.

'Did the village have electricity?'

'For 12 hours a day…and it can be any 12 hours. They don't tell us when it's going to go off.'

'Water?'

'Yes. There are handpumps.'

'Has the Swachh Bharat programme reached here yet? How many people have managed to build private toilets?'

'Very few…most of us still go in the fields.'

'What are your biggest problems?'

'We need a proper road to the village…the road we have is so broken and bumpy that when we take pregnant women to the hospital for delivery they sometimes deliver on the way because it takes us an hour.'

While my inquisition was in progress Aatish sat silently behind me, jotting down notes in his little notebook. At some point an older, balding man arrived, who seemed from his appearance to be the village intellectual. He interrupted my questions, saying, 'Nobody has done anything for this village except Sonia Gandhi…we will never forget what a difference it made to our lives that year when she waived all the loans we had taken. She is truly a great leader.'

This paean of praise puzzled me until more than a year after Uttar Pradesh gave Modi a spectacular majority in the assembly and I ran into Rakesh again in Delhi. He said that things had improved in the village after the BJP came to power and that people were happy with Modi in general. Then he said, 'Do you remember that time when you came to my village and there was this Misraji who came and started praising Sonia Gandhi?'

'Yes.'

'Well, he did it because he thought your son was Rahul Gandhi.'

In March 2017 the BJP won a mandate from the people of Uttar Pradesh that was bigger than any they had given any of the two caste parties that had ruled in the name of Dalits and other backward classes for 15 years. The BJP came back to power in this electorally most important state by winning 312 of the assembly's 403 seats. The voters of UP seemed more than ready to give Modi's slogan of change and development a chance.

Days after the UP results came *India Today* had its first annual conclave in Mumbai. And Modi was the star. On the final evening of the conclave, just before he was due to speak to us, on a giant screen came the news that he had appointed Yogi Adityanath as Chief Minister of UP. Aroon Purie's sister, Madhu Trehan, who had founded *India Today*, heard the news before the rest of us and said to me that the announcement had created a Twitter storm and that this might persuade Modi to change his mind. Wishful thinking! Even as we were gasping at what seemed like a complete betrayal of the mandate that UP had given the BJP, Modi appeared on the giant screen.

He did not mention Yogi Adityanath but talked in grandiose terms about development and prosperity and what his government had already done towards achieving these things for India. In my journal I wrote that 'his words no longer rang true'. Looking through the journal I found these words, 'Sab ka saath, sab ka vikas and radical Hindu yogis do not go together. Besides it is a seriously bad idea to make a sadhu a Chief Minister, especially since there has always been that suspicion about Modi that beneath the talk of "vikas" and "parivartan" lies a Hindutva agenda.'

After his speech that evening in Mumbai, as the conclave ended and we gathered outside the hall to drink a glass of wine and chat about politics and other things, many people taunted me for having supported Modi.

'Do you still support him?' said a colleague who had always hated him.

'This is his real face,' said a Muslim friend. 'Frankly I have no idea why people like you didn't see that this was his agenda all along.'

Yogi Adityanath was never one of my favourite people but had become one of my least favourite people when after the lynching of Mohammad Akhlaq he had demanded that his family be arrested on the suspicion that the meat in their fridge may have been beef. His family consisted of bereaved women, a son who was in the Indian Air Force and another son who was recovering from serious head injuries, and Yogi Adityanath saw them not as victims of a terrible tragedy but as the perpetrators of a crime. His comment was so repugnant that I ranted against him at some length in my column. So when the announcement of his becoming Chief Minister of Uttar Pradesh came, I began to wonder if I had misread Modi's political message all along.

I travelled extensively before and during the 2014 general election in the rural districts of UP, Bihar, Rajasthan and Maharashtra and nowhere did I meet anyone who said their reason for voting for Modi was Hindutva. It is true that in the salons of Mumbai and Delhi and in the glass and marble halls of five-star hotels I met many Indians who saw Modi as the first real Hindu Prime Minister but these were mostly people who hated the Congress Party's version of secularism because they saw it as 'appeasement' of Muslims. It was useless saying to them that more than 90 per cent of Muslims had benefited not at all from this so-called appeasement and actually lived in desperate poverty. Their views on the matter were engraved in stone and trying to erase them was an exercise in futility. But Indians of lowlier birth voted for Modi because they believed sincerely that he would bring the 'parivartan' and 'vikas' they wanted so badly.

Within hours of Yogi Adityanath being sworn in as Chief Minister, the state he was given charge of began to feel his presence. The two things he did in his first month seemed designed to make Muslims aware that neither they nor their sources of livelihood were safe any more. He began a campaign to close down 'illegal' meat factories. The meat industry was huge in Uttar Pradesh and vast quantities of buffalo meat was exported from this state to the Middle East. Only two communities in India are involved in the business of killing and skinning animals. Muslims do the killing and Dalits skin the dead animals. Upper-caste Hindus are usually squeamish about doing this kind of 'dirty work', so they get involved in the meat industry much higher up the chain.

The new Chief Minister's campaign against the meat industry caused many legitimate butchers to close down as well because the state government's inspectors could always find some reason or the other to act against them. It was not just shops selling beef (buffalo meat usually) that began to shut down but meat shops in general. Nobody has calculated how many jobs were lost because of this as the meat industry functions mostly in what is called the unorganized sector of the economy. More dangerous than the least privileged Indians losing their jobs was the message that Yogi was sending. He was going to run a state in which Muslims would have to accept that they were no longer as equal citizens as Hindus. If Dalit Hindus became collateral damage, he seemed not to mind.

Another thing he did at almost the same time as closing down the meat industry was setting up what he called 'Anti-Romeo squads' in police stations. Technically these squads were appointed to keep women safe from unwanted male attention but somehow the only men they caught were Muslim. Awful stories quickly came from UP about how policemen had gone into the homes of people on the suspicion that Hindu women might be going out with Muslim men. Since they did not consider the possibility of consensual relationships between adults, they did not hesitate to harass couples in public places if they suspected that the man was Muslim and the woman Hindu. When these things began to happen I found myself wondering if Modi's legendary 'political acumen' was an exaggeration.

To unleash a Hindu fanatic upon India's electorally most important state seemed like not just stupidity but madness. Apologists for Yogi Adityanath defended his appointment on the grounds that he was a fine administrator and this was the reason he had been elected to represent Gorakhpur in Parliament for five consecutive terms. I decided to go to Gorakhpur myself to check if this was true. Aatish came with me.

* * *

At Delhi airport we met a former Congress MP called R.P.N. Singh. He had lost from a constituency bordering Gorakhpur in 2014. He came from an old feudal family and was married to Sonia Singh, who worked at NDTV as an anchor. When we landed at Gorakhpur's ugly little tin shed of an airport he helped us get into the VIP lounge while we waited for our luggage to appear on the rickety carousel. Inside the lounge we found a man seated on a grimy armchair. Rings set with different birth stones gleamed on every finger of both his hands. From the flunkeys that hovered in servile fashion around him I gauged that he was a politician. R.P.N. Singh introduced us to him saying, 'This is the new MP from…'

He was the new, rough kind of politician that had washed into Parliament with the Modi wave. He had probably been chosen because of his humble origins. Modi was very proud of his own humble beginnings. But this new 'humble' kind of political leader abandoned whatever humility they may once have had as soon as they found themselves in positions of political power. He behaved with us as if he were a prince and we his lowly subjects. He acknowledged R.P.N. Singh's presence with a slight nod of his head and a hint of a smile on his paan-stained mouth. Us he did not acknowledge at all, so while waiting for our bags I had ample time to observe his manner and mannerisms.

He sat with his arms extended fully on the arms of the chair on which he sat. His oily head rested on the back of the chair. It was as if he had copied this stance from some portrait he had seen of an Indian prince sitting on a throne in a Bollywood film. A flunkey came in to tell him that his flight to Delhi was boarding and he nodded but did not get up for a few minutes more. A flunkey appeared carrying his bags and it was only then that he stood up and left. Aatish commented on the contrast between him and R.P.N. Singh and I said it was because Modi had created a new kind of Indian politician to suit a new kind of India. A particularly repugnant kind, I thought, even as I said this.

The Clarks Hotel in Gorakhpur had full-length images of Yogi Adityanath pasted on the glass doors through which we entered the lobby. Since his hands were held together in a namaste and he had a welcoming smile on his face, he looked absurdly like a lobby manager in saffron robes and with gold rings in his ears. I found myself wondering if these images of the man who had represented Gorakhpur in Parliament since 1998 had been there before he became Chief Minister or was this a gesture of more recent sycophancy. One way or another he should have taken serious offence at having his image plastered on the doors of so grubby an establishment.

Room 208 smelled of toilet freshener and was as squalid as I expected. Long years of reporting from small towns in India have taught me how to survive in the worst kind of hotels and this was not one of them. Since I had brought my own linen and towels it was bearable once I had removed the hotel's linen and towels and dumped them along with the cushions and smelly bedcover in a cupboard. After checking in, Aatish and I went to the dining room, which seemed cleaner than the rest of the hotel despite curry stains on the menu. We ordered spinach with corn and dal. It came with hot, fat rotis and made a surprisingly excellent vegetarian lunch.

After lunch we headed to the Gorakhnath temple, which had been governed by Yogi Adityanath for more than 20 years. He had inherited the temple and the Gorakhpur constituency from his mentor, Mahant Avaidyanath, who had been a leading light of the Ram Janmabhoomi movement. Ellen Barry of the *New York Times*, who had been on the same flight as us, was already in the Gorakhnath mutt talking, with the help of a translator, to a temple official who seemed to be Yogi's spokesman. So we wandered around the temple premises while waiting to talk to him. We went first to the temple. It was white, ugly and modern.

We went next to the temple's cow shelter. The cows looked healthy and happy and greeted visitors with little nuzzles and expectant expressions because so many devout Hindus came to feed them many times a day. The cow shelter had a lovely banyan tree in the middle and clean enclosures for the cows, so it had a charming, rural Indian air about it. That is until Aatish, always looking out for weird details, pointed out that some visitors were gathering fresh cow dung in their hands and bearing it away with reverential expressions on their faces. When we asked someone why they were doing this they explained that it was to make idols for their temples at home.

At some point of this unguided tour we ended up behind the main temple in what seemed like a farm in which the temple grew its own vegetables and grain. In one field on a large heap of rotting garbage and discarded plastic bags sat a very sad-looking cow. I dutifully reported this to the men who were running the Yogi's cow shelter and they said, 'What can we do? We have limited space and there are so many abandoned cows to look after.' I made the mistake of posting a picture of the sad cow on the garbage heap on Twitter and was immediately inundated with angry tweets.

Yogi Adityanath was very popular with an aggressive new kind of Hindu who had become very vocal on social media after Modi became Prime Minister. Among them were some Hindutva harridans who attacked in shrill, angry tweets anyone who appeared to be saying things that they considered offensive to Hindus. I came under virulent attack from them a few weeks later when I put up on Twitter a picture of Yogi Adityanath apparently drinking urine from a cow. I had no idea that the picture was doctored but apologies were no use nor were explanations that I believed the picture was genuine because I knew that cow's urine was considered holy and used in many religious ceremonies. Yogi Adityanath was so big a star in the eyes of this new kind of Hindu that some had already started speaking of him as Modi's heir.

After touring the temple premises we went back to the head office. Ellen was still chatting to Yogi's pointsman, so we waited in the veranda of a double-storeyed red brick building nearby. It consisted of a lot of empty rooms with pictures of gurus and gods in garish colours on the walls.

There, seated with his legs pulled up in a squatting position on a wooden chair, was a man in his fifties with a lined face and rheumy eyes. We got talking.

'I used to be a policeman,' he said, 'but I gave that up to join Yogiji's Hindu Yuva Vahini.'

'Why?'

'Because I believe that this is the only way to prevent Muslims from ruling India again.'

'There is very little chance of that happening. Surely you don't believe that it is even a remote possibility?'

'What do you mean not a possibility? Have you not noticed how they are already marrying our women and converting them to Islam? This is exactly how these things happen. They first steal our women and then they convert them. They have to be stopped.'

'Was that the only reason why the Hindu Yuva Vahini was created?'

'No. Of course, there are other goals but the main one is to prevent Muslims from taking over India again.'

Finally, Ellen Barry finished her interview and we entered the tiny office of P.K. Mull. He said he was in charge of the Hindu Yuva Vahini's operations in the state. I asked

him about this crusade against Muslims. Was this the main
purpose behind the creation of this Hindu youth militia?
He smiled sweetly and said, 'No, of course not. The main
purpose behind the creation of the Hindu Yuva Vahini is to
end casteism. The food in this temple's kitchen is cooked by
Dalits.' In the rest of the time I spent talking to Mr Mull he
tried to convince me that the Vahini was not involved in hate
crimes against Muslims and was really just a militia that was
trying to reform Hinduism from within. He seemed delighted
that Yogi Adityanath had become Chief Minister and said
that he deserved this appointment because he had done such
'wonderful work for Gorakhpur'.

This was something I had heard from Yogi's supporters in
Delhi as well but after seeing Gorakhpur with my own eyes I
found it increasingly hard to believe. After our trip to the temple
I suggested to Aatish that we visit the town's main mosque to
see how the Muslim citizens of Gorakhpur felt about Yogi
Adityanath being made Chief Minister. To get to the mosque we
had to walk through a bazaar that was so crowded and so filthy
that I was reluctant to step out of the car. If I did, it was only
because the car could not go into the street where the mosque
was. It was too narrow.

To get to the mosque, whose white and green domes loomed
over the bazaar, we had to fight our way through a crush of
vehicles, stray animals and skip over open drains. Clouds of
flies and other flying insects followed in our wake. By the time
we got to the mosque it was time for evening prayers, so we had
to wait till they were over. I wandered about what seemed to
be the Muslim quarter of Gorakhpur. I chatted to shopkeepers
who said that local businesses had been badly affected by
'notebandi' and that most meat businesses had closed down.

They seemed reluctant to answer political questions, so I stopped asking them.

Dusk had fallen by the time we could go into the mosque. A small group of mostly old men stood around chatting. They seemed a little afraid to talk to us. I think what reassured them was that Aatish talked to them in Urdu and looked clearly more Muslim than Hindu. In the half hour we spent talking to the men in the mosque, we gathered that they were worried about what Yogi would do now that he was Chief Minister. The Hindu Yuva Vahini was something they feared and they thought that it would become more active now. Of course Yogi was anti-Muslim, they said, and already the steps taken to close 'illegal' butcher shops had caused legitimate businesses to close down as well. They said buying meat was becoming almost impossible. When I asked if they feared that there would be Hindu-Muslim riots, a white-bearded, bespectacled old man said, 'It's not riots that we fear. When there is a riot there is violence for a few days, then everything goes back to normal. What is happening now is much worse because it is as if there is a tension that is permanently in the air and we have no idea when things will suddenly erupt.'

In my notes of the visit to the Gorakhpur mosque I found this description: 'They said that the only leader they believed in was the Prophet and that they believed Allah would look after them. But they were definitely not militant (Islamists). They generally wanted to get on with their lives but did not believe this was possible as long as Modi was Prime Minister and Yogi Chief Minister.

'On top of these tensions is the horror of Gorakhpur itself, which is such a horrible, wretched, filthy little town...so impossible to believe that it once produced poets like Firaq Gorakhpuri. Not so hard to believe that Vidia's ancestors would have been so poor that they were taken away as indentured labour from some wretchedly poor village.' The writer V.S. Naipaul's family was from Gorakhpur and when he came to India on one of his visits he said to me that he would love to go and see the village his family came from. I am not sure if he ever did but I imagine that a man as fastidious about cleanliness as he was would have found it hard to spend a single night in Gorakhpur. One night was all that I was prepared to spend here, and had there been a town close enough for us to drive to I would have preferred not to spend even a single night there.

When we got back to the Clarks Hotel, Aatish spotted a sign that said 'BAR' in big blue letters and had a blue arrow painted under it. He suggested that we go and have a drink to cheer ourselves up. So we followed the sign down to a dingy basement lit with blue and violet lights. When my eyes adjusted to the dimness of the lighting I saw a long room filled with small tables at which sat men who looked so sleazy that I said Aatish should be ashamed of bringing his mother to a place like this. If Gorakhpur could be such a dismal place after having elected Yogi Adityanath as its MP for five consecutive terms, I shuddered to think what he could do to UP and found myself truly puzzled about Modi's political instincts.

Had I misunderstood him completely? Was he really not the man he had appeared to be during the 2014 election campaign when he had spoken so convincingly of leading India towards an era of prosperity? He said all the right things in his campaign speeches. He talked of India needing to think about prosperity and not just about removing poverty and for this to happen he said India needed to take a new economic path. He also said what we all believed – that India had no business to be a poor country and that if it was poor it was mostly because of bad economic policies. But here we were three years into his term in office and nothing had happened to make us feel that India had in fact taken a new path.

As someone who remembered well how quickly things had changed when P.V. Narasimha Rao ended the licence raj in 1991, I kept hoping to see something like that happen with the advent of Modi. Rao had admitted later that he had liberalized the economy out of compulsion rather than conviction and that he had remained a Nehruvian socialist to the core. But he chose as his Finance Minister Dr Manmohan Singh, who had moved away from socialist views because he saw socialism had not worked. What he did not do, and what Modi so easily could have, was explain to ordinary people why India needed to take a new path.

Most Indians had no idea at all about the licence raj, so they did not notice that Indian entrepreneurs had been unshackled from a brutal economic dictatorship that fined them if they exceeded their quotas and licences. I remember doing a television programme in Dharavi back then, talking to ordinary people about the economy and being surprised at their answers. The conversations had gone something like this:

'Do you think government should be running businesses or giving us better governance?'

'They should be giving us better governance...look how bad our schools are, our hospitals, look at how filthy our streets are. That is what government should be concentrating on.'

'So they should not be wasting our money running big unprofitable companies like Air India?'

'Absolutely not.'

'You know that the government runs many big companies and they make no profit?'

'No.'

'Do you think that these companies would be better run by businessmen?'

'Yes.'

There were reasons why the Congress Party could not speak openly against the fundamental principles of Nehruvian socialism but Modi had no such constraints. With a full majority in Parliament he could have taken big decisions – as he proved with demonetization – but somehow he chose not to. Instead he took on the vast, leaky welfare schemes that Sonia Gandhi had started under the influence of her povertarian NGO advisors and tried to run them more efficiently. Instead of investing huge amounts of money in trying to make these welfare schemes more efficient, had he created better schools in rural India, better hospitals and better roads he could have transformed India in three years. In his campaign speeches he had talked eloquently about creating 'rurban' schemes that would provide urban services in rural India and then done nothing to make this happen.

9

Disappointment

BY the middle of 2017 my weekly column acquired a tone of despondency. I continued to support Modi but as if out of desperation. I said in almost all of them that Modi and his team of Hindutva chief ministers seemed to be doing all sorts of things that did not need to be done, and doing none of the things that needed urgent attention. Modi was the first major Indian politician to have noticed how important tourism could be as a pillar of the economy. In one of his first visits to Nepal as Prime Minister he even advised the government of our neighbouring country that tourism could be for them the most important way of lifting people out of poverty. And yet in India, instead of building the infrastructure needed for tourism, his government seemed to be doing its best to drive foreign tourists away. Along with the beef hysteria came rules about closing down bars that were too close to highways. This was as a result of a ruling in the Supreme Court but it added to the general atmosphere that there was too much interference from government in matters that should be private.

Modi's Minister of Food came up with the idea of ensuring that restaurants start controlling food portions so that there is no wastage. This was not an idea that took off nor did the ban on bars but by the summer of 2017 I began to feel as if Modi and his Hindutva warriors were turning India into a Hindu version of Pakistan. In our neighbouring Islamic Republic there are mountains as magnificent as our own and romantic old towns like Peshawar that evoke memories of travellers from long ago and forgotten trade routes. There are remnants of ancient civilizations from times before Islam arrived. When Imran Khan became Prime Minister one of the first things he talked about was how he would do his best to bring foreign tourists to see how beautiful Pakistan was. But he forgot that in countries where religious fanatics rule and things like prohibition prevail, the chances of luring tourists are bleak.

India was always different. I can remember that 40 years ago, when Imran Khan and his cousins became almost the first cricketers to come to India in an aeon, how impressed they were with how free India was in comparison to their own country. I first met Imran when he came in 1975 to play a benefit match for the Indian cricketer Abbas Ali Baig and I remember how surprised he was that Indian women danced with men in restaurants and drank openly in bars. Later, when I got to know Pakistan better and made more friends who made the short journey from Lahore to Delhi, I found that they were as startled by these things. When we talked about the tensions between India and Pakistan they would sometimes joke about how they were prepared to trade Kashmir for the right to lie on a beach in a bikini.

So it worried me deeply when from small towns on the edge of Delhi came horror stories about Yogi Adityanath's anti-Romeo squads. In Meerut a Muslim man was arrested when he went to drop his Hindu fiancée home. In a Bulandshahr village called Sohi, Ghulam Mohammad, a middle-aged farmer, was beaten to death by Yogi's Hindu Yuva Vahini goons because they suspected that he had helped a Hindu woman elope with her Muslim lover. Hindutva Twitter warriors celebrated every Muslim killing as if it were an act of valour, retribution for what Muslim conquerors did to Hindus centuries earlier. There are two kinds of Hindus. The first kind are those who are totally confident of who they are and what their role is in Indian society. The second kind are those brought up with an inferiority complex about Muslims that manifests itself as hatred and violence of the most cowardly kind. Sadly the cow crusades unleashed by Modi and his chief ministers brought out the second kind.

So in a column that appeared in the *Indian Express* on May 7, 2017, I spoke in tones of deep despondency in these words: 'A joke popular on social media these days goes like this. "Dear Pakistanis, we as a nation have become immune to the martyrdom of our soldiers because they are paid to die. You just try and kill one of our cows and we will show you the fun." I begin with this joke to make the point that India is in danger of becoming a laughing stock in the rest of the world because of our new violent obsession with cows. So enough is enough, Hindu fanatics. Stop! Stop right now if you really love Bharat Mata.'

In another column written some weeks later I went so far as to say that Modi had failed to bring about any change at all. I said all his schemes seemed to have flopped and that even his vaunted Swachh Bharat Mission was showing very little actual difference on the ground. A day after this column appeared I got an email from Parameswaran Iyer, then Secretary in the Ministry of Drinking Water and Sanitation. He said he had read my column and would like to meet me to tell me how much difference the Swachh Bharat Mission had made. Could we have breakfast in the Gymkhana Club, he said, at 8 a.m. if I was in Delhi. I said I was and we arranged to meet in the club where I had spent many childhood mornings swimming in its indoor pool and eating chips drenched in tomato ketchup on its resplendent lawns. When I was older and living with my parents not far from there, I played squash on the mornings that I did not go riding in the polo club. So for me it was a symbol of a Delhi from a long ago time, a Delhi that no longer existed. I rarely went to the Gymkhana Club any more and on the morning I went to have breakfast with Mr Iyer I must have gone for the first time in more than ten years.

I got there before him and so had time to wander about the corridors that encircle the pillared, high-ceilinged ballroom where I remember having childhood Christmas parties and teenage jam sessions. I peeped into cardrooms that seemed unchanged from when old aunties would sit around tables playing bridge with bejewelled hands. I always thought they gossiped more than they played but then I never learned to play bridge, so am in no position to comment. I noticed that the billiards room looked exactly the same as I remembered it from my childhood. On the walls of the corridor were old-fashioned portraits of club presidents and dead princes and in the dimness of the empty bar I noticed furniture that seemed to have been there since I was a child. Even the wicker chairs with their fat chintz cushions seemed unchanged. I was still lost in childhood memories when a tall, thin, grey-haired man arrived and introduced himself as Parameswaran Iyer. I already knew from his email that he had worked with Arun Singh, who was Rajiv Gandhi's Defence Minister and among his closest friends for the first months that he was Prime Minister.

'I am sorry I am late,' he said.

'You're not. I am early. I now live in a village on the edge of Delhi, so I often miscalculate how long it's going to take me to get into town.'

He suggested that we go into the dining room and get some breakfast. We walked through the main dining room into a sunny anteroom that seemed like a new addition. It was nearly empty, so we were able to talk. He ordered a masala omelette and I a poached egg. We both ordered spiced 'desi' tea and even before our breakfast arrived Mr Iyer began to tell me his story. He said he had given up working in government to travel with his daughter who was for a while a professional tennis player. He went on to work for the World Bank and lived abroad for many years. He had been on assignment in Vietnam when he heard Modi announce in his first speech from the Red Fort in 2014 that he wanted India to become conscious of the importance of sanitation and for this would be launching a Swachh Bharat programme.

This appealed to him, Mr Iyer said, because sanitation was his area of expertise, almost to the point of being a passion. He believed that there was nothing more important than sanitation because open defecation caused terrible diseases that were particularly dangerous for small children. Open defecation was an inappropriate subject to be discussing over perfectly poached eggs and hot brown toast but I did not mind because I myself have spent years wandering about India and always being shocked at the sight of people defecating in the open. That morning over breakfast Mr Iyer and I exchanged views on how damaging open defecation was for the health of small children. Those who do not die of stomach infections before the age of five usually suffer from stunting. It is dangerous for women because it is often on trips to the fields after dark and before dawn that they are raped or face other forms of sexual harassment. Little girls are especially vulnerable.

Mr Iyer told me that morning, at the first of many breakfasts we were to have, that the Prime Minister was taking a personal interest in the Swachh Bharat programme. 'He monitors progress every six weeks,' he said. He then told me that he had got in touch with me because I had said in my column that none of the Modi government's projects was doing well. He wanted to assure me that there was a huge difference already visible in the countryside. And awareness about the harmful consequences of open defecation was spreading.

As we sipped on our hot, spiced 'desi' tea Mr Iyer explained me the finer points of 'two-pit toilets'. It is the simplest thing, he said, and uses not much more water than people use in the 'lota' (mug) that they take with them when they defecate in the open. And once one pit fills up you close it and open it a year later to find that it has become manure. He showed me a picture of himself in a newly opened pit with what looked like coffee beans in his hands. My poached egg did not go down that easily when I realized it was human excrement that had dried up.

After this meeting with Mr Iyer I was inspired to find out if the ladies from my own village whom I saw on my morning walks sitting in long lines on the beach had disappeared. For nearly 20 years now, Ajit and I have made our real home in a village called Kihim on the Konkan coast. It is here that we

have our dogs and books and this place that both of us think
of as home. We come into Mumbai during the week to work
and return by Friday to rest. Other people from Mumbai have
holiday homes in Kihim but Ajit and I are almost the only people
who come even in the rainy season when the boats stop and the
only way to get to Kihim is to drive. It is my favourite season in
Kihim because the rain comes with melodrama of a kind I have
never seen anywhere else and I love to sit on the veranda and
watch angry waves come crashing up against the garden wall.
The garden has to be protected from the salty winds that come
with the monsoon, so on the wall gets erected a screen made of
what looks like fishnet. It is through this net that I watch the
drama of the sea and the rain.

Ajit has an overdeveloped interest in public hygiene and so
from the time we first moved to Kihim 20 years ago he has tried
to help the village deal with waste. For a while he succeeded
in getting everyone to invest in a little truck that came at
certain points of the day to collect garbage and separate it.
For a while he even managed to get the ladies of the village to
gather up waste plastic from the beach and turn it into baskets
and shopping bags. For a while the bins he set up all over the
village to separate dry and wet waste worked. For a while a
little truck with a gong went about the village gathering waste.
Then village politics got in the way of his fine project and it
ended.

What he never managed to do was to get village people
to stop defecating on the beach. For me this was so horrible
a sight that I stopped walking on the beach, or at least tried
to schedule my walks to avoid defecation time, but this was
difficult to do because although women came only in the early
hours of the morning, men came at all times of the day. Women

squatted in clumps of beach vegetation that grows wild along the shoreline. Men simply sat whenever and wherever they wanted on that part of the beach that was wet and empty at low tide. Some more adventurous defecators actually went deeper into the sea and did their business in the waves so that washing afterwards was not necessary. It put me permanently off swimming in the sea. But tourists showed no hesitation perhaps because open defecation is such a socially acceptable Indian reality.

After my meeting with Mr Iyer I came back to Kihim village and sent my Maharashtrian housekeeper into village homes to see if the government scheme to build private toilets was working. She came back with pictures of pretty little toilets with red and blue tiles on the walls and neat white potties but I remained unconvinced that the women squatters had vanished from the beach.

So the next morning I went on an especially early walk to catch them out. The tide was low and the sky and the sea lit with a silvery dawn light but I kept my eyes where the fat-leaved, wild shore plants grew amid the Casuarina trees. It was here that the women usually squatted in a long, happy line, gossiping to each other, beside their plastic bottles of water. Most wore long nightgowns or kaftans and when they saw me they would smile cheerfully and even look askance at my tight shorts. It took me a while to realize that they found naked legs indecent but did not think it was indecent to sit half naked in full view of passers-by.

This morning I saw not a single woman defecating in the open. I walked all the way down the beach and saw not a single open defecator. Then I turned around and walked in the opposite direction towards the fishing village of Nagaon, which at one time used to resemble a smelly, open-air toilet because there were so many open defecators at almost any time of the day. In the mornings would come the women, in the late morning would come children and later in the day and at almost any time of the day there would be a small army of open defecators on permanent view in this village. On this particular day I saw one man squatting in the wet sand where the tide had pulled away and one elderly couple squatting side by side.

When I reported my findings to Mr Iyer he said that Kihim had been declared ODF (open defecation free) but there were still some problems with Nagaon and the Collector of Raigad was aware of them. My breakfasts with Mr Iyer became a regular thing. We would meet every few weeks in the Gymkhana Club at 8 a.m. He would always order a masala omelette and I a poached egg and we would wash these down with cups of desi chai and chat about the progress being made towards ridding India of the filthy habit of defecating everywhere. Every time I spotted a defecator – and once I did on Marine Drive in Mumbai – I would report my field research to Mr Iyer and he would tell me how much progress they were making.

At one of these breakfast meetings in the Gymkhana Club he told me that the Prime Minister was planning to visit Champaran to inaugurate a conference of rural sanitation motivators who went by the name of Swachhagrahis. These are young people, he said, who are being trained to educate rural Indians about the importance of ending the practice of open defecation. Champaran was chosen because it was from here that Gandhiji had started his Satyagraha movement in 1917 to use non-violence to get the British to leave India. The centenary of this event was important to Modi. Of all the dead Congress leaders the only two he seemed to think of as his heroes were the Mahatma and Sardar Patel. Gandhiji was especially important to the Swachh Bharat movement because he was the only Indian political leader before Modi who had ever spoken out about how filthy Indian villages were. 'He looked at India as no Indian was able to...' This was V.S. Naipaul in the first of his India books, *An Area of Darkness*. Gandhiji liked to think of rural India as the real India but did not hesitate to point out that most villages were filthy. Naipaul quoted Gandhi:

> Instead of having graceful hamlets dotting the land, we have dung-heaps. The approach to many villages is not a refreshing experience. Often one would like to shut one's eyes and stuff one's nose; such is the surrounding dirt and the offending smell. The one thing which we can and must learn from the West is the science of municipal sanitation.

Champaran was chosen for its symbolic importance, Param Iyer told me, and because they wanted to link the idea of Swachhagraha to Gandhi's Satyagraha. When he told me that Modi would be addressing more than 20,000 young volunteers who would be coming to Champaran from different parts of India I said I would love to come. He said that I should come and that would really be worth my while. Then suddenly it occurred to me that the only way I could survive a night in the wilds of rural Bihar was if I could find a clean toilet.

Long decades of traveling in rural India have taught me that in small towns and villages the one thing that is impossible to find is a clean toilet. When I was younger and reporting was an adventure that opened for me things I would never have otherwise seen, I was prepared to endure filthy toilets. I have been forced to use some of the worst ones imaginable in towns more urban than Motihari (East Champaran). One of the very worst was in the temple town of Nathdwara in Rajasthan, where I once stayed in a room that had only a curtain between the bed on which I was expected to sleep and the Indian-style toilet that looked as if it had not been cleaned for a week. When I complained to the manager of the hotel he said, 'It hasn't been cleaned today because the sweeper did not come in.' He used the word "bhangi", which is as ugly a casteist slur as possible, and did not flinch while using it.

'Can't someone else do it from your staff?' I asked, asserting customer's privilege.

'Of course not,' he replied, looking truly horrified. 'It is a job only a bhangi can do and I told you he did not come today.' So I decided to spend the night on a chair in the hotel's lobby and the first thing I did the next day was to find a clean bathroom to use. Nathdwara is where the finest pichwai paintings of Krishna come from. It is also where there is one of the most famous temples to Krishna and the richest businessmen from Mumbai come here on pilgrimages, but when I went 20 years ago the hardest thing to find in this temple town was a clean toilet. The cameraman I was travelling with finally found one that was in a private home.

When Param Iyer mentioned spending the night in Motihari, memories of this visit to Nathdwara came to mind and I told him that I wanted very much to attend his conference but I would only be able to come if he could find me a clean toilet. We both laughed at the irony of my asking the maestro of the Swachh Bharat campaign and the highest bureaucrat in the Ministry of Sanitation to find me a clean toilet.

Before I left Patna for Motihari I checked into this city's single decent hotel and stole some toilet paper and soap from the bathroom. I think I was in the process of committing this small crime when Mr Iyer's assistant sent me a text message saying that they had found me a room that had a clean toilet attached. So I set off. The journey was long but painless because the road by Bihar's standards was excellent. A highway took me nearly all the way. I got to Motihari as night was falling and found that I was going to be staying in the SS Exotica Hotel. Room 202 was its finest suite. It had walls that were painted in a luminous shade of lilac and the upholstery on the couch in my suite was maroon and gold. The bed was of thick wood and the linen dodgy. This was not a problem as I had wisely brought my own, as also my own towels. But to my enormous relief the Indian-style lavatory was clean and had a flush that actually had water in it.

My suite was windowless and, despite an air-conditioner working full blast, had an airless feel about it, so I decided that instead of eating dinner in my room, as suggested by an eager member of the food and beverage department, I would be better off inspecting the venue of the conference. The idea of Indian spices cloying their way into the heavy upholstery of #202 and mingling with that musty smell of unclean carpets would, I knew, ensure that I would not be able to sleep that night.

The conference was to be held in a vast tented township that had been built in the heart of Motihari. It had vast dormitories and dining rooms and when I got there I could hear music from a live performance that was in progress somewhere among the white tents. The volunteers wore white jackets and white Gandhi caps and had come from states in different parts of India that had done better at stopping open defecation than Bihar had. They had come with the idea of inspiring young people in Bihar to do more to motivate people in their villages.

These details were given to me by the Sanitation Ministry officials who presided over the event from an air-conditioned tent. Afterwards I wandered through dusty alleys filled with young men and women in white caps and white jackets. I stopped to talk to a group of young girls who were in their late teens. They said they had travelled out of their villages in Uttar Pradesh for the first time. They were cheerful and passionate about the work they were doing.

'Until we volunteered for the Swachh Bharat movement we never knew how bad open defecation was,' said a slim, pretty girl.

'What have you learned?' I asked.

'Open defecation spreads diseases that kill children.'

'Do you feel safer now that you do not have to go in the open?'

'Absolutely. It has changed our lives. Before we got toilets in our homes, we could go only once in the day...early morning... and even then it could be dangerous. You never knew when you could be bitten by a snake or a scorpion.'

'And men?'

'Yes. That too.'

'So how do you motivate people to change their habits?'

'We use different ways. So one way is that we take a hair and put it into a glass of tea and ask them to drink it. They always refuse, so we tell them that they should imagine how much dirtier their food is because flies who have sat on excrement come and sit on it.'

Everyone I talked to said that they believed Modi was the best Prime Minister India had ever had and they were sure that he would become Prime Minister again. When he arrived the next day they started cheering from the moment that giant screens showed him landing and walking on to the tarmac with the Chief Minister of Bihar. When he actually arrived on the stage he was given the kind of reception that he got in election rallies in 2014. Cries of 'Modi, Modi, Modi' filled the white tent in which the young volunteers had gathered. When he got up to speak they listened as if to a messiah. He made an unremarkable speech about cleanliness and hygiene but ensured that he mentioned that the Swachh Bharat movement's success owed much to my breakfast friend, Param Iyer.

A small army of reporters had been flown in to cover the Champaran conference but as usually happens in Indian journalism all that they did was report the Prime Minister's speech. It was a speech that did not need covering any more because he had started making it everywhere he went. He mentioned in passing that India had a sanitation coverage of less than 40 per cent when he became Prime Minister and that this was now over 80 per cent, with more and more districts in the country becoming ODF. This was without question his most successful programme but he did not dwell on it as much as he did on other things that he believed he had gifted the people of India.

He reminded his enthusiastic young audience that it was because of him that women who earlier harmed their eyes by cooking meals over smoky fires now had gas cylinders. These were distributed through a programme called Ujjwala. The 2019 general election was less than a year away, so he made what sounded like an election speech. He had taken lately to expounding at length on the many achievements of his government and so he did in Champaran that morning. At some point our eyes made contact, because I was sitting close to the stage, but he either did not recognize me or pretended not to. I also noticed something that I often see happening to people who reach the heights of political power. His eyes had an unseeing glaze over them as if he really did not see anyone. If any of the young volunteers noticed that his speech that morning was almost messianic, they were not worried by it. They seemed mesmerized just to be in his presence. I was dwelling on this thought when the driver suddenly stopped in the middle of the highway on which we were traveling to Patna.

'What happened?'

'You see this line of cars in front of us...it's not moving. This means that there is some kind of jam further up. Let me find out.' After consulting with unknown people on his cell phone, he got out of the car and made some inquiries with other drivers. He came back with a worried look on his face.

'We will have to get off the highway,' he said. 'The road to Muzaffarpur has been blocked by upper-caste Hindu protesters who are objecting to reservations for lower castes.'

'So what are we going to do?'

'We are going to take the old Patna road that goes through Vaishali.'

So we got off the highway and drove through narrow lanes on the outskirts of Muzaffarpur. There were open drains and because it had rained these lanes were clogged with pools of wet garbage and animal waste. But the worst sight I saw on this excursion off the highway was an old man sitting on a bed outside his flooded house watching a little girl, possibly his granddaughter, defecate in the doorway of their home. No matter how disappointed I was with Modi's other plans for India, I had to admit that when it came to Swachh Bharat he had done something that really would make a difference to one of India's ugliest realities.

It took me an hour longer to get to Patna. I arrived in the Maurya Hotel feeling optimistic about India. If Swachh Bharat continued to grow stronger in its attempts to teach ordinary Indians the importance of sanitation and public hygiene, it could make a huge difference in an area that really needed change.

10

Article 370

IT was raining heavily in Delhi on August 5, 2019. It had been raining since the day before when the last tourists and pilgrims were ordered to leave the Kashmir Valley and more troops were sent up. Late that night curfew was imposed on Srinagar and every major opposition leader was put under house arrest. It was a lovely, rainy Sunday afternoon and Ajit and I had lunch with my brother and his wife in a restaurant with glass walls through which we watched the rain fall. The only thing we talked about what was Kashmir. My brother, who reads history like some people read airport novels, said that the article of accession that the Maharaja of Kashmir signed was exactly the same as the one the rulers of Junagadh and Hyderabad signed a few years later. So technically Kashmir acceded fully to India. He reminded me that V.P. Menon had been a friend of my parents when my father was posted in Bangalore in the early '50s and had gifted them his book on the integration of the Indian states. As a civil servant, he had worked with Sardar Vallabhbhai Patel, India's first Home Minister and Deputy Prime Minister, to make this happen.

The next day's newspapers in Delhi were filled with speculation that the drama that was unfolding in Kashmir was leading up to the removal of Article 370 and Article 35A. Together they provided a special status to Jammu and Kashmir and also acted as an invisible wall between the state and the rest of India. Among their provisions was one that prevented other Indians from buying land in the Kashmir Valley. This was something most Indians resented and it was something that the leaders of the BJP had fought against right from the time India became independent. The man who founded the Jana Sangh, that later became the BJP, Shyama Prasad Mukherjee, died in a jail cell in Srinagar in 1953 and this had strengthened the BJP's resolve to repeal Article 370 because it was for this that the founder of the party had died. He had been a minister in Jawaharlal Nehru's Cabinet and had resigned because of differences over Kashmir. When he died in that jail cell in Srinagar, his party believed that he had been killed because of his opposition to the Article that was the symbol of Kashmir's separate identity. Much of the autonomy that it promised was eroded over the decades but as a symbol it was powerful.

On that rainy August morning all that anyone could talk about was its removal. So when it was announced that the Home Minister would be making a statement in the upper house of Parliament that morning everyone I knew sat glued in front of their TV screens. Amit Shah was not given to meandering aimlessly in his speeches, so in a few short sentences in Hindi he declared that Article 370 was going to be repealed by a presidential order and that with it would go 35A, making Kashmir a truly integral part of Bharat Mata. It would temporarily be governed by Delhi as a Union Territory and Ladakh, which had been part of Jammu and Kashmir, would now become a separate Union Territory. His statement was received with shouts and screams and one MP tore a copy of the Constitution and had to be removed from the house by marshals. Most Indians were jubilant.

Ram Madhav, the BJP's general secretary who had been in charge of Kashmir, tweeted, 'What a glorious day. Finally d martyrdom of thousands starting with Dr Shyama Prasad Mukherjee for complete integration of J&K into Indian Union is being honoured and d seven decade old demand of d entire nation being realised in front of our eyes; in our life time. Ever imagined?' When I retweeted this saying, 'Let's not celebrate just yet Ram Madhavji. This could be a new beginning or the beginning of the end', I was reviled as a traitor, a Pakistani and a pessimist. Most Indians were jubilant that Modi had shown the courage to do what no Prime Minister before him had shown the courage to do. On prime-time television shows that evening all that anyone could talk about was his courage. Ordinary people in cities like Delhi and Mumbai and faraway Bangalore took to the streets to dance and beat drums and distribute sweets. Many of them had been to Kashmir many times either to make the pilgrimage to the icy cave shrine in Amarnath or just as tourists. And many of them hated the manner in which Kashmiris behaved as if they were not Indians.

This came up in Parliament that morning when Kashmir's history was changed by an executive order. During the debate Ghulam Nabi Azad, a Kashmiri politician who had once been Chief Minister of the state, accused the Home Minister of trying to change the nature of the Kashmir Valley. We are different from the rest of India, he said, we have our own religion, our own culture, our own language and our own civilization. This is true of every state in the Indian Union and when it comes to civilizational differences they do not exist because Kashmir's civilization was Hindu until not very long ago. The ruins of ancient Hindu temples remain to remind Kashmiris of this, and until Kashmiri Hindus were driven out of the Valley in the early '90s by violent jihadists Kashmir's culture was composite. So Amit Shah in his response to Azad's assertion of a separate identity reminded him that the temple in Amarnath was linked to the Somnath temple in Gujarat and the Vishwanath temple in Varanasi. These are Shiva temples that are called 'jyotirlingas' and worshippers of Shiva try in their lifetime to make a pilgrimage to all of them. They were built thousands of years ago by a Shankaracharya who wanted to reassert the dominance of Hinduism over Buddhism.

When Modi became Prime Minister the Kashmir Valley was in a moment of rare political calm. One reason was that there were more urgent things to think about than 'azaadi'. The terrible floods that occurred in 2014 in the last months of Omar Abdullah's term as Chief Minister devastated huge areas of Srinagar and ravaged the homes and lives of a large swathe of people, both rich and poor. For some the devastation was incalculable. A friend whose family had been in the business of making carpets and objets d'art in papier mâché lost old drawings and designs because water flooded into the whole lower floor of his shop, which is on a high point of Srinagar's main market called the Bandh. When I went to see him in the summer of 2015, nearly a year after the flood waters had receded, he said sadly that it was hard for him to put a cost on what he had lost. 'There were designs for carpets that were more than a hundred years old and they are gone now forever.'

Srinagar was in the middle of what is called its second season and I was there with an English friend and his wife. Since he was a politician he was keen to understand how the political situation was but all that anyone wanted to talk about was the flood damage. They said they had believed Modi when he came to the city soon after becoming Prime Minister a year earlier and promised a relief package of more than Rs 80,000 crore. They had heard that he had a reputation for being an excellent administrator and hoped that the money would arrive soon and be distributed equitably. But a year had gone by and it had not come.

In the inner quarters of the city, where narrow, wooden houses define the architecture of what is called 'downtown' Srinagar, I met people whose homes had been totally destroyed by the flood waters and who had received such small amounts of monetary relief that it made no difference to their lives at all. Not even the small things had happened. Children who had missed their school examinations because of being unable to go to school through flooded streets lost a year because they were not allowed to take their examinations again. They blamed this on the government of Mufti Mohammad Sayeed that had come to power in January 2015 in a coalition with the BJP. It was the first time that the BJP was part of a government in Kashmir. The coalition was made because no party had won a majority. The BJP won 25 seats and Mufti's People's Democratic Party (PDP) 28 in an 87-member legislative assembly. It was a clear division, with the Hindus of Jammu voting for the BJP and the Valley's Muslims for the PDP. The National Conference did badly in this election mostly because people believed that Omar Abdullah, the grandson of Sheikh Abdullah, had shown administrative incompetence when the floods came.

The floods were so bad that Srinagar looked terrible even a year later. And not just because of the damage caused by the floods. Twenty years of violence and political violence had taken a heavy toll, so a city that I remember from my childhood as being magical and breathtakingly beautiful now looked as if it was in an advanced state of decay. A shabbiness defined everything. Piles of construction material lay almost everywhere. Except in the area where political leaders had their homes and where rich tourists enjoyed the luxury of five-star hotels, most of Srinagar looked like a construction site. It had been allowed to decay long before those unusually heavy rains in the summer of 2014 caused the Jhelum to swell and pour its waters through the streets of the city.

The damage was so great that even rich people found it hard to rebuild their lives. Dilshad Sheikh was among those who had been unable to repair the damage to her beautiful home. In a garden full of flowers, at a table laden with Kashmiri kebabs and sweets, she told me how unprepared she had herself been on the day that the floods came. Dilshad is a legendary beauty and the sister of the Bollywood actors Feroz and Sanjay Khan. They did not want their stunning sister to become an actress, so she was married off at a very young age to a Punjabi businessman whose family had lived in Srinagar long before Partition. After her husband died, Dilshad continued to live in the family home with her three daughters.

On the day the floods came she was at home. 'When I came down that morning to pick up the newspaper,' she said, 'I noticed that there was water in the garden. It was about six inches of water and I didn't think for a minute that within an hour there would be a foot of water inside the house. By the afternoon all the downstairs rooms were under water and by the evening my daughter and I and the staff had to take refuge in the attic because the water had flooded into the upstairs rooms as well.

'It was terrifying because night had fallen by the time the army came to rescue us and we had to jump from the attic down into a small boat. I tried to refuse but my daughter said that if I didn't then the household staff would be too scared to as well and we might all drown. So I jumped...God knows how...and they took us to a hotel near here which was filled with other flood victims. There were women with small babies and hardly any water or milk or food for nearly two days.'

After telling me her story she took me into the house and we wandered through empty rooms filled with ruined furniture. She was living out of suitcases in one room on a higher floor. In the year that had gone by since the water receded she had been unable to restore the house to its former glory. If it was hard for her to repair her home, it was virtually impossible for poorer people. Many were forced to live in homes that looked like ruins because they did not have the money to repair the flood damage.

It was during that summer in Kashmir that I first heard about Burhan Wani. Every political person I met talked of him with an awe bordering on reverence. He was Kashmir's new hero, they said. He was young, they said in surprised tones, but already a legend because all sorts of myths had grown around him. Some said he had become a militant because his brother was killed by the Indian army. Others said that he had joined the armed struggle with the idea of fighting a jihad to turn Kashmir into an Islamic state. Whatever his reason for becoming a militant, what was clear was that he was so popular that ordinary people gave him shelter in their homes. This was why the police could never find him.

When I turned to Google for more information about this new Kashmiri hero I came upon recruitment videos that seemed to have been copied from those of the militant group the Islamic State. They showed a young man in combat fatigues wearing a green bandana with Arabic letters on it that seemed to be a saying from the Koran. In his arms he held a machine gun and around him stood other young men similarly attired and armed. In these videos Wani, who was leader of the Hizbul Mujahideen, made it clear that he was fighting not for Kashmir's freedom but to create an Islamic state.

Hizbul Mujahideen is a group that was created by Pakistan's military intelligence to give the movement for 'azaadi' an Islamic character instead of the secular one it had when it was led by the Jammu Kashmir Liberation Front (JKLF). But the demand to make Kashmir an Islamic state was new. Videos of Burhan Wani were being widely circulated on social media, so the Government of India should have been forewarned that something new and dangerous was happening in the Kashmir Valley. There should have been an urgency in creating a coherent policy of handling this new situation. There should have been at least an urgency in delivering the promised package of flood relief. When I got back to Delhi I went to see Ram Madhav to ask him about this.

Ram Madhav was the most educated general secretary that the BJP had appointed in a very long while. Both Modi and Amit Shah were men of rough education who seemed to have a serious aversion to intellectuals and intellectual pursuits. Ram Madhav was the opposite and went out of his way to cultivate writers, journalists and thinkers. Not since L.K. Advani had I met a member of the BJP who actually read real books instead of Hindutva pamphlets. So when he was put in charge of Kashmir he made it his job to learn about the history of India's oldest political problem.

I went prepared to give him details about how the total failure to help those who were ruined by the floods could open a new chapter of rage and violence. He said, 'Yes. I know. The package has been sanctioned by the Prime Minister's Office but has been stuck in the Finance Ministry.' It was the first sign I saw that Modi was relying too heavily on bureaucrats and not using his massive mandate to push through important political decisions.

In my journal, on September 15, 2015, I recorded that I went to one of the regular 'dialogues' that Ram Madhav organized and that the main speaker was the National Security Advisor, Ajit Doval. I felt convinced that the Modi government had a proper plan to deal with Kashmir despite the Rs 80,000 crore package being so senselessly delayed. I wrote in my journal: 'Doval outlined an entirely new approach to Kashmir by saying that the first objective is to reduce the space that Pakistan has occupied internationally on Kashmir. So it is with this objective that the meeting with Hurriyat leaders became a reason to cancel talks with Pakistan. They must talk to the elected representatives of the people of Kashmir, he said, so that we can delegitimize Hurriyat. This, he said, was part of a wider plan to increase India's space in the debate...I got the feeling that he is working on a clear strategy that is the opposite of the one followed by Sonia-Manmohan.'

After seeing Burhan Wani's recruitment video I shared the view that a tough new policy was needed instead of the namby-pamby one that had been followed by the last government. I also shared the view that India needed to keep Pakistan out of any discussion on Kashmir. It is a domestic problem. What I did not know was that Modi's Kashmir policy was built on such flimsy ground that it would swerve from jackboot to kid gloves at the slightest turn of events. What I did not know was that there was virtually no real policy made during the months of peace in the Valley that lasted for two whole years. Not only was there no policy for peace, there seemed not to be even a policy for war.

So when Wani was killed in an encounter a year later and young Kashmiris took to the streets to throw stones at Indian security forces, nobody seemed to know what to do. Wani was so much more dangerous in death than in life that a wiser government would have been careful not to target him. He was just 22 when he was killed in an encounter in a village called Bumdoora near Kokernag on July 8, 2016. His killing seemed to have been carefully planned. Later, the Chief Minister, Mehbooba Mufti, who inherited Kashmir from her father who had died in office, said that had they known Wani was in the house from which security personnel were being fired at, they would have been careful not to kill him. But she seemed to say this only because of the way in which Kashmir turned overnight into a place of angry, violent mobs. They threw stones at Indian security personnel and once more was heard in the Valley that old, ugly slogan: 'Indian dogs go back.'

When Wani was taken for burial the number of people following his funeral procession was said to be between 20,000 and 200,000. Funeral processions mimicking his were taken out in most Kashmiri towns as acts of defiance. Police stations were attacked, as were transit camps in which small numbers of Kashmiri Pandits were living in a failed attempt to bring them back to the Valley. They had been forced to flee in the early '90s because the violent groups leading what was then not a jihad but just a movement for a vague idea called 'azaadi' warned them to leave Kashmir or be killed. When Hindus started being killed, they left en masse on a dark January night in 1990. It was the only instance of ethnic cleansing ever to take place in India but shamefully has never been given the attention it deserved. Once the Valley was cleansed of nearly all of its Hindu population, Kashmir began the process of becoming a virtual Islamic state. Cinemas, bars, liquor shops and video libraries were forcibly closed and a new kind of Islam began to spread that was harsher than the easy-going version that Kashmir had known.

Wani and the young men who supported him were the children of this new kind of Islam. Inevitably, it was not freedom that they began to fight for, but for Kashmir to become fully Islamic. Women who had never bothered to cover their heads in the old Kashmir now wore full hijab. Those who belonged to a women's organization called Dukhtaran-e-Millat (Daughters of the Faith) covered all visible female flesh. On their hands they wore black gloves and on their faces hijab so severe that it revealed only their eyes. It was easy for young men like Wani to believe that with so much Islamization already in Kashmir, taking it towards becoming a full Islamic state would not be hard. After he was killed, the Pakistani ambassador to the United Nations raised his death in the Security Council and described him as a Kashmiri youth leader. His links to jihadi groups in Pakistan became increasingly clear but he remained a hero in the eyes of many young Kashmiri men. Like him, they joined armed groups in the jihad that now spread like a cancer through the Kashmir Valley.

Had the government in Srinagar been headed by a politically wise Chief Minister, it is possible that the situation would not have got out of hand. Mehbooba Mufti was not that leader. So the slide towards chaos continued. When it became too alarming and too hard to handle, Modi suddenly announced a complete change in his policy. He threw away the jackboot and started to talk about returning to the Kashmir policy followed by an earlier BJP Prime Minister, Atal Bihari Vajpayee, who had said that his policy would be based on 'insaniyat, kashmiriyat, jamhuriyat.' Humanity, Kashmiri identity and democracy. It was with this policy that Vajpayee had managed to bring peace in Kashmir. But he had been Prime Minister in a time when the movement for 'azaadi' sought no more than a higher degree of autonomy for the state. What Modi was up against was jihadi terrorism.

The young man who replaced Burhan Wani as leader of the Hizbul Mujahideen was called Zakir Rashid Bhat. He released his own recruitment videos in which he made his motives absolutely clear. He said, 'When we pick up stones or guns, it should not be with the intention that we are fighting for Kashmir (as a nation). The sole motive should be for the supremacy of Islam so that Shariah is established here.' The situation by then had deteriorated so seriously that in a column that appeared in the *Indian Express* on April 23,2017, I wrote, 'The Kashmir Valley has become a warzone today because of radical Islam. This is the exact same genre of Islam that caused the terrorist attack in Paris last week.'

At about this time a video went viral on social media in which young boys were seen attacking Indian security personnel with stones and taunting them in a way that was upsetting to anyone who watched. Modi would have had the support of most Indians if he had taken harsher steps to control the situation. Instead, by August that year when he made his annual Independence Day speech from the Red Fort, he announced a softening of his Kashmir policy. He said that Kashmir could only be won over with hugs and not with bullets. Had this been part of a clear policy it may have made sense but there was no evidence of a policy.

It had begun to seem as if neither the Government of India nor the government in Srinagar had any idea what to do next. In Delhi every time I met a high official or a high BJP functionary, they said confidently that they knew exactly what to do. The high officials in Modi's government were the most disturbing.

They talked of Doval as if he were some kind of higher being when it came to matters of national security. He knew exactly what to do, they kept saying grandly, without convincing anyone other than themselves and perhaps the Prime Minister.

As someone who has been writing about the Kashmir problem since the early '80s when Farooq Abdullah was anointed as Sheikh Abdullah's heir, I have been witness to many mistakes by policymakers in Delhi. Modi seemed to me to be making yet another mistake. But none of the high officials who surrounded him seemed to think so, nor did anyone in the BJP. They sensed that things were not going too well when Mehbooba Mufti spent months trying to decide if she should take up the post vacated by her father's death or not. In this time there was no Chief Minister in charge of one of India's most politically volatile states. A high official in Delhi, who shall remain nameless, said, 'She says that she is still in mourning.'

'But then why doesn't she let one of her more competent ministers like Haseeb Drabu or Muzaffar Baig take her place?' This was so obvious a question I felt foolish asking it.

'Yes, that would be the best thing,' the high official said with clear exasperation, 'but you know what these inheritor type of politicians are like. They don't want anyone whom they see as competent to replace them even temporarily.'

'But this is Kashmir. Can you afford to let the slide into chaos continue?'

'You know that it's just a handful of people who are doing this? We think it's no more than about 500 people in south Kashmir who are causing the problem. The average Kashmiri wants peace…'

'I know that,' I said, 'but this was true from the beginning of the problem. I can remember that even when the Pandit exodus happened most Kashmiri Muslims were devastated that they were leaving. Many tried to physically stop them by offering to protect them if they were attacked.'

'But that was at the height of the azaadi movement in the '90s. It's different now. People are tired of the terrorists. Have you seen the video that has gone viral on social media of an armed militant being attacked by ordinary Kashmiris?'

'No.'

'I will send it to you. And by the way, there have been fewer incidents of stone pelting because we have taken a tough stand. If it wasn't for you human rights type of journalists who keep reporting about the victims of pellet guns and making it sound much worse than it is, we might not have any stone pelters.'

'There were none till Burhan Wani was killed,' I pointed out, adding, 'there was a tourist boom in Kashmir for more than a decade.'

This was true. So peaceful were things in the Kashmir Valley that when my friend Nadira Naipaul said to me that she wanted to see Kashmir because her grandmother was Kashmiri, I said we could go any time. She pointed out that she was of Pakistani origin. Pakistanis are strictly forbidden from entering Kashmir. But she held a British passport and there was so much peace in the Valley that I did not think we would get into trouble. We were talking over an evening drink in the discreet, elegant lounge 'for residents only' that hides behind the Bukhara restaurant in the Maurya Hotel in New Delhi. She was sitting opposite me beside her husband. I noticed that Vidia (V.S. Naipaul) did not look pleased at all. He looked up briefly from the martini he was sipping. I noticed that his eyes, always half closed, seemed to become even more closed so that he looked almost oriental. He was in a wheelchair because of serious back problems and more dependent on Nadira than ever, so I whispered in Punjabi that she better get permission from her husband before I started booking tickets and hotels.

To my astonishment she rang up the next day and told me to go ahead. She said that Pradeep, a butler they had befriended in the Maurya, had agreed to take extra care of Vidia and so we could leave as soon as possible. It was late November, a time between seasons when the hotels in Kashmir were mostly empty because the summer tourists had gone and the winter tourists had not yet come. So I got two rooms easily in the old Oberoi Palace Hotel that in its new incarnation was called the Lalit. I had seen it in its worst days in the '90s when it fell to such ruin that weeds grew out of its empty rooms and wild grasses climbed out of broken roofs. Its once exquisite gardens were so ravaged in that long decade of violence that it brought tears to my eyes every time I drove past.

Tears and memories. For I had also seen it in its full glory in the '70s and '80s when summer never seemed to end in the magnificent halls and lobbies of this former palace. I remembered evenings filled with loud music from its disco. I remembered sunlit gardens so packed with tourists during the day that we Kashmir old-timers would often escape to Gulmarg and Kokernag to trek and fish in places where the tourists did not go. We who knew Kashmir before Bollywood turned it into every Indian's honeymoon fantasy were snobbish about 'the hordes' that began to come to Kashmir in the late '60s and early '70s. It was discovered by them from films like *Kashmir Ki Kali* and *Jab Jab Phool Khile*. There had been earlier movies shot in Kashmir but they were in black and white and usually told unhappy tales of soldiers and wars.

When I came to Srinagar in those long-gone days, I preferred staying in houseboats that smelled of walnut wood and flowers.

I loved sitting on their carved wooden decks and watching
sunsets on the Hari Parbat. I loved the shikara shops that floated
by all day, selling flowers and fruit and Kashmiri trinkets. For
me this was an essential part of the magic of Srinagar. My
grander friends like the Oberois and the Patnaiks always stayed
in the Palace and on most evenings I would join them for drinks
and dinner. The Palace was so high above the Dal Lake that the
sound of the azaan and music from pleasure boats came up as
if from far away. The Maharaja of Kashmir must have built
it high above Srinagar to maintain a discreet and necessary
distance from his subjects. It managed to retain its dignity and
magic long after it had become a hotel.

The magic died only when the insurgency began. This was
such an unexpected shock – both the coming of violence and
the dying of magic – that it took a long time for those of us
who had grown up in the old Kashmir to get used to it. From
a time when the Valley was empty because of the violence, I
remember an interview with Dr Karan Singh, who would have
been Maharaja if Kashmir had remained a princely state. We
talked in the garden of his other palace that had the same
wonderful view of the Dal Lake as the Oberoi Palace. It was
a day of light winds and bright sunshine and the lake looked
like a vast glass painting of gilded shadows. I asked Dr Karan
Singh what he thought the future of his former kingdom would
be, and he looked sadly down at what is truly one of the
most glorious views in the world and said, 'I don't know. But
whatever the future is I hope that it will retain the special scent
that only Kashmir has.' We talked in Hindi and he used the
word 'sugandh' for scent and for a moment I thought his eyes
filled with tears.

* * *

The last time I stayed in the Oberoi Palace was in 2003, when the hotelier Lalit Suri (who bought it from the Oberois) finished the enormous task of restoring a palace that had for more than a decade been a broken ruin in a wilderness. The restoration was amazing. So he invited a small group of people up from Delhi to see what he had achieved, before he reopened his new Lalit hotel to the public. Among his guests were travel agents, journalists, friends and socialites. There was much music and laughter and drinking and dining in the two days we spent in the new Lalit Palace Hotel. And it was easy to erase those memories of when the gardens had become a desolate wilderness. I told Nadira this story as we flew into Srinagar. I said I had not been back to stay in the Palace since then and that was ten years ago.

At Srinagar airport a man who could have been an official or a tout came up to Nadira and told her that she would have to register as a foreigner. I told him she was my sister and definitely not a foreigner. It helps that as good Punjabi women, even if from opposite sides of the border, there is a vague sort of family resemblance between us. It helped that we talked to each other in Punjabi and I think it helped that he may have recognized me when I told him my name. In any case we managed without further obstacles to enter Srinagar and drive safely to the Palace.

It was late afternoon. The city seemed empty. Nadira wanted to see 'everything' in the two days we had, so we dumped our bags in the rooms we were given next to each other in a corridor that seemed alarmingly spooky and a little too far from the lobby. I had succeeded in bringing Nadira into Srinagar but was worried that if any of the militant groups got wind of the fact that the sister of a Pakistani general and the wife of a Nobel laureate was in Srinagar, we might have a problem. In this distant corridor they could have whisked her away unnoticed. But the view from my room was of a beautiful Chinar tree whose leaves had turned orange and yellow and gold for the season, so I put all gloomy thoughts out of my head.

We set off to do the touristy things I had not done in years. We went to the Shalimar Bagh and took pictures of its empty fountains and its trees coloured in shades of autumn. Nadira said there was a Shalimar Bagh in Lahore that was almost exactly like this one. I said Mughal gardens were always the same everywhere. We went up to the Pari Mahal and were persuaded by a local photographer to have pictures of us taken, posing together against the backdrop of mountains and lakes. Then we went back to the hotel and carried the bottle of wine we had brought up from Delhi to the bar. Someone had advised us to bring our own wine to Srinagar under the mistaken impression that the prohibition imposed by the Islamists was still in force. I believed whoever it was who told me this because I had been in the city in the early '90s when bearded goons had wandered into the hotel I was staying in and ordered the bar closed. Small gangs of these jihadists had gone around Srinagar forcibly closing liquor shops, bars, cinemas and video lending libraries.

To my happy surprise the bar in the Palace hotel was well stocked with liquor, both foreign and Indian-made foreign. We drank our wine in peace because we had the bar to ourselves. Then we went to the restaurant, where I introduced Nadira to Kashmiri food. We had Kashmiri kebabs and Haaq, a special spinach that only grows in the Dal Lake and is served with fat Kashmiri rice. Then we sat in her room and talked late into the night over more glasses of wine.

I first met Nadira some years before she married Vidia. We met in Lahore when she worked for the *Frontier Post* and this newspaper organized its own exercise in bringing peace between India and Pakistan. I was among a group of journalists and scholars invited from India. We did not know then that the owner of the *Post*, Rehmat Shah Afridi, was almost a jihadist himself. Osama bin Laden, the one-time leader of the terror group al Qaeda, was a guest in his home in Khyber Pakhtunkhwa in the years before he travelled back to Afghanistan to start his jihad against western civilization. Rehmat Shah was passionate about solving the Kashmir problem but in a way that would make it part of Pakistan. We travelled from Lahore to Islamabad and Peshawar, and Nadira and I became good friends along the way. So when she came to Delhi she stayed with me.

One of the things we did whenever we met was to gossip late into the night about love and life and politics, and since we had not done this for a long while we talked late into the night catching up on each other's lives. Then I went off to my room, noticing in the short distance that there was nobody else staying in this wing. Nadira took a sleeping pill. She had jet lag. I was not so lucky. I woke in the middle of the night because of loud thumping noises that sounded as if furniture was being moved. I was sure that it was not furniture being moved but Nadira being kidnapped by some militant group. I tried to call her but she did not answer her phone and I was too scared to go out into the corridor in case my fears were true. I managed somehow to sleep through the rest of the night and woke early to knock on her door to make sure she was still there. She was.

So we went down to the lake and posed for pictures in a shikara, like proper tourists. Then we shopped. I looked for shawls and papier mâché souvenirs. Nadira was more interested in food. She was impressed by how cheap morel (gucchi) mushrooms were and spent what I thought was a small fortune buying them to take home to London. The Valley was so peaceful in that November of 2013 that I even risked taking

her out of Srinagar to see the magnificent ruins of the Martand
Temple in Anantnag.

Two days later, at Srinagar airport, we were treated to a first-
hand experience of that peculiar mix of diligence and stupidity
that defines Indian security systems. Nadira was ahead of me in
the queue and was waved through every checkpoint although
she carried a bottle of water, a tube of mosquito repellent and
a matchbox in her purse. I was stopped because they found a
tweezer in my bag. I tried to argue, as I always do, that there
was no possibility of this harmless implement being turned into
a dangerous weapon. It was no use. I had to surrender it while
Nadira watched from the other side of the barrier. When I made
it across she showed me the banned items she was carrying and
said, 'No wonder planes get hijacked from this airport.'

This was six months before Modi became Prime Minister. So
what did he do wrong that the situation deteriorated so badly
that some people said things had gone back to the way they
were in the '90s when the violence began? How did things get
so bad that a year after Burhan Wani was killed a Kashmiri
Superintendent of Police called Muhammad Ayub Pandith
could be brutally killed on the last Friday of Ramzan. He was
praying with other believers in Srinagar's main mosque when
some people got suspicious about his identity. Eyewitnesses
later said that he was dragged into the street, stripped naked
and beaten to death. In the year before this horrific killing, the
toll of security personnel killed by the faceless jihadists of the
Kashmir Valley was the highest in eight years.

We knew by then that Modi was the sort of leader who
wanted history to remember him as the Prime Minister who
brought peace not just to the Kashmir Valley but between
India and Pakistan. When he brought the BJP into a coalition
government with Mufti's PDP, he believed that it could be a

time of healing the wounds that had festered so long. What he seemed not to have had was a B plan, so when Mufti died and his place was taken by his politically limited and administratively incompetent daughter, things fell apart.

In the last weeks of 2018 I was invited to the Military Literature Festival in Chandigarh to participate in a panel discussion on Kashmir. I had not been to this city since I came here for another literature festival to promote my book *Durbar* six years ago, so I decided to drive. It was a lovely, early winter day when there was sunshine and blue skies as soon as I left the polluted streets of Delhi. The highway was now in a more advanced state of construction than I remembered, so the squalor of the towns and villages that I drove past was concealed beneath the wide road on which I travelled. The highway restaurants that had once been filthy, dusty eateries with primitive cooking facilities were now shiny and new. Gone were the barefoot child waiters in rags, gone were the chickens scrabbling about in the dirt and the grimy tables. The new highway had inspired them to improve, so they were now proper restaurants in little gardens, with names like Zhilmil Dhaba and Vaishno Dhaba, on the older road to Chandigarh that I saw below me at a distance as we sped along the highway. I spent the night in Chandigarh in the Taj Hotel that was filled with wedding parties and tourists. Faded memories of the Punjab insurgency came back to me. Chandigarh was where I would stop for a few hours on the way to Amritsar and the Golden Temple.

If that insurgency could end then there was no reason why there could not some day be an end to the insurgency in Kashmir, I found myself thinking as I drove down Chandigarh's sun-filled, spotless, orderly streets to the lake where the Military Literature Festival was being held. At the height of the insurgency in Punjab, it had felt like there would never be light at the end of the tunnel and that the secessionists would one day win their independent country called Khalistan. Kashmir was peaceful then and full of tourists, and now it was Kashmir where the tunnel seemed dark and endless. In both stories the problem was created by bad policies made by prime ministers in Delhi. Modi could have begun with a clean slate in Kashmir. He had not.

The panel discussion on Kashmir was held under a shamiana on the edge of the lake. Every other panellist was a retired general with experience of serving in Kashmir, with the exception of A.S. Dulat, who had once been head of the Research and Analysis Wing (RAW) and had more experience of dealing with Kashmir than perhaps anyone else. He tried to speak of the nuances and the complexities of the problem. But the military men were blunt in their assessment of what had gone wrong. They said that policymakers in Delhi had simply never paid any attention to making a strategy and that sadly this had been true also of Modi's tenure. It is not a problem, they pointed out, that can ever be solved without a proper strategy but there seems to be nobody in Delhi who has time for Kashmir until it explodes. They agreed that Modi had a real chance to make a new strategy and they were disappointed that he had failed to do this.

As whatever limited strategy there was for a new beginning in Kashmir began to unravel had come the news earlier that year that an eight-year-old Gujjar girl had been locked up in a Hindu temple and drugged, starved and raped for days. Her tiny body would have already been broken by what was done to her but to make sure she was dead her rapists had taken her out of the temple and smashed her head with a stone.

The first news of this came to me from Farooq Abdullah. A new book by my old friend Karan Thapar was being released in the garden of the British High Commissioner's residence in New Delhi and among the glamorous haute Lutyens guests was Farooq. He was sitting in the row ahead of me and since Shashi Tharoor, who was going to be reading from the book, was late we got a chance to talk. I asked him the question I always ask him when we meet: 'How is Kashmir?' This time he did not give me the usual answer, which was always a shrug and words to the effect that nothing had changed. This time he said, 'Forget about saving Kashmir and think about saving India. Do you know what they did in Kathua? Do you know what will happen in the Valley when the news spreads?'

It spread fast. And to make the horror of what happened to the little girl, who liked to ride horses and sing songs, more horrible was that it became a Hindu-Muslim thing. Fine Hindu intellectuals in Delhi who had been the first to raise their voices when something horrible happened this time announced that they saw a plot to frame innocent Hindus. Lawyers in Jammu protested when the temple priest and his nephew were arrested and in most of the mainstream media there was an attempt to play down the incident. Soon the little girl's smiling picture in her printed purple frock disappeared. Soon even her name was erased because of a law that prohibits identifying child victims of rape. Once this happened the story died. A woman lawyer who had taken up her case pro bono became a heroine for a few moments and was feted in conferences in Delhi and Mumbai while in the Valley huge mobs came into the streets and stoned Indian security personnel. The rape and murder of this little girl was the final blow. If anyone in Kashmir had believed that Modi would do something new to solve India's oldest political problem, they stopped believing after this.

Not just because of the Hindu-Muslim nature of the response to the horrible rape and murder but because by early 2018 it was clear that in Modi's last months in office he would appeal to his Hindutva base if all else had failed. This process that had begun with the appointment of Yogi Adityanath as Chief Minister of Uttar Pradesh now accelerated into more talk of cows and temples than development and change.

On that rainy morning of August 5, 2019, all this was forgotten and Modi was once more a hero in the eyes of most Indians. There were many cynics and sceptics who tried to say that the timing of his repeal of Article 370 was suspect and that it came when it did to distract attention from the economic despair that his Budget had caused. But there were many more who pointed out that he had no choice but to do what he did to make it clear to Pakistan that Kashmir was a domestic problem for India and none of its business. Imran Khan made his first visit as Pakistan's prime minister to Washington in July and had managed to persuade US President Donald Trump to offer to mediate between India and Pakistan to resolve the Kashmir problem. This was probably because Trump, who had cut American aid to Pakistan for being a 'deceitful, subversive' country, now needed Pakistan's help to end the war in Afghanistan. It was America's longest war and he needed it to end before he stood for re-election in 2020.

Would Modi have ended Kashmir's special status in any case? Probably. But perhaps later in his second term.

11

Desert Wanderings

HARD as it seemed after Modi won his second term, he had lost considerable popular support by the middle of his first term. The first electoral shock came in the last days of 2017 when the BJP almost lost Gujarat. It seemed inconceivable that Modi as Prime Minister could lose a state that he never lost as Chief Minister but it did almost happen. To discuss this I went to see a high BJP official. His office was new and shiny. It had long glass windows that looked on to a manicured lawn and old trees. Inside there were shiny, new sofas of faux leather, glass tables, fancy computers and television sets. Was he worried, I asked.

Taking his eyes off the computer screen he said, 'No.'

'Why not?'

'Because our biggest asset is Rahul Gandhi...he is a dope.'

'The dope did well in Gujarat. His endless visits to temples and all that talk about him being a Hindu who wears a sacred

thread seems to have worked for him. For the Congress to have
risen from the dead is no small thing.'

'Well, we still don't think he is any match for Modi.'

After this conversation I went to South Block to see an
official in the Government of India who had once said to me
that in his view Modi was 'God's gift to India'. Not much
had changed in this sandstone edifice in the 40 years that
I have been coming here to meet the men who rule India.
When I first came here in the '70s the corridors smelled of
vetiver from the khus screens that shaded the entrance in
summer. Air conditioners were rare in those days and in any
case frowned upon by our socialist leaders. So they were
installed only in the offices of the high officials who sat in
South Block but not in public areas. The vetiver screens
worked well to cool the corridors that made up the entrance
to this seat of government but also made them seem darker
and murkier. They were now gone and in their place was a
brightly lit entrance, where I was metal-detected and ordered
to surrender my cell phone. I had left my handbag in the car
as a precaution.

After it was established that I constituted no risk to the
security of the highest officials in the Government of India I was
led up a flight of worn stone steps to a waiting room that had a
mural on its ceiling painted by a Maharashtrian painter in the
'20s. Some British official in concession to the Hindu way of
life must have ordered this casteist artwork that despite being
politically inappropriate to our egalitarian times had survived.
It showed low-caste Hindus in servile mode and high-caste
Hindus as exalted beings. It also showed the stages of a good
Hindu's life – from being a student and a householder to finally
when he leaves for the forest, having given up the joys of the
material world for more spiritual pursuits.

After studying the mural in some detail I studied the dreary room in which I waited and marvelled at the deep imprint that socialist times continued to leave in the decor of our government offices. The sofa on which I sat was ugly and badly made. The red gladioli that wilted in a government issue vase seemed plucked from a municipal garden and everything in the room had about it a second-rate quality. I was still dwelling gloomily on these thoughts when I was summoned into the high official's office by a peon who bore a slip in his hand.

The official, an elderly man, sat behind a large desk and seemed unperturbed by the results from Gujarat. He told me that in his view there was no way that Modi could be defeated because his government had done so much wonderful work for the people. 'I monitor every programme digitally,' he said, 'so when a poor family is given a loan to build a house I know immediately. I know when the house comes up because a little light goes on where it exists. I know when a family has been given a gas connection for the first time and I know when electricity reaches a village where people have never seen a light bulb. I know when a rural road is built. No government has done more work than this one ever.'

Later that day of the results from Gujarat, BJP spokesmen appeared on prime time and exhibited similar bumptious confidence. With wide smiles on their faces they quoted the title of a famous Bollywood film to say, 'Jo jeeta vahi Sikander.' He who wins is the only one who can call himself Alexander. The Prime Minister himself appeared at the celebrations of this tenuous victory in the BJP's head office. And later that day was seen smiling graciously at the wedding reception of cricketer Virat Kohli and Bollywood star Anushka Sharma. It was the most glamorous reception in India that day and everyone would have seen him there looking confident and happy.

But the truth is that it was not till the BJP nearly lost Gujarat that questions first started to be asked about the possibility of Narendra Modi not getting a second term. Modi had been Chief Minister of Gujarat for three successive terms and had won the state so convincingly since 2002 that he had acquired an aura of invincibility that few other chief ministers had. It was on the strength of his record there that he decided to aim for a higher role. So for the victory in Gujarat to have been so slender as to almost be a defeat came as a shock. The difference between the BJP's tally and the tally of the supposedly moribund Congress Party was just 20 seats – the BJP got 99 seats in the 182-member legislative assembly and the Congress Party 77, and should have made alarm bells ring in Delhi. But the smugness that had defined the Modi government since he became the first Prime Minister in 30 years to come to Delhi with a full majority remained unshaken.

If Rahul Gandhi had grown from being a spoilt princeling to a possible Prime Minister it was with the help of the BJP. Months before the Gujarat election he went off on a visit to the United States. Unlike his many mysterious visits to unknown foreign lands this particular visit was given more than usual publicity by the Congress Party almost as if this was his coming-of-age party. During this visit he made a speech to Indian students in Berkeley University. It was a dull speech filled with the usual tired platitudes about poverty and liberal values and criticism of Modi's failure to deal with India's problems. It would have gone unnoticed if Smriti Irani, Modi's Minister for Information and Broadcasting, had not suddenly appeared on every news channel to rant and rave against it. She used to be an actress by profession, and a good one, so when she delivers a diatribe she delivers it well.

She called Indira Gandhi's grandson a 'failed dynast', sneered at him for his 'failed journey' and then berated him for not accepting the verdict of the people of India. Suddenly, everyone I knew was going to YouTube or Google to search for Rahul Gandhi's Berkeley speech. It made headlines across the country. What people began to read from Smriti Irani's feverish denunciation of Rahul Gandhi was that the BJP's managers were no longer as sanguine about Modi's possible challenger as they pretended to be. Why else would they have chosen a minister to comment on an innocuous speech in a university that most Indians had not heard of? Discreet inquiries in media circles revealed that this new aggression against the scion of the Nehru-Gandhis was being orchestrated by the BJP president himself.

Amit Shah, like Modi, was a provincial politician. But Modi had managed to enhance his political and linguistic skills, so he seemed more sophisticated. He also had a dignity in his demeanour that his closest confidant lacked despite having been projected as Modi's 2IC (Second in Command), as they say in the military. He had never managed to achieve the status that L.K. Advani had when he was BJP president and Atal Bihari Vajpayee was Prime Minister.

Another lesson that they could have learned from Vajpayee was to never attack India's imperial Dynasty. He made this a matter of policy because he knew that no matter how low their ratings fell they had a hold on voters that no other political family did. So during the election he lost in 2004 when I asked him whether he had any problems with the fact that his main opponent was a foreign woman, he smiled and said, 'None at all.' I remember saying to him after the cameras were switched off that he should have made it absolutely clear that he had serious problems with a foreigner becoming Prime Minister and he gave me one of his cryptic smiles and said that the more attention he drew to Sonia Gandhi the stronger it would make her.

Amit Shah seemed to believe the opposite. He seemed to believe that the way to recover any ground that Modi may have lost was to continue to talk about Rahul Gandhi in the hope that when people saw that it was a choice between these two, Modi would seem like a messiah. There was a degree of truth in this as I discovered on a tour of rural Rajasthan in early 2018. It was not a tour to assess the popularity of Rahul Gandhi but in the desert villages through which I wandered I found that my guide always asked about him. He was a supporter of Modi and liked to hear people laugh when Rahul's name was mentioned. There was less than a year left for elections to the Rajasthan legislature and he was worried that the BJP could lose a state it had won spectacularly in 2014.

I was in Jodhpur to attend the seventieth birthday of Maharaja Gaj Singh. It was an occasion for Bapji, as everyone calls him, to celebrate with his old friends and with those who over the years had supported his beloved Jodhpur in its journey from being a decaying desert backwater to one of the most hauntingly magical Indian cities. Umaid Bhawan has become almost more popular than Jodhpur because in its magnificent gardens and halls of marble and stone there remained trapped so much grandeur and beauty that every Bollywood star and Mumbai businessman seemed to go there to organize a 'destination wedding'.

Bapji's wife Hemlata was in Welham School with me but after school I met her again for the first time when I came to Umaid Bhawan in the '70s. She was a young bride then and had just given birth to her son and Jodhpur's heir, Shivraj. I was travelling with an English friend of Bapji's from Eton. What I remember most about this visit was that Umaid Bhawan was a magnificent ruin. Its fine corridors reeked of bats and its beautiful rooms were filled with dusty mounds of furniture and mouldering carpets. After Independence, India's new socialist rulers took a special kind of revenge on the princely states and nobody seemed to hate them more than the Nehru-Gandhi dynasty perhaps because in socialist India it was the Nehru-Gandhis who became India's royal family.

In 1971 Indira Gandhi formally derecognized the princes, breaking a treaty they signed with the Government of India when they merged their states into the Union. In exchange for this they were guaranteed privy purses and certain privileges which Mrs Gandhi wanted to end. When she got rid of them it was a hugely popular move. The princes were on the wrong side of history but managed to retain enough popular appeal in their former kingdoms to be able to win elections. This made them even more unpopular with local officials who revelled in their descent from feudal grandeur to supplicants in the new socialist durbar. They knew that it was they who were the new rulers of India and enjoyed wandering about ruined palaces demanding that some object or painting be sent to them forthwith. In the case of Jodhpur there was also the problem that Bapji became Maharaja due to his father's untimely death in an air crash, when he was barely five years old. His widowed mother decided to send him to school in England to keep him away from enemies in the Jodhpur court.

It was many years later in the early '70s that he returned home for good after completing his education in England.

When I first saw Umaid Bhawan it would have been less than a handful years after his return. Had someone told me then that it would one day become one of the most beautiful palace hotels in the world I would have thought they were mad. But this was what it had become. And for Bapji's birthday he had taken over most of its rooms for his friends who had come from all over the world. There were writers, film-makers, businessmen and that eternal rock star, Mick Jagger. Long days were spent on lazy lunches in sunlit gardens and evenings at dinner parties and concerts in forts and palaces that retained the forgotten magic of princely India.

Bapji took his responsibilities as the Maharaja of this desert kingdom very seriously and had done much to help his former subjects deal with their most pressing problem. Water. To solve a problem that had given his former kingdom the terrifying Hindi name 'marubhoomi' (land of death), he had assembled a group of water experts and with their help set up a foundation called Jal Bhagirathi, which worked in villages where water was desperately needed and where government schemes to supply it had either failed or never reached.

The foundation's main job was to help revive ancient systems of harvesting rainwater and to help individual families build their own tanks to do that too. It was with Jal Bhagirathi's officials that I travelled into rural Rajasthan. We drove straight from the airport to villages more than a hundred kilometres in the deep, sandy wasteland of rural Jaisalmer and Barmer. Tarun Goyal from Jal Bhagirathi was my guide that day and an ardent supporter of Modi. So we spent the long drive to the first village, Ranjeetgarh, talking about politics. He said he spent most of his time 'in the field' and that although he met people who were very dissatisfied with the absence of 'parivartan' and 'vikas', the minute he asked them if they would rather have Rahul Gandhi than Modi they either laughed or remained silent. 'You will see,' he said, 'you will see.'

We seemed to drive forever to get to Ranjeetgarh. The landscape soon lost all signs of urbanization, except 4G signals, and became more and more sandy as we drove off the highway on to narrow, broken rural roads. At some point even these vanished into sand dunes. We had to abandon our Toyota SUV and climb into a rickety Mahindra jeep to drive through sand dunes that seemed like they would any moment submerge us in their soft, pale gold sand. Finally, we had to abandon even the jeep to walk the last stretch to the village through sandy fields in which the only plants that grew were fat, stumpy cacti.

Tarun told me that although this part of Rajasthan had almost no water at all there was much we could learn about water conservation from the people who lived in these parts. 'I have seen women wash their children with no more than a few inches of water, which they then re-use to wash their clothes and utensils. They have no choice but to conserve water because there really is none. This is one of the reasons why Jal Bhagirathi chose this area for our work.'

Ranjeetgarh was not so much a village as a settlement of a group of people usually from the same caste. In Rajasthan a settlement of this kind is called a 'dhaani'. This 'dhaani' consisted of a scattering of small huts in the sand. Visitors were so rare that everyone from the village seemed to have gathered to meet me. The men sat on sheets spread on the sand. The women in colourful skirts and with their faces veiled squatted at some distance on the sand with children who were mostly barefoot and malnourished. It was the men who answered my questions. They said that not a single person – man, woman or child – was literate in this Dalit village. There were no schools within walking distance, they explained.

'So none of these children go to school?' I asked.

An elderly man with skin the colour and texture of brown leather took on the role of village spokesman. He had once been a soldier, he said, and learned to speak Hindi. The rest of the 'dhaani' spoke only Rajasthani.

'We would send the children to school,' he said, 'if there was one nearby.'

'What about a hospital? What do you do if someone gets sick?'

'The nearest hospital is 20 kilometres away.'

'What about jobs?'

'The only jobs are in the stone quarries 50 kilometres from here. We walk six kilometres to the highway every morning and take a bus there and then we come back in the evening. Half of our daily earnings go on transport. We voted for Modi this time because we believed him when he said that he would bring "achchhe din". But nothing has changed. Nothing at all.'

'So it has always been this way, hasn't it?'

'Yes.'

'So why are you angry with Modi?'

'Because when he promised parivartan,' he said, 'we believed him. And we still believe him. He is working hard. It is the state government that we blame for nothing having changed. We haven't seen our MLA once since the last election. We will probably see him next when he comes in a few months to ask for our votes and we will not give them to the BJP this time.'

'But you still believe that Modi is a good man?'

'Yes.'

'What do you think of Rahul Gandhi?' This question came from Tarun, who had been waiting impatiently to ask it. And as he predicted, there was general laughter from the gathering.

Then one elderly man with deep lines on his face said, 'We blame Modi for only one thing, though. We blame him for this Aadhaar card business. Look at my hands...the lines have disappeared from them because of working in the stone quarries, so the machine (bio-metric) never recognizes me and I don't manage to register.'

There were other complaints. But above all of them was the complaint that the village had absolutely no water other than what they collected in the new 'taanka' (tank) that they had built with the help of Jal Bhagirathi. But this year the rains had failed completely, so they were forced to buy water from tankers at prices they found hard to pay. They had hoped for help from the government but it had not come. It was a complaint I heard all day as I wandered through remote villages in the deep interior districts of Jaisalmer and Barmer. People admitted that it was not as if life had been easier in Congress times but it was because they believed that Modi really would bring 'parivartan' that they were disappointed. When I asked if there had been no change at all since Modi became Prime Minister, they said the change had been digital. They now received all government benefits in their bank accounts but they were not happy about this.

The people I met were all small and marginal farmers and they said that for them to go to the nearest bank to get their government benefits meant that they had to take a day off from farming. 'Then, when we get to the bank, the queues are so long that sometimes our turn doesn't come at all, so we come home and have to go back again the next day. It can sometimes take three or four days to cash a cheque so small that some people spend half of it travelling to and fro.'

'So Modi has made life more difficult?' I asked in a small Muslim village.

'Yes. If there were more banks there would be no problem. If the banks were closer to our village there would be no problem.'

Since this was a Muslim village I asked if there had been any incidents of vigilantism over cows. They said that they were lucky that there had been none but they had heard about the lynchings in other parts of Rajasthan and many Muslims they knew had given up dairy farming because of this. This was soon after a Bengali construction worker, Afrazul, had been burned alive in Rajsamand. He was asleep when his Hindu killer woke him and started beating him with iron rods before burning him alive. The killer, Shambhulal Regar, got someone to make a video while he was committing this brutal murder. After the killing he explained in the video that he murdered a complete stranger to save Hindu women from 'love jihad'.

Muslim communities across India began slowly under Modi's rule to wonder if his talk of 'sabka saath, sabka vikas' (in partnership with everyone, and development for everyone) was a charade. What began to worry his Hindu supporters was that a lot of the things that had been promised them were also a sham. A 'jumla'. The word means 'sentence' in Urdu but credit for it becoming an important part of the political lexicon goes to Amit Shah. When asked by a cheeky reporter where the Rs 15 lakh were that Modi had promised to deliver in the bank accounts of every Indian after he brought 'black money' back from abroad, he smiled and said, 'Oh that was just a chunawi jumla.' Just an election promise. He may not have meant to turn this into a weapon to be used against his boss but it became one. Modi began to be sneered at as a 'jumlebaaz', which loosely can be translated into 'trickster', as the last year of his first tenure began.

12

Media Management

IN the first weeks of 2018 it began to seem as if Modi was losing touch with the popular mood. When political leaders begin to lose touch with the people, their most important feedback usually comes from journalists. Nearly losing Gujarat should have alerted him to the need for more communication with the media but this did not happen. His communication with the people remained through his monthly monologue on radio, *Mann Ki Baat*, but with the media there was so little contact that I knew almost no journalist in Delhi who had met him even in those informal groups that had interacted with him in his first months in office.

My own attempts to meet him failed completely. If he saw any journalists at all it was only those who told him that all was well. These were nearly all from that genre of journalists who had long given up real reporting for peddling power in Delhi. Real journalists began to be treated as if they were the enemy or as pawns in the hands of the Dynasty. Some indeed were, so the charge was not baseless. But there were many real journalists in Delhi who tried to tell real stories about what they had seen on their travels. They began to discover soon just how allergic the Prime Minister was to even mild criticism. Things got so bad that reporters covering the government were frightened to use their cell phones when they were inside a government building because these could be used to trace their sources and this often resulted in the sources never taking their calls again. It did not take long for rumours to spread that there was more pressure on the media than 'ever before'.

The newspaperman who first said this to me was old enough to remember the Emergency. We were talking in the quiet corner of a restaurant that was not frequented by officials or politicians but he seemed scared and began the conversation by saying in a nervous whisper, 'We haven't met. We are not having this conversation.'

'Understood. But when you say there is more pressure than ever before, have you forgotten total press censorship during the Emergency?'

'No. I haven't. I remember but I also remember that once there was censorship we knew what we were dealing with and that this made it much easier to deal with. What is happening now is press censorship of a much more insidious kind.'

'Tell me.'

'Well...if they think you are against them then they make sure that your access to sources in government dries up completely. Do you know that reporters covering the government now keep spare cell phones that cannot be traced to them to talk to sources. Do you know that editors have lost their jobs if they are seen to be anti-Modi?'

'I have heard. But as someone whose column was nearly shut down by Sonia Gandhi because she didn't like what I was writing, I find it a little hard to believe that things are worse.'

'Believe me they are.'

This narrative gained credibility when Smriti Irani used her discretion as Minister of Information and Broadcasting to send out a circular warning journalists that if they spread 'fake news' their accreditation would be withdrawn. Naturally, this official missive did not make clear who the arbiter of fake news would be. The circular was withdrawn by the Prime Minister's Office before it could be implemented but the damage was done. It confirmed everyone's fears that this was a government that did not like journalists at all.

If Modi made this clear by not meeting journalists and never holding a press conference, Amit Shah made it clear by showing open hostility whenever he met journalists. It had not always been this way. When Modi's government celebrated its first year in office, Amit Shah, who at the time was president of the BJP, called a group of us for a little dinner party at the Constitution Club. We gathered in a long hall filled with the scent of hot rice and Indian spices and I found myself sitting on Amit Shah's immediate right. Around the rectangular table sat journalists from print and television. I noticed some who were not exactly on good terms with Modi. But the BJP president talked to everyone and answered all questions with an amiable smile on his face. I even managed to have a private chat with him to warn him that the 'parivartan' everyone expected was not happening fast enough. He listened with good grace.

I am not sure if these meetings with the press continued but I was never invited to another cosy dinner. The next time

I met Amit Shah was more than a year later at a conference that the India Foundation, a Delhi-based think tank, had taken to holding annually in a Goa resort. Shah had by then acquired a forbidding haughtiness but I took my chance to go up to him and ask if I could come and see him in Delhi. He gave me a cold stare before saying curtly, 'If you want to.' His words were unwelcoming enough for me to not make an effort to meet him again.

Shah's demeanour was not just haughty but peculiarly menacing and in the interviews he routinely gave friendly journalists he exhibited a belligerence not usually seen in politicians. He was also unpopular with most people in the media because of rumours that he actually threatened journalists openly if he thought they were not being kind to the Modi government. A colleague who shall remain nameless told me this story. 'I was sitting with him and heard him call up a minister and tell him off for giving an interview that he had not approved. I heard him say that he had been appointed to work for the government, not to speak out of turn, so could he in future keep his opinions to himself.'

It is hard to know if he did this sort of thing more than once but soon in newspaper offices and TV studios began to spread rumours that if Amit Shah did not like something you may have written or said then you could lose your job. Around these rumours slowly developed a narrative whose basic message was that Modi hated 'intellectuals'. The first time I heard this said was at an event organized by the leftist news portal The Wire at Delhi's India International Centre. Historian Ramachandra Guha was being interviewed by Karan Thapar and I went along for want of anything else to do that evening. The interview was on a stage and was conducted in front of an audience of leftist intellectuals, many of whom had been shining lights in the Durbar that existed before Modi became Prime Minister.

The practice of cultivating friendly 'intellectuals' was started by the Congress Party and continued when Atal Bihari Vajpayee became the first BJP Prime Minister. He was a poet and loved the company of people who could talk to him about poetry and literature and so cultivated the same leftist intellectuals who made up what came to be sneered at, in Modi's time, as the 'Lutyens elite'. This was before he renamed it the 'Khan Market gang'. Modi entertained nobody in the Prime Minister's residence or, if he did, these dinner parties were kept a complete secret. He also seemed to make it a point to avoid people with intellectual pretensions. So it was inevitable that people who thought of themselves as public intellectuals like Guha began to charge the BJP with being 'allergic' to intellectuals. Karan, who had months earlier lost his show on India Today TV, was very much part of this 'Lutyens elite' but no leftist. If he was doing this interview for The Wire it was because he found himself in the sort of limbo TV journalists are condemned to when they are no longer seen on national television.

The 'dialogue' he had with Guha that evening had as its theme the failures of the Modi government. Modi's alleged attempts to control freedom of expression were mentioned more than once during the course of this dialogue without anyone noticing the irony of loudly attacking Modi's failures within spitting distance of the Prime Minister's residence. I found myself wondering if either Karan or Guha would have shown the courage to attack Sonia Gandhi in the days when she was India's de facto Prime Minister. Modi's government had done no more to control unfriendly journalists and intellectuals than Congress governments had, but because he had isolated himself so completely from the media he allowed

the narrative of his government to start being written by his
opponents.

They did this with aggression and credibility because the
movement to malign him was led by two former BJP ministers,
Arun Shourie and Yashwant Sinha, both of whom had expected
to be in Modi's cabinet. As I mentioned in an earlier chapter, I
had met him for coffee weeks after Modi became Prime Minister
for the first time and he had said that I should not support him
in my column. He is not going to be good for India, he had
said, because he does not understand what needs to be done.
He might do a few 'big things' but the real reforms he needs to
make will not happen.

Some months later I happened to be at a small lunch
organized by the Swedish ambassador. Shourie was among the
guests. He had by then allowed bitterness to corrode him so
deeply that we had barely begun our first course of prawns
in perfectly ripe avocado when he started to denounce Modi
and his government for being a complete failure. I have known
Arun for many years as a friend and editor and it disappointed
me to hear him speak with so much bitterness. But I knew that
the reason for it was that he had turned his former admiration
for Modi into total contempt.

Yashwant Sinha was as bitter. He had been kept out of
Modi's Cabinet on what he considered the flimsy grounds
that he was over 70. He said in interviews that he regularly
began to give that Modi appeared to be a man who thought
people became brain-dead after that age. Those who knew
Modi better said that he had made this rule because without
it he would have been forced to have BJP leaders like L.K.
Advani and Murli Manohar Joshi as senior ministers and this
he believed would be a disaster because both men were long
past their prime.

Shourie and Sinha teamed up to raise their voices against Modi loudly and clearly. The charges they threw at him were serious. They accused him of destroying all of India's democratic institutions and Shourie warned grimly, at another event organized by The Wire, that if he won a second term it would be the end of Indian democracy. By 2018, when Modi was at his weakest, they joined hands with everyone who opposed him and Arun began to advise opposition parties on strategies to defeat him. By the time of the general election in 2019 it was said that he was among Rahul Gandhi's most trusted advisors on his campaign. I was never able to confirm this but found it easy to believe that he might be because of the emphasis that Rahul put on trying to pin corruption in the Rafale deal on Modi. Arun was convinced that there was such huge corruption in this deal that it would end up being a bigger scandal than any other defence deal.

Modi's isolation as Prime Minister cost him not just his well-meaning critics but also his friends. In Mumbai I found myself constantly running into people who had helped him win in 2014 but were bitterly disappointed that he dropped them immediately after winning. Why did Modi not notice that as Prime Minister he needed friends much more than he ever had before? Why did he not notice that by isolating himself he was allowing other people to take charge of a story that should have been his to write? The more I thought about this the more I noticed that he was starting to suffer from what I think of as the 'Messiah syndrome'. It is a syndrome that makes political leaders forget that they are in office only at the will of the people. They begin to see themselves as having an old-fashioned divine right to rule. Instead of concentrating on their administrative duties they develop delusions of being above mere mortals.

Modi could have been forgiven for having a Messiah syndrome. His political successes were spectacular. After becoming Prime Minister it was his personal appeal that helped the BJP win elections in nearly every major state. This was no small achievement. But instead of being treated as par for the course, these victories began to be celebrated in a style that was dangerously reminiscent of despots, not democratic leaders. If the victory was stunning, as in Uttar Pradesh, Modi would drive through Delhi in a cavalcade of cars bedecked with garlands of marigold. If he saw people lining the streets, he would open the door of his vehicle, step on to the footboard, and raise his right hand as if in benediction. Then he would drive into the splendid new party headquarters that the BJP had built after he became Prime Minister and walk ceremoniously on to a stage on which beside him sat only the highest officials of the party. Usually, instead of members of his Cabinet, the person given the position closest to him was Amit Shah, who never pretended to affect the humility that politicians should have.

The humility Modi affected before becoming Prime Minister seemed to disappear totally and even his admirers started to whisper about how 'messianic' he was beginning to sound. Having personally been an admirer and a vocal supporter, I started paying more attention to his body language when he addressed public meetings and began to notice that he seemed to feel the constant need to remind those who came to listen to him that it was he who had bestowed upon them the bounties they had: You have bank accounts now because I made this possible. You get money in these accounts because I insisted on this. Corruption has come down by half because of me.

The only thing that he gave anyone else credit for was when he reminded them that India's respect in the eyes of the world had risen 'not because of Modi but because of 125 crore Indians'. His isolation slowly made him lose his sense of what would appeal to the people and what would not. So in the middle of his last full year as Prime Minister he released a video that was meant to be a testament to his physical fitness but ended up making him look alarmingly weird. In it he was seen barefoot and wearing an Indian version of sports gear, a short black kurta worn with knee-length tight cotton shorts. He wore a scarf around his neck that hung all the way down the kurta. Dressed in these clothes he walked round and round a tree in his garden, jumping from stone to stone on a circle of stones that were set in a small pool of water. The commentary said that he used the elements of fire, water, air and light in his fitness routine because this was the Indian way. There was no explanation for why he later walked backwards on bare feet at so strange an angle that he looked like a marionette.

When this fitness video went viral on social media even his admirers began to wonder if his judgement had become impaired. A journalist who had abandoned the profession to become a member of the BJP said, 'It's hard to know why he needed to put that video out…what was he trying to prove?' On social media there were many who were much more vicious and for the first time since he became Prime Minister jokes started being made about Modi. More worrying than the weird fitness video was his obsession with always being photographed alone even when he visited states in which the Chief Minister was present at the event he attended. Most pictures used on private channels were anyway taken by cameramen working for state-controlled Doordarshan, so their pictures seemed designed to make him look larger than life. This was what they had always done with every Prime Minister but propaganda of this kind did not work any more. It was puzzling that Modi, with his passion for digital technology, had not noticed that the Internet had made propaganda irrelevant.

Propaganda was so much from another time that he would have done well to close down the Ministry of Information and Broadcasting altogether, but instead of this thought occurring to him he continued to use it to build his own image as a higher being. So when he went to Assam to inaugurate the longest bridge in India on the Brahmaputra river, he was shown by Doordarshan cameras driving on it alone. There was no sign of the Chief Minister of Assam or of the engineers who built the Bogibeel bridge. As he drove in solitary splendour along the entire length of the bridge he appeared to wave to an invisible crowd.

There were people below somewhere but Doordarshan cameramen are trained to focus on the leader, so he seemed to be acting rather than waving to a real crowd. The Congress Party's managers spotted this and flooded social media sites with merciless memes. Who was he waving to, asked mocking tweets. Where were the people? When he went to inaugurate 'the tallest statue in the world' of Sardar Patel in Gujarat, he posed alone beside one of its giant feet and looked like such a small white speck that he was ridiculed for it. When people start laughing at political leaders it is often a sign that they are no longer invincible.

I had personally seen this happen more than once. Long before Indira Gandhi lost her own seat in 1977, because of the Emergency, jokes had started being made about her and her son. They said the party symbol which at that time was a cow and calf was really a depiction of her and her son Sanjay. When Morarji Desai, who became Prime Minister that year, became the butt of jokes about his habit of drinking his own urine every morning, it became clear that even if his government had lasted a full term he would find it hard to become Prime Minister again.

As long as the BJP's electoral victories continued this did not matter, but by the middle of 2018 there seemed to be a sharp change in the popular mood. I felt it in remote villages and in the shiny halls of Delhi and Mumbai. Modi was lucky that Rahul Gandhi still looked like a goofy, cartoon politician, but although he may not have acquired the gravitas that he should have as leader of India's oldest political party he began to use the media well to burnish his image. His advisors saw that one of the things that had harmed Modi was that he had not held a single press conference after becoming Prime Minister, so they encouraged Rahul to talk to reporters almost every time he spotted them.

He continued to misunderstand his own message and muddle up his lines but managed to use even this to his advantage. 'Yes. I make mistakes,' he took to saying with a cheeky smile, 'I am only a human being. Only Modi makes no mistakes.' This went down well with the media. Most 'Lutyens' journalists were on his side anyway because they understood him better than they did Modi. I have always found it hard to understand why, but have noticed from long years of covering Indian politics that my fellow journalists have a reverence for our Imperial Dynasty that comes close to servility. For the 'chaiwala' from Gujarat they had only disdain. BJP spokesmen now began to attack Rahul daily, confirming that he was being taken more seriously by the day.

The most virulent attacks came from the BJP president, who imitated Modi's style of speaking and his manner. But no matter how hard he tried to mimic the man who had lifted him out of the obscurity of provincial politics and exalted him as the leader of India's biggest political party, he never managed to fit the role. He appeared to believe that his only job at his many, many public meetings was to praise Modi and the achievements of his government, so his speeches, when he was not attacking Rahul, consisted mostly of a list of things that he believed Modi had done. His attempts to speak forcefully made him sound more belligerent than convincing. And because he lacked the kind of charisma Modi had, he never developed the popular appeal that he tried so hard to cultivate. He tweeted daily about the vast crowds he addressed and thanked the people of whichever state he was visiting for their 'love and affection' but on the ground there were hardly any signs of it.

Within the BJP, even lowly party workers began to snigger about how the day Modi lost power the first man to be thrown out of the party would be its president. When I asked BJP leaders about this they would immediately defend him for being a 'great booth manager' and credit him with being around because of this ability to win election after election after election.

When the BJP started to lose elections in 2018 the BJP president should have lost some of his arrogance. The opposite happened. He began to tour the country at a furious pace and address political rally after political rally as if he were Prime Minister himself. His speeches became more belligerent and his attacks on 'Rahul baba' and his family more vicious. A line he used most often on these tours was, 'Oh baba (little boy), you dare to ask Modi for an account of what he has achieved in 48 months when you have given this country no account of what your family has done in 48 years.'

It was mostly because of the importance that senior BJP leaders, including Modi, began to give the Gandhi family that

Rahul came to be seen in 2018 as Modi's main challenger. There was no indication that his becoming president of the Congress Party in December 2017 had altered its bleak prospects until the party managed to win the parliamentary seats of Alwar and Ajmer in Rajasthan. These were both constituencies that had seen Muslim cattle traders and dairy farmers lynched by fanatical Hindu vigilantes and this could have been one reason why the BJP lost. But for Congress candidates to win with huge margins seats that they had lost to the BJP just three years earlier was the first indication that Modi winning a second term was no longer a certainty.

When this was followed months later by the loss of Gorakhpur and Phulpur in Uttar Pradesh, questions began to be asked more seriously about whether Modi's popularity was beginning to wane. These were not seats that were won by the Congress Party but by an alliance of two political parties whose only reason for being was that they represented some of the lowest castes in India. Mayawati's Bahujan Samaj Party was the voice of the Dalit community in Uttar Pradesh and the Samajwadi Party, led by Akhilesh Yadav, represented low-caste peasants. Akhilesh was a political heir at the head of a party that was as much a private firm as the Congress Party had become but the Yadav caste he represented continued to be loyal to him. The only time that they switched loyalties was during the 2014 general election when the Modi wave swept away most of the Samajwadi Party's base, leaving it with only five members in Parliament. All five were related to the man who created the party, Mulayam Singh Yadav.

So when the alliance between Mayawati and Akhilesh Yadav won two seats, including Gorakhpur which had been won by Yogi Adityanath for more than 20 years, questions

inevitably arose about Modi's chances of winning a second
term. Questions also began to be asked about whether he
had in fact brought the 'parivartan' and 'vikas' that had been
such a compelling factor in his winning a full majority in
2014. The word 'parivartan' (change) had more power during
that election campaign than any other and was understood
in rural India differently from how it was understood in
Lutyens' Delhi.

In Delhi the word 'parivartan' frightened the ruling class to
death. I remember conversations with members of the reviled
'Lutyens elite' that nearly always went something like the one I
had with the wife of a senior political leader. She was an elegant
older lady who kept her head covered in traditional style and
whose husband had once been a powerful minister. We talked
in a bungalow filled with antique furniture, surrounded by
photographs in silver frames of her husband in the company of
Indian prime ministers and world leaders. 'Modi is a murderer,'
she said, taking a delicate sip of tea. 'When I meet him I don't
shake his hand because it has blood on it.'

'What happened in Gujarat in 2002 happened many times
before in many Indian states, so why is it only he who has a
permanent blot against him? Why not Rajiv Gandhi for what
happened in 1984?'

'I don't know why…1984 was a long time ago. I'm not really
sure what happened anyway.'

'Well, more than 3,000 Sikhs were killed in three days.
Senior leaders like Chandra Shekhar and I.K. Gujral went to
Narasimha Rao, who was Home Minister at the time, and
pleaded with him to call the army. He did nothing.'

'But Rajiv Gandhi did not personally supervise the killings.'

'He could have stopped them. Not only did he not do this
for three whole days but he justified them in that famous speech
about the Earth shaking when a big tree falls.'

'Maybe he did that but in the case of Gujarat I know people who called Modi and begged him to stop the violence and he did nothing. His ministers have been convicted and sent to jail for what happened.'

'True. And Rajiv Gandhi did not allow a proper inquiry to be held into what happened to the Sikhs.'

'It's not just Gujarat that bothers me about Modi, it's other things. I think if he becomes Prime Minister he will change the country forever.'

'How?'

'There is a political culture in Delhi that we are used to and I am sure that he will destroy it.'

'Like allowing political leaders to live in houses like this?'

She looked nervously around her fine drawing room and said, 'Yes. I am frightened that it is these things that he could change. I don't like all this talk of "parivartan". God only knows what he means by it.'

'Maybe he means the end of power remaining totally in the hands of a ruling elite.'

'Maybe he does. Every country has ruling elites. That is what keeps the balance.'

Other people like the Congress Party's Mani Shankar Aiyar had fewer qualms about their reasons for hating Modi. He is a 'chaiwala', he famously said during the 2014 election campaign, and the Congress Party will be happy to offer him a job of selling tea outside our office. He compounded this first mistake by calling him 'neech' (lowly) during the campaign in Gujarat and once more Modi made huge political capital out of this. As he did when Mani went to Pakistan and said in a videotaped conversation that Pakistan should help Congress oust Modi.

India's ruling elite has been the ruling elite from the time the British left and the thought of losing their access to power and privilege terrified them. This elite includes judges, lawyers, writers, bureaucrats, public intellectuals, journalists, movie stars and socialites. They were all uncomfortable with a man who not only did not come from the traditional ruling elite but who did not even speak English, making it impossible for many of them to understand what he was saying. In the old-fashioned English clubs in which they congregated over imported whiskey and wine on most evenings they mulled gloomily over the possibilities that Modi would change everything. When all he did after becoming Prime Minister that first time was to leave them alone they found other reasons to hate him. It was this group from which most rumours emanated of how Modi was 'destroying' all the institutions of democracy and how he was planting RSS men in places where they could change textbooks and 'saffronize' the education system.

Ironically, it was in India's public education system that real 'parivartan' was most desperately needed. Indian children continue to be victims of a colonial system of mass education that teaches them so little about their own country that they grow up half-ashamed to be Indian. Their parents send them to schools in which the medium of instruction is technically English but it is so hopeless a pidgin version of this language that they learn to neither speak, read nor write in it. If they learned their own languages as they did before the British came to rule India, it would not matter. They could learn English as a foreign language, as do children in most other countries, but in the process of being taught badly in a foreign language they lose touch with their own.

They are also deprived of knowledge of the country for reasons of a false idea of secularism. By the time I left school I knew more about English history and literature than my own and spoke only English even though the only language I spoke for the first years of my life was Punjabi. At least in the school I went to I learned to read and write English well. This is not true of most Indian schools and the worst sufferers are those who are forced to rely on state schools. The linguistic and knowledge skills they leave school with make them virtually unemployable, so this was an area in which Modi could have brought 'parivartan' without anyone complaining. It did not happen.

* * *

There was an attempt soon after he came to power to create an alternative to the leftist, supposedly liberal, viewpoint that had dominated the public square. This was done under the aegis of the India Foundation and was led by Ram Madhav. After Modi became Prime Minister I went to see him in the fine new office of the India Foundation in a new building in an old and expensive quarter of Delhi. He had his own private office in an open-plan hall in which many people worked behind fancy computers. I told him I had come to see him in the hope that Modi would be able to do something to create the institutions of classical studies and languages that were necessary if there was ever to be an Indian renaissance. He listened attentively and when I mentioned that there were certain classical Indian languages that would soon disappear because only a handful of scholars knew them any more, he said that even with his own mother tongue, Telugu, there were reasons to worry.

Then I told him about a proposal that one of the great American Sanskritists, Sheldon (Shelly) Pollock, had given the Sonia-Manmohan government. It was a detailed proposal to create an institute of classical languages. It had remained buried in some government office, I told him, but as I said this I noticed that the mention of Shelly's name had disturbed him. After a pause he said, 'Our people tell me that he has done harm to India.' I knew exactly who he was talking about and told him that he should pay no attention to anything 'these people' said because all they had ever done was attack any western scholar who dared learn Sanskrit. Shelly was head of the Sanskrit department in Columbia University and had done more for Sanskrit by starting the Clay Sanskrit Library than most Indian scholars had. He would be considered a great rishi in ancient times just for this. But I realized that Ram Madhav was no longer listening. No institute of classical languages ever got built and the man who had hounded Shelly and denounced all he had done was soon to be seen at important RSS events seated in the front row.

The cultural 'parivartan' never happened but Ram Madhav made an effort to create an atmosphere from which the idea of an Indian renaissance could begin to germinate. In the winter of Modi's first year as Prime Minister I was invited to the India Foundation's annual 'ideas' conference in Goa. As were a large group of other people who were not considered part of the 'Lutyens set'. On the eve of my departure for Goa I met the editor of *Open* magazine, S. Prasannarajan, at the launch of my son's new novel and he said jokingly, 'So the fascists are going to the beach tomorrow.' Prasanna was joking but those of us who had dared support Modi openly were already being called fascists by those who spat at the mention of his name. I supported him openly in my column and lost a lot of friends for doing this.

The conference was held in a lovely beach resort that sprawled over many acres of gardens going down to a private beach. There were villas set amid dancing palm trees and luscious gardens. There were restaurants and swimming pools, so nobody needed to go to the beach or even leave the premises unless they wanted a taste of local colour. The entire resort was taken over by the India Foundation. The lobby was open on all sides like a pavilion, so salty, warm breezes blew through it, and I saw India Foundation placards and banners and volunteers with distinctive saffron scarves around their necks. While sipping my welcome coconut drink I noticed my old friend and comrade in journalism, Swapan Dasgupta, and Shaurya Doval, both of whom were on the board of the India Foundation.

That evening a feast was laid out in one of the gardens. There were tables laden with dishes from all over India along with spicy Goan seafood and European food for those who wanted it. The only thing unavailable was liquor, so those of us with a taste for an evening glass of wine or two abandoned the garden feast for snacks and drinks in the bar. We talked, inevitably, of how Modi was doing as Prime Minister and a consensus formed that his biggest flaw till then was that he had not moved fast enough on bringing about desperately needed reforms in the economy. We agreed that without this there was no chance of creating the one million new jobs that India needed annually. He had spent most of his first six months in office travelling at a frenetic pace to foreign countries. Almost as if he needed field trips to learn how to deal with the leaders of the world. This exercise in foreign travel was ostensibly to convince foreign investors to come and 'Make in India' and to show the leaders of the world that India now had a real Prime Minister instead of one who was appointed by Sonia Gandhi. Indians are mostly too poor to travel abroad, so they see foreign travel as an unaffordable luxury even if it is undertaken by their leaders. Modi's whirlwind foreign tours had become the butt of jokes and sneers. Congress supporters took to calling him an NRI (Non-resident Indian) Prime Minister, a label once pasted on Rajiv Gandhi who travelled even more in his first months in office.

There may not have been jokes about Modi's foreign travels had there been signs of real 'parivartan' at home. For this to happen the most important change that was needed was for the Prime Minister to curb the vast powers of the bureaucracy. Nobody hates the word 'parivartan' more than the Indian bureaucrat and they are masters at preventing change wherever they see signs of it beginning to happen. But instead of curbing their immense powers Modi seemed to become increasingly dependent on bureaucrats. And not just those who worked for the Government of India. He took to holding regular videoconferences with the chief secretaries of states to discuss the progress of the programmes that he had initiated. I heard from one BJP chief minister that this reliance on chief secretaries was annoying. 'I have sometimes been holding an important meeting with my chief secretary when he has excused himself because of the Prime Minister's video conference. It's not on.'

So that evening in the bar we gossiped about things such as this but in general there was a consensus among us that Modi's first few months in office had gone well. 'It's nice to see the Prime Minister of India being taken seriously by the leaders of the world,' a BJP MP said, sipping his Scotch.

'Yes. It is.'

'But he needs to move faster on the economic front,' said a journalist who had been an old supporter of the BJP.

My own contribution was to say that I had just been in Srinagar and noticed real discontent building up because the flood relief package of Rs 80,000 crore had not yet been disbursed.

'You must tell Ram Madhav this.'

'Yes.'

'He is in charge of Kashmir.'

'Yes. I shall try and catch him between sessions tomorrow.'

The next morning I woke early for a quick jog on the beach and noticed that it was a perfect, balmy Goa day. I would have loved to spend it lying on the resort's beautiful, private beach but there were sessions to attend. Sessions that began with a blessing from Sri Sri Ravi Shankar. I saw this as an indication that the India Foundation was not afraid of sending the message that it functioned in a country in which 80 per cent of the people were Hindu. If this was indeed the plan it unravelled early that morning when a Belgian Indologist and Hindutva sympathizer called Koenraad Elst had to be sent home in disgrace because of his remarks on Islam.

It was not what he said about Islam that was wrong so much as the offensive manner in which he said it. A Muslim diplomat stood up halfway through Elst's speech and walked out. Ram Madhav, who was seated in the front row, intervened and the session was abruptly ended. The next thing we knew was that Elst had been put on a flight back to Belgium. The conference was intended to create a new idea of India but definitely not one in which there would be no room for Muslims.

The other sessions at the conference were about nationalism and India's heritage. The people who spoke about these things were not necessarily scholars but the one thing they had in common was that they were not leftists. Most had some degree of allegiance to the BJP or the RSS but they were not overtly members of either the political party or the 'cultural' wing of it. I attended this annual conference in Goa for the next three years but stopped going when it became clear that they were just talk shops and not designed to actually come up with solutions for such serious problems as saving India's ancient languages or decolonizing the mass education system – a British legacy that Congress prime ministers had never bothered to Indianize or change.

If no Indian renaissance began to happen under Modi it could also have been because his alma mater, the RSS, had no idea of what needed to be done. Having talked at length to many of its leading lights I learned years ago that their idea of India was limited to revivalism and religion. The only exception was Ram Madhav. But after Modi became Prime Minister he was given charge of Kashmir and the north-eastern states and this was so huge a political burden to handle that he had little time for doing much else.

Modi himself was too busy doing the things he understood better. He had grown up in a poor family, with memories of a mother who spent her entire day inhaling smoke from cooking on a primitive stove. This seemed to have left a scar on his heart because one of the first things he did was to request rich Indians to give up their subsidy on gas cylinders. The response was overwhelming and he was able to use the money saved to provide gas connections in the poorest rural homes under what he called his Ujjwala Yojana. Posters bearing his face and that of a smiling village woman appeared all over the country to make the point that this was a scheme that he had personally devised.

His critics sneered that the cylinders he provided to rural homes were rented out for weddings and not used by the woman of the house. But on my travels in villages that had remained almost unaffected by the 21st century it never ceased to surprise me to see kitchen stoves working on gas. He also expended his personal energy on other schemes that would benefit the poorest of India's citizens like building 'pucca' houses for those who lived in huts of mud and thatch and he took pride in the fact that after his government came to power they had ensured that every home in India without electricity was connected to electricity grids.

13

Final Months

THE *India Today* conclave was held for the second time in Mumbai in 2018 in the same Grand Hyatt hotel's vast basement conference hall where it was held the year before. While trying to register as a delegate and collect my entry pass I noticed a businessman friend who was having the same problem I was with the girls at the registration desk. They were not convinced that we were valid delegates. I thought it might be because of the way the businessman was dressed. He wore a bright red jacket and trousers of an equally unusual hue and with his shock of white hair looked more aged hippie than tycoon. I knew him to be an ardent supporter of Modi, so while waiting for someone from *India Today* to come and help me convince the registration girls of my credentials I chatted to the businessman.

'Still a Modi supporter?' I asked.

'Yes. Definitely. But he has made mistakes. Demonetization was the biggest of them but this cow business is also too much. Who are these vigilantes who are killing Muslim traders and dairy farmers? Why don't you journalists do some investigative journalism?'

'We don't need to. They admit to being supporters of the BJP. And judging from the huge tilaks on their foreheads and the saffron scarves they wear, they must be. Also they speak BJP language.'

'Nonsense. How can you be sure that they aren't Congress goons pretending to be BJP to discredit Modi?'

'If they could be that organized,' I said, 'then it's hard to understand why they aren't organized enough to win a few elections.'

'That is because Rahul Gandhi is a moron.'

'You know that the keynote speaker in the first session today is Sonia Gandhi?'

'Yes. That is why I am here so early in the morning...since I am in semi-retirement now I rarely wake up this early.'

Kaveree Bamzai, who worked at the time for *India Today*, appeared at this point and took less than a minute to convince the girls at the registration desk to let us in. A wide stone staircase led to the conference hall that glittered and shimmered with huge flashlights as if we were in an enormous TV studio. This was what it in fact was. All the sessions were filmed and shown live on the India Today group's two channels. Near the stage there were tables covered in white table cloths at which already sat Aroon Purie's wife, Rekha, their two daughters, their friends and other VIP guests. Behind the tables, to the end of the hall, stretched chairs tightly packed in rows. I knew that if I did not manage to get a ringside seat at one of the front-row tables it would be more worth my while to watch the proceedings on television. So I grabbed the first empty chair I saw and ignored the *India Today* usher who tried to tell me that I was sitting at a table reserved for speakers or sponsors or something. He did not get much of a chance to continue trying to send me away because a hush suddenly fell and Sonia Gandhi appeared in a pale green silk sari with a shawl draped over her shoulders.

Our eyes met and she looked coldly away, as did the little coterie of tired-looking middle-aged men who accompanied her. I knew most of them but like their boss they too had taken to pretending to have never met me. The last time I had got within chatting distance of Sonia was three years earlier when the celebrated writer Khushwant Singh died. He had been of great help to me when I tried to publish my first book, so as soon as I heard that he had passed I went to pay my last respects. His ground-floor apartment in central Delhi's Sujan Singh Park was full by the time I got there. Family and friends crowded into his small drawing room, whispering mournfully to each other, but there was almost nobody in the anteroom in which they had laid his body. I went in and said my personal goodbye and an atheist's little prayer to wish him well on the journey he was taking. As I was walking back into the drawing room I almost bumped into Sonia. She mistook me for a member of the family and smiled and did a polite namaste on the way into the anteroom but on the way out realized that it was me she had been polite to, so she then pretended not to see me as she walked past.

We had once been friends. But our estrangement began after she became a politician, much as it had when Rajiv became Prime Minister. Before he was killed I managed to explain to him that when I wrote about him in my columns and disagreed with his policies, it was a disagreement with the Prime Minister of India. He understood. She never did. The estrangement deepened after she became Congress president and the most powerful political leader in the land. I did not approve of her policies and she did not approve of what I said about them. After she virtually destroyed Lavasa, I found it hard to forgive her. If she had tried to be nice to me I would have probably responded with rudeness. So her cold stare that morning was only what I expected. What was less expected was the standing ovation she was given by the businessmen gathered at the conclave that morning. In the front row there were rich and famous men with names like Godrej, Wadia, Bajaj and Goenka and they all stood up and clapped.

Nobody had supported Modi more fervently than India's biggest businessmen. They supported him more than they had any other Prime Minister because his campaign speeches in 2014 were music to their ears. He spoke of how government had no business to be in business. He spoke of making India a country in which it would be easier to do business than anywhere else in the world. They believed him and saw him as the man most likely to become India's Margaret Thatcher and Ronald Reagan rolled into one. When the 'suit-boot' jibe made him revert to exactly the sort of economic policies that Sonia Gandhi had pursued in the last years of her tenure as India's de facto prime minister, they were not just disappointed but angry.

So when they saw Sonia that morning they greeted her as they would have a beloved friend whom they had lost touch with because of their own betrayal of the friendship. She smiled and accepted the standing ovation as if it was long overdue. When she stood up to go to the stage to make her keynote address I noticed that she looked frail and walked with uncertain steps. Rumours of her being on the verge of dying from some mysterious disease had circulated for many months. These were confirmed by her regular visits for medical attention to a country that everyone assumed was the United States but nobody knew for sure. Nobody was sure either whether she was suffering from cancer or some other serious ailment in her pancreas. Since she had never lost her hair or shown other signs of chemotherapy, everyone concluded that she did not have cancer but a pancreatic tumour.

That morning the only sign of ill health was that she looked thinner than usual and her skin had the pallid colour people get when they have not been outdoors much. In every other sense she seemed in fine fettle. She made a better speech than I had ever heard her make before, interspersed with little jokes and self-deprecation. She said she was relieved to have given up being Congress president, after 20 long years, because one of the things she looked forward to was not having to speak in public again. 'It does not come naturally to me, which is why I have been called a reader, not a leader.'

After praising the men and women whom she called India's 'founding fathers and founding mothers' she painted a truly gloomy picture of present-day India, saying that the 'open, liberal society' that had existed was under threat from an 'alternative, regressive vision'. She described what was happening as a carefully crafted plot to re-imagine India by fanning bigotry and rewriting history. Alternative voices were being silenced, she said, and institutions destroyed. 'Fear and intimidation are the order of the day...something even more sinister is happening. Our very DNA is being re-engineered.'

Then seated in front of a backdrop that said 'Sonia Gandhi, the Great Unifier', she spent an hour answering questions that Aroon asked. She mocked Modi's 'achievements' every chance she got and said that most of the programmes that were working well were those that had been started by her government. It was important to remember that Congress governments had done a lot of work in their time and it was not as if there was some kind of 'black hole' till Modi came along, she said. When Aroon asked her why she believed the Congress had lost the election, she said it was entirely because of 'marketing'. They had failed to market their achievements and in this department Modi had shown that he was far better than anyone else. There were also false promises made, she said, that fooled the people into believing that their lives would change dramatically under Modi. This had clearly not happened, she said, with a smile.

When Aroon reminded her that one of the factors that had worked in Modi's favour were the scams that had defined the last years of her government, she admitted that there had been some but pointed out that they were exaggerated far beyond their actual scope. I noticed that most of the audience looked at her with a reverence that was undeserved but that most Indians continue to feel for our only real royal family. Sonia sensed the adulation and she sensed that the winds were blowing in a new direction, so she predicted that Modi's 'achchhe din' slogan would do what Atal Bihari Vajpayee's 'India Shining' had done in 2004. Her last words before she departed with her little coterie were, 'We are going to come back. We are not going to let them come back.'

The audience cheered when she said this because by March 2018 not only was the economy not showing any signs of the boom these businessmen had hoped for but it was doing worse than expected. Later when I asked friends in the audience what they had thought about her speech, the consensus was that she was looking more like a leader than ever.

'Look at the dignity with which she spoke.'

'Look how elegantly she was dressed. And let's face it, Modi has made such a mess that we are quite looking forward to her returning to power.'

'But it won't be her,' I pointed out, 'it will be her son.'

'Well, so what? He is already looking more like a leader than he did before. So it's just a question of time before he learns the ropes. And look at the family he comes from…they have ruled India for so long, so they know what to do.'

'What do you think has been the biggest mistake Modi has made?'

'Demonetization.'

Businessmen are usually afraid to speak openly about political matters and political leaders but that morning nobody I spoke to seemed at all afraid to speak out against Modi. The conclave was taking place soon after the BJP lost Gorakhpur and Phulpur and this was another reason why people seemed to feel confident enough to speak openly against Modi. There was also the shadow of Nirav Modi hanging over this conclave in an ominous way. It was being held weeks after the world discovered that this diamantaire to the rich and really famous had fled to an unknown country because of an inability to pay back the loans he had taken from public sector banks. When the story broke it turned out that he had managed to bribe bank officials, mostly at the Punjab National Bank, into continuing to give him loan after loan despite his showing no sign of paying back the thousands of crores of rupees he had already borrowed.

At the conclave's gala dinner that evening I met a journalist from a financial newspaper who said to me conspiratorially that he had just talked to Nirav Modi. 'Where is he?' I asked him.

'In the Bahamas,' he said. 'I managed to get through on his cell. I am surprised that the government has not managed to find him.'

'Nor has the media. Reporters went looking for him all the way to New York and didn't manage to find him there.'

'He is a clever man,' the journalist said with a laugh. 'They won't be able to bring him back ever.'

'Do you know him well?'

'Well enough...I've interviewed him a couple of times. He is not a bad man but a bit twisted because you know that he was about five when his mother committed suicide. He was in the room when she jumped out of the window.'

'That is terrible,' I said, 'but it doesn't excuse the fact that he was a bank robber in the guise of a businessman.'

The Congress Party had used the Nirav Modi story as yet another rock to fling at Modi. Before absconding the jeweller had shown up in Davos, where Modi came for the first time to address a special session. Before his session or after, he posed with Indian businessmen for a photograph and in this photograph standing almost directly behind the Prime Minister was Nirav Modi. This was the last time he was seen in public and because the Congress Party was at this point sensing that Modi was at his weakest they used 'chhota Modi' (little Modi) like a weapon against his surnamesake.

So little was going right with Modi's tenure by those first months of 2018 that his political obituaries were being written by pundits in newspapers across India. Most of the writers of these obituaries were men and women who had hated him even before he became Prime Minister, and because he had done nothing to cultivate the mainstream media he got no support when he most needed it. BJP supporters on social media, and there was a small army on the move daily, attacked any journalist who made the slightest criticism of Modi by charging them with resenting the fact that their perks had been taken away. By this they meant that there were no more trips to foreign lands on the Prime Minister's plane, as used to happen in the past. This army of semi-literate trolls had not noticed that when prime ministers take journalists with them on foreign tours it is usually to win their support, not to give them a free ride.

Modi had harmed himself by keeping this unnecessary distance from the media. And by 2018 Rahul Gandhi realized that he could take advantage of this weakness and so made it a point to be much more accessible to journalists than he had been when his mother's government was in office. He started holding regular press conferences where he chatted with journalists with charm and informality, and so by the time the doubts about the Rafale defence deal began to become public he had a large army of friendly journalists who were more than ready to listen to his charges of corruption. Rahul seemed to have been fooled by the support he got from the media and became increasingly reckless in the charges he made. Almost every time he addressed a public meeting he said, 'Modi has taken Rs 30,000 crore of your money and put it in the pocket of his friend Anil Ambani.' He did this without noticing that most of the people he addressed did not think of Modi as a thief. He did not see that it was simply not possible for Modi to have 'stolen' Rs 30,000 crore from a deal that was worth Rs 56,000 crore.

Ambani was one of nearly a hundred Indian businessmen who were listed to make Rafale parts once the fighter jets started being produced in India. But it was as if Rahul Gandhi had either not grasped this or because he was deliberately trying to ruin Ambani, already in financial trouble, by making him into a whipping boy. The problem was that he was unable to come up with any evidence that Rs 30,000 crore had in fact been stolen and given to Ambani, so his allegations began to sound silly and a little hysterical.

It was as if he was trying to prove that Modi was a thief to erase the memory of the scandal that had besmirched his father's reputation as Mr Clean. What had happened then was a different story altogether. Rajiv Gandhi had banned arms dealers from becoming agents in defence deals in what he said was an attempt to end corruption in a sector that was truly corrupt. I remember well how Delhi in the '70s and '80s swarmed with arms dealers. I knew some of them and they became enormously rich very quickly. Their newly acquired riches became the subject of much gossip in social Delhi. There were also foreigners, many of them French, who cultivated military men and high officials to sell whatever equipment it was they were selling. Bribery and corruption were nearly always involved, so when Rajiv Gandhi announced that he was banning all agents he was called Mr Clean by the media.

Foreign journalists were so bedazzled by his looks and his charm and his beautiful Italian wife that stories about an Indian Camelot were published in important western newspapers. Rajiv and Sonia could do no wrong for the first three years that he was Prime Minister. Not even the massacre of more than 3,000 Sikhs in the first three days of his tenure besmirched his name. Nor did the horrible tragedy in Bhopal that killed more than 15,000 of the city's poorest citizens because poisonous gas leaked out of a Union Carbide chemical plant. The worldwide head of this American company was in India at the time but was allowed quietly to leave. Rajiv did not get blamed for this. Nor did his government in Madhya Pradesh whose Chief Minister fled the city when he heard about the industrial tragedy. Rajiv was untouched by both these events because in the eyes of most Indians he was almost as perfect as the god Rama. He was young and good-looking, which are almost as important prerequisites for political leaders as they are for movie stars.

This state of affairs lasted until halfway through his term in office when Swedish radio broke the news that the arms firm Bofors had paid bribes to Indian officials to win the deal to sell its Howitzers. Immediately rumours began to spread that it was his Italian wife who had ruined him. Rumours spread that when the deal was signed in Stockholm between Bofors and the Government of India, Sonia's brothers-in-law had been present. My journalist friend Chitra Subramaniam risked her life and her marriage to follow the story until she found evidence that Bofors bribe money was paid into the accounts of Sonia's best friends, Ottavio and Maria Quattrocchi. The mud from Bofors became hard to shake off long after Rajiv died.

Long before the election campaign began, Rahul Gandhi started yelling 'Chowkidar chor hai' (the watchman is a thief) at his press conferences and public rallies. It was a catchy slogan and for a while it may have had resonance but it did not convince ordinary voters that Modi was a thief. In the eyes of most of them Modi was such a patriot that they could not imagine him making money out of a defence deal.

When Bofors happened the story really was different. I remember wandering about rural northern India and coming upon semi-literate and illiterate voters who felt personally wronged that the 'biggest thief in India is sitting in the Prime

Minister's house'. Inevitably the 'foreign woman' got more blame than a son of India, so little ditties started to be sung at election meetings that sneered at Rajiv for being a son-in-law of Italy. No matter how hard Rahul Gandhi tried to achieve the same sort of consensus on Modi, he failed. In the Lok Sabha during the debate on the Rafale deal, his handful of MPs (44) flung paper planes at the treasury benches instead of taking the debate seriously. When Rahul's sister formally entered politics with a rally in Lucknow in which she and her brother rode through the streets on the roof of a truck, Rahul carried a toy fighter jet in his hands. But these antics failed to convince ordinary voters that Modi was a thief mostly because nobody in Rahul Gandhi's team was able to establish that bribes had been paid to anyone.

At the height of their efforts to establish that Modi was a thief came the Valentine's Day attack on a paramilitary convoy in the Kashmiri town of Pulwama. Modi's Kashmir policy was confused and blundering but the attacks on security personnel by masked, stone-pelting Kashmiris had created a rift between the way the average Kashmiri saw what was happening and the way the rest of India saw it. Videos of young Central Reserve Police Force (CRPF) men responding only with smiles when they were assaulted and mocked by mobs of Kashmiri boys went viral on social media every time they were uploaded. Slogans like 'Indian dogs go back' had been heard in the Valley for years but were not as offensive as they became in this time of social media.

Kashmiris in any case were unpopular in the rest of India because of the belief – mostly based on wrong information – that Indian taxpayers had spent a fortune on giving Kashmir's citizens subsidies of all kinds. So when 40 CRPF men were killed on February 14, 2019 by a suicide bomber who recorded a video claiming that he was from the Jaish-e-Mohammed before he used his car to blow up the bus in which the troops were travelling, a pent-up volcano of rage erupted through India.

When the bodies of the young soldiers were brought to their homes, ordinary people came out in huge numbers to join their funerals in towns and villages across more than 16 states in India. They shouted angry slogans against Pakistan. In the salons of Delhi and Mumbai even 'secular', educated Indians began to question why India had never responded militarily to the many attacks on Indian soil by Pakistani jihadist groups. The question most asked was why a Congress government had not retaliated militarily even after the terror attacks on Mumbai on November 26, 2008. When that terrible event happened Modi was Chief Minister of Gujarat and appeared on Rajat Sharma's programme, *Aap Ki Adalat*. When Rajat asked him what he would have done after the attack on Mumbai if he had been Prime Minister, he said, 'The first thing I would have done would have been to stop sending love letters to the leaders of Pakistan. I would have made them pay for what they did.'

The Valentine's Day massacre of unarmed young men returning from leave was the worst act of jihadist terrorism after he became Prime Minister. But despite what he had said after 26/11, everyone thought that at the very most there would be another 'surgical strike'. Two years earlier, when a military camp was attacked in the Kashmiri border town of Uri, he had ordered an attack into Pakistan. The army fired missiles across the Line of Control at what the military intelligence identified as jihadist staging posts in Pakistan Occupied Kashmir (POK).

Ajit and I were in Delhi two days after the Pulwama attack for the wedding of the daughter of Raian Karanjawala. Raian was one of Arun Jaitley's closest friends, so the wedding was in the garden of Arun's house on a chilly, bleak day that reflected the general mood. The wedding ceremony was still going on when we arrived and the garden was nearly empty except for a handful of early guests who stood around the bar. Vijay Dhar was among them. His father, D.P. Dhar, had once been among Indira Gandhi's closest advisors. Vijay himself had been close to Rajiv, and as one of the few prominent Hindus who continued to live in Srinagar he kept a keen watch on what was happening in Kashmir.

'What do you think Modi will do?' I asked soon after the usual pleasantries.

'Nothing.'

'Surely he will have to do something...there is real anger across the country.'

'Yes. I know. But he won't do anything because he will be told by his advisors that any escalation could result in war. And the Pakistanis are mad enough to use nukes.'

The garden filled up slowly with guests. Nearly all of them were people who had served in some capacity or the other in the Government of India. When I spotted A.S. Dulat, I cornered him and asked what he thought would be India's response. Like a good spy he kept his views to himself at the best of times. His response to my question was an enigmatic smile, but when I pushed him for an answer he hinted that he thought there would be some kind of escalation in tensions but that it would stop short of a real war.

Everyone I talked to that day, whether bureaucrat or politician or journalist, said almost the same thing. Modi would not risk a war, they said, he could not afford to with a general election around the corner. As we were leaving, Ajit noticed that Arun was lying on a daybed on his veranda and that small groups of people were going in to ask after his health. He had just returned from New York, where he had a surgery to remove a cancerous tumour on his leg. Ajit said we should go in and say hello and so we did.

At some point Arun said that he wanted to tell me something that he did not even want to say in front of Ajit, so I had a few moments alone with him. He told me that what he was going to tell me was something that he never wanted to see in any of my columns or in a book. So I shall keep what he said private, but as I was leaving I asked if India was going to respond to the attack in Pulwama. 'Just wait and watch,' he said with a grim smile. He had just returned from a special Cabinet meeting, so it was clear that he knew something that he could not talk about yet.

This convinced me that something was likely to happen. But when I talked to a Pakistani friend in Lahore he said that the general feeling there was that nothing was likely to happen. 'Nothing can happen,' he said, 'because our military guys would have no hesitation in using one of their tactical nuclear weapons if there is a war. They know that they cannot win a conventional war, so they feel this is their only option.'

'It's hardly an option.'

'It's crazy because Lahore would be destroyed as well if they target Amritsar but there is talk of these tactical nuclear weapons all the time.'

'Here there is talk of terrorist camps being attacked,' I said.

'Well, if that is all that happens you would be doing us a favour,' said the Pakistani friend.

On the morning of February 26, when I checked Twitter I noticed tweets from a couple of TV journalists that said that Indian fighter planes had gone deep inside Pakistan to attack a jihadist training centre in a town called Balakot. I also noticed tweets, including one from Kashmir's former Chief Minister Omar Abdullah, wondering which Balakot this was. It was a careless tweet because he should have known that the other Balakot was actually in India on our side of the Line of Control. The tweet that confirmed that Indian fighters had in fact crossed deep into Pakistan and attacked the Balakot that is in the province of Khyber Pakhtunkhwa came from Pakistan. A tweet from the official handle of the Government of Pakistan said, 'Indian aircrafts intruded from Muzaffarabad sector. Facing timely and effective response from Pakistan Air Force, released payload in haste while escaping, which fell near Balakot. No casualties or damage: DG ISPR Major General Asif Ghafoor.'

It was much later that the Government of India confirmed that Indian fighter aircraft had entered deep into Pakistan and bombed a site in Balakot that was a Jaish-e-Mohammed training camp for jihadists. Indian government spokesmen called it a pre-emptive, non-military strike, and if Modi's opponents had been wise they would have congratulated him on the strike and then carried on with the election campaign. They were foolish enough to start demanding proof of the airstrike and foolish enough to start attacking Modi personally with all sorts of mostly silly charges.

Leading this campaign was Rahul Gandhi, who seemed to become increasingly hysterical in every speech he made. He started his attack on Modi by charging him with shooting a promotional film in Jim Corbett National Park on the day of the attack in Pulwama. 'I stopped everything I was doing that day,' he took to shrieking in every speech, 'but Modi continued making his promotional film.' Then came a revival of the charges of his having 'stolen money' from the Rafale deal and 'put it in the pocket of Anil Ambani'.

He sounded more and more desperate as the election drew closer and Modi sounded once more as confident as he had during the 2014 election campaign. Rahul's sister Priyanka – long considered the Congress Party's ultimate weapon – declared that she was now a full-time politician days before the attack on Pulwama. She had always been a media star, so every major TV channel followed her to Lucknow and covered every detail of her first visit to the capital of Uttar Pradesh after she was appointed a senior general secretary in the Congress Party.

Some journalists were so excited by her official entry into politics that they stayed up all night outside the Congress Party office to report her every move. So we discovered that she had worked into the early hours of the morning. They gushed about how her resemblance to her famous grandmother was the reason why there were traffic jams in Lucknow on the day of her first official tour because people stopped their cars in the middle of the road to take pictures of Indira Gandhi's granddaughter. They filed long TV reports speculating about why she had chosen not to make a public speech. Her brother did, at the end of their long drive through the streets of Lucknow, and as usual sounded uncomfortable with the Hindi language and uncomfortable with public speaking.

So even before the attack on Balakot fired up patriotic passions across India, when he was compared to Modi, he looked like a sullen, diffident schoolboy. After Balakot he began to sound like an angry, diffident schoolboy. It was as if he had begun to sense that the election was unlikely to throw up a result that would put him ahead in the race to become India's next Prime Minister. In the alliance that he was part of, virtually every single person who led one of the 21 political parties saw himself (and, in two cases, herself) as India's next Prime Minister.

So Rahul's chances were not good in the first place, but because he led India's oldest political party and because he alone in the alliance could claim to be an 'all-India' leader he was projected by the media as Modi's main rival. Somehow, though, gravitas always seemed to elude the heir to India's oldest and most powerful political dynasty. No matter what he did.

Priyanka, who was appointed a senior general secretary with an office in the party headquarters that had once been Rahul's, made widely televised visits to Varanasi and other parts of India and gave speeches in better Hindi than her brother but mostly talked about her family. It reminded ordinary Indians that the mighty Congress Party of our freedom movement had under Sonia Gandhi become a private limited company. Sonia was president of the Congress Party longer than even those who had been president in its glory days. She was so successful that she not only revived it when it was at one of its lowest ebbs in its long and illustrious history but managed to win a second term for the Prime Minister she appointed. This was no small achievement. Nor was it a small achievement that as a foreigner who spoke only servants' Hindi before becoming a politician, she learned to speak Hindi well enough to make public speeches. Why she never encouraged her son to become better at this most widely spoken of India's languages remains a mystery. So even when Rahul Gandhi was making a public speech he ended up making some stupid blunder or the other, mostly because his Hindi was so limited.

This became a serious problem when he announced what he declared was the most 'historic' anti-poverty plan in the world. In the last week of March 2019, while addressing an election rally in Dehradun, he announced that if the Congress formed the next government in Delhi it would ensure that the poorest 20 per cent of India's population would get Rs 72,000 'straight into their bank accounts' every year. This was going to be the biggest universal basic income scheme in the world. In Hindi the acronym for it was NYAY (Nyuntam Aay Yojana), which means 'justice'. It was to rectify the 'anyay' (injustice) that Modi had done by giving all the people's money to his '15 rich friends'. 'If Modi can give money to the rich,' he said grandly, 'then where is the harm in the Congress giving money to the poorest of the poor.' The scheme was going to cost Indian taxpayers an estimated Rs 3.6 lakh crore a year. This meant spending more on it than the Indian government did on health, education and subsidized food, petrol and fertilizers.

Congress Party cheerleaders in the media hailed the scheme as a 'gamechanger' even if Rahul Gandhi found it hard to make up his mind about exactly how much each poor family would get. He got so muddled with announcing the figures in Hindi that he went from telling India's poorest citizens that they would get Rs 72,000 a year to Rs 72,000 a month. It was left to Congress Party spokesmen to explain that the actual amount would be Rs 6,000 a month for families that were earning less than Rs 12,000. And that not every poor Indian would qualify to receive this munificence. They tried to explain how they would identify the beneficiaries but it soon became evident that the scheme had been so poorly planned that nobody was sure about anything that it involved. What disappointed me personally was that men like P. Chidambaram gave it full support.

My own awareness of the futility of schemes of this kind came directly from a conversation I had with him long ago. He was Finance Minister in the H.D. Deve Gowda government in the '90s when I travelled with him to his constituency to interview him for a television programme. It was a Hindi programme called *Ek Din, Ek Jeevan* (One Day, One Life), so I spent the day travelling with him through dusty villages and grimy towns. As dusk was falling we arrived in a small settlement. The light was perfect, so we stopped in a barren field and I asked him my last few questions for the interview. While we talked a very old, very wrinkled woman approached him with her hands folded in supplication. She spoke in Tamil, so I am not sure what she said but noticed that he seemed to become increasingly irritated with whatever it was. When she finished what she was saying he turned to me and said that she was complaining about her Rs 100 monthly pension always being late and about how she had to travel a long way to collect this pathetically small amount. Her sons had moved to the city and she was dependent on this tiny pension to stay alive.

When she limped away sadly he turned to me and said with real anger in his voice that it was madness to create huge, centralized welfare programmes because thousands of crores of rupees went into running schemes that delivered almost nothing to beneficiaries. The money would have been much better spent on delivering services that were more decentralized and accessible. The reason why I remember this particular conversation vividly was that it was the first time I became aware of the futility of the sort of huge centralized anti-poverty programmes that had been in existence ever since Indira Gandhi won what came to be known as the 'Garibi Hatao election' in 1971. Mrs Gandhi was a clever politician and managed to turn the opposition's charges of corruption and inefficiency against her into a slogan that ended up winning her a huge majority in Parliament. 'They say remove Indira and I say to them remove poverty.' In Hindi it had a ring to it that was almost musical and very catchy: 'Woh kehte hain Indira hatao, main kehti hoon garibi hatao.'

The NYAY scheme that her grandson announced with such fanfare was so much like the many grandiose schemes that his grandmother and mother had created to 'alleviate poverty' that it ended up being called Garibi Hatao 2.0. His father, Rajiv, had admitted once when he was Prime Minister that these programmes were not the solution to removing poverty because less than 15 paise out of every rupee spent actually reached the beneficiaries. If he had won a second term it is possible that he would have found better ways of dealing with India's hideous, shameful poverty. It is possible that he may have done what the Congress Prime Minister who replaced him did, which was to end the licence raj and allow India's shackled private sector to flourish and bloom. P.V. Narasimha Rao started moving his government away from Nehruvian socialism and central planning mainly because he inherited a bankrupt economy. But it worked.

Indian businessmen were so bound down by quotas and licences under Nehru and his daughter that many admitted that it had been easier to do business under the British Raj. Nehru believed fundamentally that the way forward was to emulate the Soviet Union's methods and so he created a Planning Commission and five-year plans and an economy that fined businessmen who produced more in their factories than their quotas permitted. His daughter raised taxes to 97 per cent to fund the massive welfare schemes she created in her efforts to prove that she was on the side of the poor. This ended up leaving poverty pretty much intact under the benign, centrally planned economic dictatorship created by father and daughter.

The India in which I grew up was a place where everything was in short supply because even daily necessities like bread and milk were produced only by the state. The poor remained poor, illiterate and desperate but there were not many rich Indians in those socialist times. If there were any lurking in the shadows, they tried to live humbly to evade the prying eyes of the income tax department. The only people who flourished in the days of the licence raj were political leaders and high officials. They lived in vast bungalows and never lacked for the things that ordinary Indians longed for. In emulation of the Marxist ways of the Soviet Union and Maoist China they lived in enclaves that may not have been as grand as the Kremlin in Moscow or the Forbidden City in Beijing, but when compared to the living standards of the average Indian they were.

Had Sonia Gandhi continued along the road laid out by the first Prime Minister she appointed, it is possible that absolute poverty would have disappeared from India altogether. She chose instead to go back to Nehruvian socialism and reinvent massive, leaky welfare schemes in the hope that this would ensure that her son inherited India as his birth right. The first of these schemes was MGNREGA that on paper guaranteed every rural family a hundred days of work a year but on the ground was little more than dole. Instead of building rural assets like schools, hospitals and roads, thousands of crores of rupees of taxpayers' money were frittered away on sham, seasonal jobs.

As Modi himself memorably said in the Lok Sabha, 'People were paid to dig ditches and shift mud from one ditch to the other.' Had he shown real political courage he would have scrapped MGNREGA altogether but he did not and instead ended up spending more and more money on a scheme that was designed to keep poor people in perpetual poverty. Nobody can rise above the poverty line, as low as it may be in rural India, on a hundred days of work a year.

Rahul Gandhi chose to continue along the path set by his mother, hence NYAY. His supporters believed that NYAY would win India back for the Congress. Rahul's main charge against Modi from the time he became Prime Minister was that he served only rich Indians. From day one he charged Modi with working only for his '15 rich friends.' Nobody ever learned who exactly these 15 rich Indians were, but even when Modi cancelled 86 per cent of India's currency in an overnight coup Rahul's charge against him was that he had done this to take 'money from the poor and give it to his 15 rich friends.'

When he called a press conference to release the Congress Party's manifesto for the 2019 general election, Rahul's exuberance about his NYAY was palpable. 'Garibi pe vaar, 72 hazaar.' The final assault on poverty will be Rs 72,000 a year. At the high table beside him sat his mother and other senior leaders and in the audience sat the newest member of the Gandhi family to enter politics, Priyanka, who clapped loudly as her brother addressed the press. Immediately afterwards she tweeted a link to the manifesto. When I went to the link I found a picture of Rahul Gandhi looking very white and wearing a white kurta amid a gathering of dark, colourfully dressed tribal Indians. The picture was posted under this headline: 'Election 2019 presents a stark choice to the people of India.'

In the text that followed there was this paragraph, 'The last five years have been disastrous for the people of India. The youth have lost jobs. Farmers have lost hope. Traders have lost business. Micro, small and medium enterprises have lost their confidence. Women have lost the sense of security. Deprived communities have lost their traditional rights. Institutions have lost independence.

'The harshest blow is that our citizens have lost their faith in the words of the Prime Minister and his Government. He has given us only grandiose promises, empty slogans, failed programmes, false statistics and an overall climate of fear, intimidation and hatred.'

14

Modi 2.0

WHEN campaigning began for elections to the 17th Lok Sabha I decided that I would go first to Behror, where Pehlu Khan was beaten to death on April 1, 2017. I had watched the video of this frail, old man being beaten to death and written about it in my column more than once. But I had not personally investigated what happened to the men who lynched him. The story was reported badly when it was reported at all, so I decided that the only way to find out what was really happening was to go to Behror. I set off from Delhi early one hot morning and drove past the deceptively modern glass and steel city of Gurgaon. It had been renamed Gurugram after Modi became Prime Minister to honour Dronacharya, who in the Mahabharata was the archery tutor to the royal family. Revival of India's ancient past was a serious project under Modi, so when it was found that modern Gurgaon was where Dronacharya had lived in Mahabharata times it was renamed Gurugram.

Little else was done by the BJP government in Haryana to improve this enclave of gleaming modernity, so if you looked behind the tall glass buildings that lined the highway it was easy to see that they barely concealed India's ancient squalor. Behind the façade of shiny, new malls and cinemas are filthy little streets that have not a semblance of municipal governance. No sooner does Gurugram end than the old India becomes clearly visible. Stray cattle loiter on the edge of the highway and crowded, squalid bazaars appear in which shops seem to rise out of dirty drains and rotting garbage.

Behror is a perfect fit with this urban landscape. As soon as I got off the highway I stopped in the main bazaar and asked if this was where Pehlu Khan had been killed. The greasy, squat shopkeeper I addressed my question to grinned and said, 'No. He was killed in the next street...'

'Were you there when it happened?'

'No, but I heard about what happened and can tell you he deserved what he got.' Another shopkeeper had joined our conversation by this point and he said, 'He was a cattle smuggler and the police knew this but wouldn't catch him because they are scared to catch Muslims.'

'He wasn't a cattle smuggler,' I said, 'he was a dairy farmer. And had bought the cows in Jaipur and had papers to prove this.'

'No. No. He was a smuggler and his son had been caught once before and beaten up for doing this. If you hurt Hindu sentiments by killing cows then this is what will happen to you.'

'What happened to the people who killed him?'

'They were arrested but they could be out on bail.'

This reminded me that the BJP government in Rajasthan at the time had been reluctant to make any arrests despite the video that proved Pehlu Khan was beaten to death. It reminded me that the Home Minister of the state had gone so far as to say that both sides were responsible for what happened. My old friend, Vasundhara Raje, was Chief Minister at the time and I remember being sickened by how little she had done to give Pehlu Khan's family the solace of justice. But she was no longer in the post in 2019 and the government was now being run by the 'secular' Congress Party. I was keen to see if more had been done to atone for the horrible lynching of a wretchedly poor dairy farmer. After my conversations with the shopkeepers in the bazaar I went in search of the police station where the case against the killers had been registered.

It was in a yellow-washed cottage that looked as if it may once have housed lower-grade British officials. It also looked as if it had not been repaired or painted since the British left. What may once have been quite fine rooms had been divided into ugly little cubbyholes in which police officials sat at badly made desks. When I asked in the first room about Pehlu Khan, the official gave me a cold stare and said, 'You need to ask the SHO (Station House Officer) about that but he is busy just now, so you can wait over there.'

He pointed to a cubbyhole that seemed a little grander than the others. In the middle of the courtyard stood an old banyan tree that lent grace to this dismal police station. I went and stood outside the open door of the SHO's office. When he spotted me he asked what I wanted and when I said that I was looking for information on the Pehlu Khan case he said, 'Go next door to the filing room. They will help you.'

Next door was yet another cubbyhole with paint peeling off the walls and shelves that were carved out of them. On these shelves lay mounds of mouldering files wrapped in red cloth. In the office were two young girls and an older man. He seemed to be in charge. When I told him that I was looking for the names of the men charged with killing Pehlu Khan he directed the girls to find the file. They spent 20 minutes or so opening and closing files before finally giving me two names that they said were of local men: Vipin, son of Sanjay Yadav, resident of Nainsukh mohalla, and Ravindra, son of Jaypal Yadav, resident of Jaitpura mohalla.

'These were the only two from Behror,' the official said, 'the others came from outside.'

'So are they under arrest?'

'No. They are out on bail. The case continues against them.'

He seemed reluctant to give me any more help. So I went in search of Vipin Yadav in the Nainsukh mohalla, which happened to be just metres away from the police station. I wandered past stray cows eating out of an open garbage bin, past drains that had greyish, soapy water in them and stopped at the first few houses that appeared at the end of the lane. A man sat outside and when I asked him if he could point me in the direction of Vipin Yadav's house he said he had never heard of him. I said he was the man arrested in connection with the lynching of Pehlu Khan. This was a name he did know and said I should go towards the college where there were houses that belonged to some Yadav families. So I did.

When a group of students appeared from behind the college gates I stopped to ask them if they knew where I could find Vipin Yadav. They said they had heard of him and that he was a student in their college but they did not know where he lived. 'You should try at the courthouse,' one of them said. So it was there I went. Lawyers sat on wooden benches outside the entrance of the courthouse drinking tea. They said the lawyer who was appearing on behalf of Pehlu Khan had not come for a while. But I should go inside and check with the 'reader'. The courthouse was a collection of yellow-washed barracks with low ceilings and small windows. Groups of lawyers sat under a shed. They directed me to the PP (public prosecutor), who they said I would find in ADJ-2 (the assistant district sessions judge's court). I found myself in a building with tiny rooms and a narrow veranda, at the end of which was a small room that was the office of the PP. A man who looked like he might be his clerk lounged lazily. It was hot. He offered me water from the bottle he was drinking from and called the PP on his cell phone.

'There is a woman here who says she is a journalist from Delhi,' he said to the PP on the phone. 'She is asking about Pehlu Khan...oh, okay.' Then turning to me he said, 'He says you should wait. He will be here soon.' I waited for half an hour and realized that it was pointless and that I would be better off going in search of Pehlu Khan's family. The clerk did not stop me from leaving. It was as if he knew that the PP was not going to be coming for a while.

Pehlu Khan's village is near Nuh in Haryana. I took the road that he was on when he was stopped by the mob that lynched him. I drove past wheat fields and small, ugly villages and got to Alwar. From here I was directed by local people to turn left if I wanted to go to Haryana. Lining the road were villages in which the most prominent signs were of private schools with names like Children's Academy and Little Flower. The villages all looked the same. They were dirty, crowded and unattractive. In one village there was some sign of colour from fruit shops that all seemed to be selling fat, yellow Indian berries called ber. I stopped and took pictures on my phone because it was such a relief to see a village that looked better than the others if only because of the fruit. It took me four hours to get to Nuh and another half hour to get to the village of Jaisinghpur.

Pehlu Khan's house was on the edge of it beyond a drain on which a couple of stone slabs had been laid to make a foot bridge. His wife, Zebunia, sat on a string bed in the courtyard. Children played on the dirt floor with a couple of baby goats. A gleaming new tractor stood in the middle of the courtyard. A young girl in a black salwar-kameez breastfed her baby. She said her name was Jafreen and that she was one of Zebunia's three daughters-in-law. Zebunia seemed used to journalists wandering by. She said in a faltering voice that she had only found out about her husband's lynching three days later. He was already dead in the hospital in Behror where they took him.

'Someone in the village saw that video of him being beaten up online. They called me to see it. I never saw him alive again. Now with him gone I depend on what my sons earn from working as helpers on trucks. It's not much but we have given up dairy farming since what happened…'

'Do you have land?'

'No.'

'But you have a tractor?'

'Someone gave it to us…someone from Dubai. We loan it out to those who have land. My son will tell you everything.'

While we talked a child was sent to find her son. Some minutes later arrived a skinny, frail young man who looked like he was barely out of his teens. He said his name was Arif. He said he was with his father when they were stopped by the mob. He told his story without emotion and as if he had told it so many times that he was tired of telling it. 'We had two milch cows and their two calves. We bought them from the fair in Jaipur and had all the papers to prove this. The men who stopped us said they were from the Bajrang Dal. They tore the papers up and took away the Rs 70,000 we had in the truck. Then they saw my father's beard and said...you are Muslims. That is when they started beating us. They used belts and hockey sticks. People watched but nobody helped us. The police took half an hour to come. Then they took us to the hospital. My father died there two days afterwards. My brother and I were badly injured. There was blood pouring down into my eyes and I lost consciousness. This was on April 1, 2017.'

As I drove from Pehlu Khan's village to Delhi I found myself haunted by Arif's words, and images of what had happened to his father filled my head. I remembered that I had seen the video of the mob beating him on social media. I remembered watching it many times because I found it hard to believe that the young men in jeans and T-shirts in the mob were fanatical enough to beat a man to death simply because he was Muslim. I remember wondering how Vasundhara Raje had been unmoved by what had happened. In the 40 years that we had been friends I did not think that she was incapable of compassion until Pehlu Khan was lynched. I remember calling her to ask why she had not gone to Behror and seen for herself what had happened. Why she had not criticized her Home Minister for saying that there were mistakes made on both sides. I remembered that her answer had disappointed me. She had said, 'We arrested people immediately. What more could we have done?'

There was much more she could have done. She could have made it clear to her officers that she was horrified by what had happened and that they must ensure that justice was done. Not only did she do nothing, the Prime Minister did nothing either.

* * *

It was in the week before Modi was due to arrive to file his nomination papers that I returned to Benares. Changes became visible as soon as we came out of the airport into the white glare of a hot day in March. I had warned Ajit, with whom I was travelling this time, that he would see some very unplanned urban ugliness on the way into the city. But the ugly little urban villages through which I usually drove on the way to Benares had disappeared under a brand new elevated highway.

Our driver, Piyush Kumar, pointed out, in case we had failed to notice the change, and said, 'This has been built since Modi became the MP of Benares. Do you remember that before this you had to drive through those crowded bazaars? You will see that he has done many things to improve Benares.'

'Are the Ghats clean now?'

'They are better than before.'

'And the river?'

'He is trying to clean it...there are improvements but you know that it takes time for people to change their habits.' At the end of this short conversation I realized that Piyush was a Modi devotee.

We were staying in the Taj this time. Ajit had not been to Benares in more than 40 years and so I thought staying in the Ganges View Hotel on the Assi Ghat would be too much for him. The hotel itself is charming and quaint but you only need to step out of it to be hit in the face by the worst thing about Benares: its filth. I remembered the Assi Ghat as being magical when seen from the terrace of the Ganges View Hotel and utterly repugnant when having to walk down the narrow lane that leads to the river. Not only was it nearly always paved with excrement, both human and bovine, but it was usually lined with humans who lived in a state of such unrelenting filth that they no longer understood its difference from cleanliness. I remembered that the first person I usually passed when I came out of the hotel was a mendicant (sadhu) with matted, unwashed hair who lived with a monkey who played the role of his wife. On most days I would see her picking lice out of his hair and beard. Neither the mendicant nor the monkey seemed to notice the stench of excrement or the filth of the road that they had made their home. I did not think Ajit would form a good impression of Benares if sights of this kind confronted him every time he stepped out of the hotel. The Taj was in the cleanest part of Benares, away from its squalor, and away from the daily traffic of funeral processions wending their way through the old city to the Manikarnika cremation ghat, where they said pyres had not gone out for centuries.

Ajit was keen to pray at the Vishwanath Mandir, so that was where we went first. While driving towards the old city I noticed that it looked cleaner than before. The usual heaps of rotting garbage at every other turn were missing and the streets themselves seemed cleaner. I remembered that every other time I had been here I had been forced to wear closed shoes because the filthy streets made this absolutely necessary. I also remembered that there were times when the stink of rotting garbage was so strong that it made me wish I had not come. So it was something of a pleasant shock to see that these normal Benares sights were not evident.

Himanshu Tripathi, whose ancestors have been the mahants of the Vishwanath temple for generations, met us at the Taj. He led us on his scooter into the narrow lanes of the old city. Its cluttered, impossibly narrow lanes were as crowded as ever but I noticed that the heavy bunches of dust-coated wires that blotted out the sky in earlier times seemed to have disappeared or at least been considerably reduced. As if answering my question the driver said, 'They have put the wires underground now. Modi has done a lot of work for Benares.'

'So do you think he will be Prime Minister again?'

'For sure. He is a good man who is working hard for the country.'

When we got closer to the temple I noticed heaps of rubble and a crater filled with the debris of broken houses. I had heard from Himanshu Tripathi that they had demolished ancient temples and the homes of many of the temple's priests to build a 'karidaar'. Corridor. But was surprised by the extent of the demolition. When we got to the temple he pointed to the tall, narrow building that had been his family home for more than a hundred years and said that that they had so far refused to allow their home to be demolished but there was a lot of pressure being applied in different ways. When I asked if their reason for not moving was that the government was not paying them enough compensation, he said that this was only one of the reasons. The main reason, he said, was that they needed to live close to the temple so that they could supervise the daily prayers and the demands of pilgrims.

When I tried to find out the need for a corridor I was told all sorts of ugly rumours that in general implied that Modi was doing this to benefit rich VIP visitors to the temple. As I listened to the grievances of the temple priests I remembered that in 2014 they had been among Modi's most ardent supporters. When Yogi Adityanath was made Chief Minister of Uttar Pradesh they were delighted and truly believed that he would usher in a golden age of Hindu rule. When the demolitions began the priests of the Vishwanath Mandir went to him and asked for his support to save their homes. He told them he could do nothing because the corridor was something Modi wanted done. I asked why they had not tried telling Modi their woes and was told by Himanshu Tripathi that the government officer in charge of running the temple had made sure that they never got close to the Prime Minister when he came to the city.

The pooja that had been arranged for Ajit and me was elaborate and went on for what seemed like more than two hours. By the time it ended, dusk had fallen and preparations began for the aarti, which had left a deep impression on me on a long-ago visit on Shivratri with my friend Mapu. I am not a religious person and ritual usually bores me even more than religion, but back then it was as if I were witnessing the beginning of worship because this particular aarti had such a primordial quality about it. I discovered later that it was based on rites that were prescribed in such detail in the Samaveda that even the flowers used to decorate the altar of Vishwanath were mentioned in detail.

Golu Bhaiya (Himanshu Tripathi) led us to an entrance of the innermost sanctum that gave us a ringside view of the cleaning of the sanctum after the last ritual and its detailed preparation for the aarti. Priests with naked torsos washed and cleaned the sanctum and then decorated the shivling representing Vishwanath with lilies, scented lotuses, roses and sacred leaves. All this while Golu Bhaiya continued to whisper to me his grievances against the officials running the temple. And against Modi. It was hard for me to believe that this was the same man who in 2014 had been so filled with hope that Modi would transform India and Benares.

The decoration of the sanctum took a long time. Long enough for him to tell me that his grievances were not just personal but reflected the feelings of those who had spent their entire lives in the city. 'It is not just because they are trying to break down our home that I am sad,' he said. 'I am sad because they seem not to know that in trying to turn Benares into Kyoto they could be destroying its entire character. What is Benares if you break down the alleys that knit the old city together? Just because you want to build a VIP guesthouse near the temple?'

'Is that the only reason for the corridor?'

'It seems to be the only reason. Modi has brought many foreign leaders here to see the Ganga aarti and he wants to make it easier for their cars to come right up to the temple from the ghats.'

'But hasn't he also brought Benares more tourists?'

'What will they see if Benares itself disappears? They have broken thousands of small temples and shrines to build this corridor. They are destroying the very character of the city.'

'But where did this idea to build a corridor come from in the first place?'

'It was an idea that some bureaucrats came up with when Indira Gandhi was Prime Minister. But she took one look at their plan and declared that she could not go ahead with it because she did not want to destroy Benares.'

Golu Bhaiya only stopped recounting his grievances against Modi when the aarti began. It was as powerful as I remembered it from that long-ago Mahashivratri. The priests in the inner sanctum – there were about ten of them – began by repeating 'Om' in a way that broke it into syllables. Then in concert they repeated the word until it became a crescendo that they developed by ringing their bells and beating a 'dumroo', which is the drum associated with Shiva. Finally came the brass oil lamps that they held up and moved in remarkable harmony. When this ceremony ended I saw that it had moved Ajit in exactly the same way that I had been moved when I first heard this aarti. When it was over and we walked back over wet marble floors to the temple's main entrance, Golu Bhaiya pointed to an ugly pink arch that had been erected over it and asked how much I thought it would be worth.

'I have no idea,' I said.

'It's made of plywood and would have cost no more than a couple of lakhs. But we hear that the amount spent on it was more than Rs 40 lakh. I tell you this to make the point that there is a lot of money being made in the name of pleasing Modi. This arch was erected just before his last visit.'

The next morning I went to Jayapur, the village Modi had adopted after becoming the MP from Benares, and about which I wrote in the first pages of this book. On the longish drive through typical squalid, suburban small-town Indian settlements, I found myself becoming increasingly depressed about whether India would ever achieve the changes that seemed to have come so easily to countries much poorer in Southeast Asia. I remember rural Thailand when it was almost as poor and squalid as most of India is today. And I remembered that within 20 years the squalid little villages that I drove through on my way from Bangkok to Hua Hin became transformed into clean and charming villages with proper roads, bazaars and living spaces. I have for the past 20 years gone to Thailand almost every year because of a spa in Hua Hin that I visit for a few days of restoration and relaxation.

When I first went to Hua Hin in the late '90s it was a small fishing village whose main tourist attraction was a palace that was the seaside home of the Thai royal family. The beach on which the spa, Chiva Som, was built used to be almost deserted in those days. When we walked from the spa to an old railway hotel at the other end of the beach, almost the only people we met on the way were Buddhist monks in saffron robes who stopped every now and then to bless the Thai tourists who bowed low when they saw them. The railway hotel had been taken over and restored by the Sofitel group, and it was at that time almost the only hotel in Hua Hin. In the small main shopping centre a few streets away from this hotel were a handful of shops that sold export rejects from Thai factories that made gym clothes and shoes for Adidas and Nike. Beyond the bazaar lay a street of seafood restaurants that were as basic as basic gets.

In the 20 years that I have been going to Chiva Som I have seen Hua Hin become a beautiful, elegant town to which western tourists flock. Many, many hotels have come up, as have glittering new shopping malls and restaurants that serve western and Thai food. Chiva Som has become one of the most famous spas in the world and its beach that once was so deserted as to seem almost like a private beach is now no longer private at all. There are new restaurants and hotels on it. Foreign tourists who come in bigger and bigger numbers every year have paid for the transformation of Hua Hin. Its entire economy survives on tourism.

When Modi became Prime Minister he often talked about how he would like to see tourism develop into a major pillar of the economy. But for tourists to come, there needs to be a degree of public hygiene and public services that for some reason India seems unable to develop. So although he had brought many important foreign leaders to Benares to witness the Ganga aarti and although he had made Benares so fashionable that Bollywood stars and Mumbai's richest businessmen now visited regularly, he seemed to have not been able to do much to improve its squalid surroundings.

On the way to Jayapur we drove through urban villages of unspeakable squalor. By an odd coincidence I had with me a friend called Uma, with whom I had first travelled to Chiva Som in the first week of 1999. It had just opened and she, always in search of new spas, had discovered it almost before anyone else. On the drive to Jayapur that morning I asked her if the filth and degradation upset her and she said that it was not much worse than most of small-town India. The highway on which we drove was being widened, so building material lay in heaps, adding to the sense that we were driving through a particularly disorderly, disgustingly unclean construction site. When we turned off the highway towards Jayapur the squalor of our surroundings increased because, along with the fields and drains littered with plastic bags, there was now that older Indian squalor: the rancid odour of rotting garbage, the pungent smell of cow dung and the revolting stench of human excrement.

When we came upon a mango grove and a clean village Uma said that she had always imagined that this was what northern Indian villages looked like. I said they did, once upon a time, but they had long been subsumed by an urbanization that had brought a measure of prosperity but without the services that urbanization usually brings. Again, it was Modi who was one of the first Indian prime ministers to notice that rural India needed urban services. Had he achieved anything like this in his model village? Most of his MPs had paid no attention to his scheme urging them to adopt one village in their constituencies and turn it into a model village. Had he succeeded in Jayapur?

When we got to the village that I had last visited two years earlier, the first thing I noticed was that the main road was now paved. The last time I had been there it was still being built. I also noticed that a new bank had opened on the edge of the village. The village also seemed cleaner than when I was last there. Under a mango tree we spotted a group of men having their heads and beards shaved by a village barber. 'They are all shaving their heads,' the driver observed, 'there must have been a death in the family.' We asked a man on a motorcycle the way to the house of the sarpanch and he told us to follow him. He led us through alleys that became unpaved ribbons as we got deeper into the village and then down a particularly narrow alley in which he pointed to a large, double-storeyed house and said, 'That is the sarpanch's house. That's him sitting over there.'

After talking to the sarpanch about the new school that had opened for girls and about how else the village had benefited since it was adopted by Modi, we wandered back towards the mango tree under which the barber was at work. There were about ten men in the group, young and old, and when I asked how the winds were blowing in this election one of the older men said, 'In this village it is "Har, har Modi, ghar, ghar Modi".' In every home there is praise for Modi. When I asked if they had no complaints about his record of the past five years another man said, 'You won't hear any complaints in this village because we have seen government schemes work for the first time ever.'

That evening in Benares I took Uma and Ajit to the Ganges View Hotel on the Assi Ghat. They were surprised that it was not as dirty as I had led them to believe. The old mendicant sat in his spot at the steps of the hotel but his monkey was not there, and even he seemed to have cleaned up a little. The cloth on the pavement on which he displayed the religious items he sold seemed cleaner than before, and I noticed that the ghat had been cleaned up in general and that a pavilion had been erected upon it that was not there in 2014.

We went into the Ganges View Hotel to say hello to Shashank Bhai, whose family home it used to be before it became a hotel, and his analysis of the changes Modi had brought to the Assi

Ghat was mixed. He said it was cleaner than before but there were also too many people coming there. 'It's quiet now,' he said, 'but in another hour or so there will be so many people here and so much noise that you won't be able to bear it.' I did not know then that the Ganga aarti had now become so popular because of Modi that it was performed on every other ghat every evening.

Golu Bhaiya had arranged a 'bajra' (barge) to take us to see the main aarti from the river. We sat on the roof of the barge on a mattress covered in a white sheet and, as we drifted towards the ghat where the aarti traditionally takes place, he set up a litany of complaints against Modi. Both Modi and Yogi had been a terrible disappointment, he said, and although he would win again he would do so only by a very small margin. Hundreds of other barges gathered around once the aarti began, and although it was dramatic and beautiful we agreed that it looked better on television than it did in real life because there were too many mosquitoes and too many people to contend with.

We discovered just how many when we got back to our car on the Assi Ghat. Our car was unable to leave the ghat because of a traffic jam in which we remained stuck for more than an hour before deciding to take another route that took an hour longer but at least the traffic moved. Modi had changed Benares but were the changes the right ones? Instead of trying to build a corridor would it not have been better for him to make the ghats into pedestrian zones? Would Benares survive becoming an Indian Kyoto? Would the Ganga ever be clean? I left Benares the next day with my head filled with questions. And my ears resounding with the mantra I had heard from those people under the mango tree in Jayapur: 'Har, har Modi, ghar, ghar Modi.'

Epilogue
Hope Against Hope

THE title of this chapter reflects my exact feelings about the first months of Narendra Modi's second term as Prime Minister. In his first campaign in 2014, Modi promised parivartan as the most significant thing he would bring to India. It was a time when the political landscape was bleak and the economic landscape bleaker, so the promise of change found resonance, more so than his other promise of vikas. The promise of development is one that all Indian political parties make at election time and ordinary voters have long become used to it being an empty assurance. But the idea of parivartan was very compelling because everyone from the poorest, most illiterate voter to the richest, most privileged Indian knows well that the thing India needs most is change.

Everything needs to change. Politics needs to change because it has for too long now been more about making money than about public service. Most political parties have become private limited companies headed by heirs who would find it hard to hold down a proper job if they had not been bequeathed political parties by indulgent parents. The most powerful of these in that election of 2014 was Rahul Gandhi as he was heir to India's oldest, most powerful political party. It was the party that had led India's freedom movement. It was the party that had once been led by men whose shadows continue to tower over India's bleak political landscape. Among them appeared the dwarfish shadow of Rahul Gandhi, who after spending a decade as a very privileged parliamentarian showed no signs of being worthy of the exalted position to which he was anointed by his mother. So when Modi, the son of a man who sold tea at a rural railway station, appeared on the national political stage he seemed like the best thing that had happened to Indian politics in an aeon. People wanted to believe him when he said he would bring change and so invested all their hopes in this possibility.

Their determination to continue believing in Modi was why they put up with extreme hardship, bankruptcy and, in some cases, permanent ruin in the wake of demonetization that Modi announced with ominous melodrama halfway through his first term. People forgave him this draconian move because they believed he was sincere in his determination to end corruption and 'black money.' When this draconian, painful exercise was followed months later by the introduction of the GST that was so complicated that many small businesses closed because they simply could not afford accountants, they forgave him this too. Modi failed in his first term to create anywhere close to the 12 million new jobs that India needs every year to meet the demands of new entrants into the workforce, but they excused him even for this.

The economy spent most of Modi's first term reeling from the shock of his two most disruptive examples of parivartan. On the political front the best change, in public perception, was that he managed to run a government that remained untainted by the sort of scandals that had been the hallmark of most Congress prime ministers for decades. Other than this perceived parivartan, Modi brought almost no change in the political culture of India. Under him, leaders continued to behave like feudal lords instead of democratically elected representatives of the people. Like those of Congress times, Modi's ministers also continued to live in vast colonial bungalows in Lutyens' Delhi and behave, as Indian 'socialist' politicians have always done, like rulers rather than servants of the people.

Modi declared in his first speech from the Red Fort that he considered himself the Pradhan Sevak (prime servant) of the Indian people and not as their Pradhan Mantri. But, except at public meetings at election time and in his monthly radio chats, ordinary Indians had no access to their 'sevak'. Modi was so isolated in the lofty realms of high office that even journalists had little access to him. He never held a single press conference in his first term and so obscure and invisible was the man who managed his media relations that most journalists in Delhi did not even know his name. Only journalists considered friendly were given access when Modi felt it was time to grant an audience to some obsequious reporter.

The most important political change he could have brought would have been to deepen the roots of democracy by abandoning the socialist, feudal political culture that defines Indian politics from its heights to its grassroots. This was a change Modi did not achieve. What he did achieve was a visible improvement in delivering the vast welfare programmes that Congress governments had devised over the years to keep up the façade of 'socialism' in the eyes of India's poorest citizens. People respected him in his first term also because he showed humility, sincerity and a dedication to making India a better country.

It was humility that seemed to disappear after he won his second term in office. I noticed this almost from the moment the term began. On the evening of May 23, 2019, when the results of the election had all come in and it became clear that Modi had won a full majority, with more seats than he had in 2014, I watched the victory party late that night. After a long day in and out of TV studios analysing the results on endless panels of 'experts', I watched at home on television as his cavalcade of black cars drove into the BJP headquarters. Party workers had gathered before a stage decked with marigold garlands and strings of shiny lights and they cheered hysterically when they saw him step on to the stage in a shower of rose petals. He turned towards them without a smile on his face in the manner of a deity receiving the obeisance of devotees. The only other person with him on that stage was Amit Shah. In the demeanour of the two men what was missing was any sign of humility.

What I remembered most from the victory speech he gave was his praise of the man who had been his fellow traveller in politics for decades: Amit Shah. Within days Shah was made Home Minister of India, thereby making him the second most powerful political leader in the country and Modi's anointed heir. Shah soon began to show that not only did he despise humility as a sign of weakness, he saw arrogance as a sign of strength. I personally noticed this for the first time during one of the early sessions of the new Lok Sabha, to which Shah was elected for the first time. There was a debate in which

Asaduddin Owaisi, leader of the All India Majlis-e-Ittehadul Muslimeen, was trying to make a point. Suddenly, India's new Home Minister stood up and said to him rudely, 'Learn to listen, Mr Owaisi. You must cultivate the habit of listening.' It was not just his words that were offensive, it was also his tone. By then it was becoming clear that Shah was the new face of the Modi government.

In Modi's first term the face of his government had been Arun Jaitley. In his second term Arun was in such poor health that he was hardly seen in public and not heard at all. Both he and Sushma Swaraj, External Affairs Minister in the first term, belonged to an older, more genteel generation of BJP leaders – a generation that was educated and sophisticated. And because Arun was so powerful in Modi's first term he inducted into the party people like himself, and was always available to journalists who needed explanations on government policy or actions. Arun died on August 24, 2019, almost exactly three months after Modi became Prime Minister for the second time. Everyone said that Modi had lost an irreplaceable member of his team. This became increasingly obvious as the days went by.

It was on August 5, weeks before Arun's and days before Swaraj's death, that Shah stood up in the Lok Sabha and announced that Article 370 of the Indian Constitution, which gave the state of Jammu and Kashmir a special status and more autonomy than other Indian states, was being abrogated. He also announced, with an air of nasty triumphalism, that India's only Muslim-majority state would no longer be a state with its own legislature, but a Union Territory to be governed from Delhi. The move was hugely popular in most of India because most Indians believe that it is on account of its special status that the Kashmir Valley has become a hotbed of jihadist violence and secessionism.

Personally, I agreed that it was time for Kashmir's special status to go but believe it could have been done without locking down the Valley for more than 100 days and counting. It could and should have been done by convincing Kashmiris that it was in their best interests for Article 370 to go since the secessionist movement that began with autonomy as its goal had become one that sought to create an Islamic state ruled by Islamic law. India cannot afford to have its only Muslim-majority state turned into a mini caliphate. But the abrogation of Article 370 could have been done with more grace. There was no need for it to be used as a test of patriotism in the election campaign that came soon after to win the states of Maharashtra and Haryana.

The man who led the campaign was the Home Minister because Modi spent the first few months of his second term travelling the world. Shah became his spokesman not just in the campaign to win Maharashtra and Haryana but also in the manner in which he gave an endless spate of interviews. In every interview and in every speech he made he dared the Congress Party to reinstate Kashmir's special status if they ever came back to power. It became so dangerous to oppose the abrogation of Article 370 that Hindutva activists filed a case against me and other speakers at a literary festival in Kasauli because at a discussion on Kashmir one of the panellists, Radha Kumar, said that Article 370 should be restored and the Government of India should apologize to the people of Kashmir. It was not something I said but a case was filed against me as well.

* * *

Just six months into Modi's second term in office, a palpable menace has crept into India's political atmosphere. The sense that the state can harm anyone it wants has grown after the Home Minister started using citizenship as a weapon. He has announced an exercise to identify and register Indian citizens across India. But before this exercise could begin the Modi government passed an amendment to India's citizenship law that makes it possible for Hindus, Sikhs, Buddhists, Jains, Parsis and Christians to be put on the fast track to Indian citizenship if they have come from Pakistan, Afghanistan or Bangladesh fleeing religious persecution. Technically this is a 'humanitarian' provision but in fact it is India's first Nuremberg law since it specifically excludes Muslims.

Within days of this amendment being passed by Parliament and signed by the President, explosions of rage began to happen across India. They started in Assam, where the Assamese have long feared that their culture, identity and language have been damaged by the dominance of Bengali Hindu and Muslim migrants. The protests spread quickly to West Bengal and within a week to Delhi's Jamia Millia and the Aligarh Muslim University before becoming a nationwide agitation. Both these institutions have mostly Muslim students. The sense that the amendment and the citizens' register were deliberately targeting Muslims has grown with the Prime Minister himself making speeches in which he said that he could identify the protesters by their clothes, the implication being that they were obviously Muslim from the way the dressed.

Shah's speeches long before the amendment to the Citizenship Act had obviously racist tones. He took to regularly describing infiltrators as 'termites' and threatened to hunt them down and throw them out one by one. He made it clear that he meant only Muslim illegal immigrants because he nearly always added that Hindus, Sikhs, Buddhists, Jains, Parsis and Christians need have no fear of being thrown out of India. The Home Minister's speeches worried me because I could see that he was weaponizing citizenship.

But I had no idea that it would affect me personally until one fine day in August, just after Arun Jaitley died, my son received an official missive from the Home Ministry declaring that he needed to prove that he had not obtained his Overseas Citizen of India (OCI) card fraudulently. He was given 24 hours to explain why he had 'concealed' the fact that his father was Pakistani. The rules to get this Indian equivalent of dual citizenship now state clearly that nobody with a Pakistani parent or grandparent is entitled to this privilege. But when I had applied to get Aatish a Person of Indian Origin (PIO) card in 1991 when it was first introduced, the officials who recommended that I get this for him rather than an extension of his multiple entry visa said nothing about this clause.

Aatish was born in London in 1980 when getting British citizenship was automatic, so we got him a British passport. Soon after my relationship with his father ended badly, I brought him to India and requested that he be given a multiple entry visa since he was a child and I was his sole legal guardian. It was when he turned 18 that I went back to apply for an extension of this visa and he was given a PIO card instead. When this was converted into an OCI card in 2016 he said his father, who was by then dead, had British nationality. Pakistanis are allowed dual nationality and as far as Aatish knew his father had a British passport. The transition from PIO to OCI was done online and was almost automatic.

There had been no problems ever about his coming and going from India until he wrote an article in *Time* magazine in the middle of the 2019 Lok Sabha election that was critical of Modi. A campaign immediately began on social media to declare that he was a Pakistani and a 'jihadist' and it did not take long for the Prime Minister himself to declare that he came from a Pakistani political family. His father was Governor of Punjab when he was shot dead by one of his own guards for trying to save an illiterate Christian woman from being hanged under Pakistan's ludicrous blasphemy laws. He was killed in 2011, so there would have been no way to find out whether he had surrendered his British passport.

Within four months of Modi becoming Prime Minister for the second time, Aatish was deprived of his OCI card and has been warned that he may never be able to come home again because he had 'lied' to the government. It soon became clear that he was not the only person who could lose the right to be an Indian citizen. Other dissidents began to get warnings and threats, and as the days have gone by the stamp of the Home Minister has been put on almost everything that the government does. Even as I write the last chapter of this book I find myself wondering if India is now on the verge of changing irrevocably into an illiberal democracy instead of one that prided itself on its liberalism and tolerance.

The India in which I grew up was a country that was desperately poor and painfully short of almost everything but it was a country in which the fundamental principles of democracy were cherished. It was not a country in which citizens were made to feel like they had less rights than others because of their faith. Since the beginning of Modi's second term it can no longer be said that Muslims have the same rights as other citizens. In almost everything that the government has done, whether in Kashmir or in its determination to make a National Register of Citizens, it has been made clear that if you are Muslim you could find it difficult to call yourself Indian.

So much has changed for the worse in so short a time that all that anyone can do is hope against hope that India does not continue to move towards totalitarianism. As things are, it has already become a country in which businessmen who do not kowtow face the threat of tax raids. Dissidents who do not give up dissidence for obedience risk being treated as traitors and journalists who do not sing the praises of Modi face retribution. So all we can do is hope against hope that Modi does not bring to India the kind of parivartan that would destroy all the qualities that made India the world's most noisy, chaotic, diverse and liberal democracy.

December 2019

Index

277

Acknowledgements

This book would not have been possible without the help of Krishan Chopra, Siddhesh Inamdar and Shruti Debi.

About the Author

Tavleen Singh is among India's most influential political journalists and commentators. She is the author of *India's Broken Tryst, Durbar, Kashmir: A Tragedy of Errors, Lollipop Street: Why India Will Survive Its Politicians* and *Political and Incorrect*. She writes widely syndicated weekly political columns in English and Hindi.